D0951085

SOME THINGS ARE
UNBREAKABLE

Some Things Are Unbreakable

Kate Willette

Coal Creek Press

Seattle

Copyright © 2006 by Kate Willette.
All rights reserved.

ISBN 978-1-4303-0796-9

Front cover photograph © Royalty-Free/Corbis.
Rear cover photograph © 2005 David Hanson.
Book design by Bruce Hanson.

Published by Coal Creek Press, Seattle, Washington USA
and Lulu.com.

To Bruce, Emily, and Heather:
Beloved ones, this is for you.

PROLOGUE

August 9th, 1986

It's the warmest day of the summer, and I am a bride. The wedding party and all the guests have changed into bathing suits and sunglasses; we are in Seattle, sailing through the Montlake Cut from Lake Union to Lake Washington, where we'll spend the next few hours gently cruising through this sparkling afternoon. We'll eat salmon and pasta and wedding cake. We'll dive into the blue water and come up laughing.

My groom is a tall, sweet man named Bruce. He has a passion for high places and challenge, which is why we'll be leaving tomorrow for a ten-day-long honeymoon hike through the back country of Olympic National Park. I will follow his long legs for forty miles through wilderness, but that is tomorrow.

Right now I am watching as the two halves of the Montlake bridge separate and rise grandly upward, like enormous crossed swords. Cars stop on either side and wait as our little rented yacht glides solemnly through. Our out-of-town guests are smiling and leaning on the rails, pointing at the Cascade mountains to the east. I am imagining our marriage: children and peace, work and rest, our lives together. Everything is still possible.

Until recently, reversing paralysis after spinal cord injuries was not a major issue because injured people usually died fairly quickly. People who survived rarely lived longer than two to three years ...

Luba Vikhanski

HISTORY OF PRESENT ILLNESS: The patient is a 45-year-old man ... He was airlifted to Harborview Medical Center Emergency Department
SOCIAL HISTORY: The patient lives in Bellevue, Washington with wife and two daughters ages 10 and 12.   (Harborview Medical Center Chart)

ONE

Day 1: March 7, 2001: 4 pm

I'm in the kitchen with a former student who's over for help with her pre-calculus. Downstairs Emily is watching a video, and Bruce and Heather are skiing at Snoqualmie Pass. Tonight he'll take the girls to choir practice while I go to a reading my friend Carole is giving at the University Book Store; she's just published her first novel. It's early spring, sunny and almost sixty degrees outside, a miraculous day for Seattle in March. I'm showing Shanti how to use her graphing calculator to find the intercepts of polynomial functions when the phone rings.

It's a ski patroller, who tells me that she's afraid she has some bad news. Bruce was in a skiing accident and is being taken to the hospital. What hospital? She's not sure ... Harborview. In Seattle. Okay. He's actually fine, everything is fine, except his toes were kind of tingling, so they wanted to be sure ... okay. She has Heather there, do I want to talk with her? Of course.

Heather sounds nervous, but I'm not concerned. Her dad is a graceful, expert skier and there's no way this could be anything serious. A broken leg, maybe. A sprain. The ski-patroller comes back on and asks whether I want her to bring Heather home or to the hospital. I give her directions to our house, hang up the phone and go back to my student. There's an odd moment after I tell her what just happened, then we shrug and go back to the math. We were almost finished anyway.

After she leaves, I go downstairs and there is Emily, watching the part of The Little Princess where the father regains his memory and recognizes his daughter at the last possible moment. I pause the video and tell her about the phone call. I say that we have to drive to the hospital and pick up Daddy as soon as Heather gets home. She looks at me carefully. Is this all okay? As far as I know, it is.

4

Back upstairs, I call Kris, my boss and friend at Plymouth Church. She's the minister in charge of education, and I'm the part-time coordinator of youth ministries. No, no reason to be alarmed, but yeah, Harborview. Weird. I'll keep you posted.

I open the phone book and call Harborview. I tell them my husband is on the way and give his insurance information and everything else they want to know. I ask them how to get there; I've heard of Harborview but don't really know where it is. I-90 to I-5 North, take the James Street exit, up the hill to 9th Avenue, turn right, you can't miss it. Okay.

A car pulls in the driveway and Heather climbs out, still in her ski clothes. The ski-patroller is named Jill, a small, slim, freckled woman with smooth, reddish hair. I have my arms around Heather on the passenger side, and I look a question across the top of the car at Jill. She meets my eyes, and hers are very sad. She makes a small face that I can't quite read. I thank her, and Heather says goodbye. Something is wrong with Heather's voice; she sounds frail and uneven. I kiss the part in her hair and reassure her; she'll be okay when she sees that Bruce is fine. We stash her skis and boots in the garage, and I tell her to change her clothes so we can go to the hospital and get Daddy.

The girls are in the car, and I'm in the kitchen putting some snacks into my bag in case we have to hang around the emergency room for very long. Pretzels, bottled water, jelly beans, cheese sticks. I look around just before I leave the room, and for a few seconds there is a wisp of awareness: the next time I'm standing here, everything might look different. It passes, and I go cheerfully out to the car. Driving across the bridge, I ask the girls how the heck we're going to get both Daddy and his big long skis into our little Toyota.

The first wait in the Harborview ER lasts about an hour and a half. Kris has sent our parish nurse, Karen, up the hill to hang out with us. Karen is a retired nurse whose job is to help out when members of the church have health issues. With us also is a social worker who looks anxious and harassed, a drab, dark-haired woman with big hands that constantly wring at each other. She comes out from the mysterious "No Admittance" doors every twenty minutes or so to ask if we're alright. She apologizes for the wait and tells me that someone will be out soon to talk with me.

Finally she comes to get us. Both girls and Karen and I follow her into a cramped and not very clean private room. The doctor will be right in. She twists her hands together and looks at Karen. Something I don't understand passes between them, and Karen suddenly volunteers to take the girls to buy some pop from a vending machine. They leave the room just as a young, dark-haired doctor with an accent I can't place comes in. He sits down in a chair and pulls it close so his knees are almost touching mine. The social worker stands by the door.

"Your husband's injuries are very serious." This is his opening statement. I don't say anything. "There is a possibility he won't walk again. We are listing his condition as serious at this time." There are more words, but I only hear them as sounds. It's as if he's suddenly switched to a non-human language. I ask if I can see Bruce, and beyond that I don't think I speak at all. The doctor gets up and leaves the room, and then I say to the social worker, in a voice that comes from way in the back of my throat, "Get my kids."

They come in with Karen, holding cans of Diet Coke, and the social worker leaves us alone. I'm on the floor, on my knees, and I tell them this impossible, impossible news.

Emily shrieks, "Paralyzed? From the neck or from the waist?" She is tracking better than I am. I don't know, I haven't even asked. The doctor said only that he probably wouldn't walk, so I tell her I think the waist. Without missing a beat, she says, sobbing, "He can still hug us."

The three of us hold on tight then. I tell them again and again, "He is still Daddy. We are still a family. He is still Daddy." The sobbing and shaking goes on for a long time. Every little while, one of us starts to breathe normally, and then it rolls over us again. They are whimpering like exhausted toddlers, and they keep looking longingly at the door.

"Mama, I want to go home," one of them whispers.

I open my mouth to say that we can't leave until we see Daddy, and then Karen volunteers to take them home and stay with them at our house until I can get there. She'll have to walk with them down the hill to church where her car is, will that be OK? Sure. It's Wednesday night, which means that a lot of our best friends are down there having dinner and getting ready to do some adult study groups while the kids go to choir. Our old life.

Harborview ER is busy. A baby screams on and on. His mother gazes at him, lying on his back in her lap, and just shakes her head. A TV plays game shows loudly from one corner. Under my feet are thin dirty carpets. Around me people sleep in the molded plastic chairs. It's a wide-open space with hideous fluorescent lights, no place to hide. I

6

drift out and blindly circle through the dim hallways, past banks of elevators and rows of doors to locked offices. Parking Enforcement. Financial Counseling. Patient Relations. Night is falling outside, the beautiful spring day almost over.

Back at the ER, I go to the desk and ask to make a phone call. I have to tell his dad, Dave. I can't remember the number, though I've known it for fifteen years. They try to look it up on the internet and can't find it. I have them search for Paul's number. Paul, Bruce's youngest brother, will know how to get hold of Dave. I'll only have to say it once.

"Paul, it's Kate."

"Kate!" Minnesota-hearty voice. "How's it going?"

"Paul, we're in trouble." Suddenly I can't breathe. "Bruce was in a skiing accident."

"Oh, God." I can hear him reeling, can almost see him sinking into a chair. "How bad?"

"Bad." OK, say the words. No. Yes. "They're saying he might not walk."

"Oh, Kate. Oh, God."

I whisper, "I need Dave to come here."

7:15 pm

Some friends who'd been at church come up, a group of three or four with anxious faces, looking for me. "Jocelyn," I say into my friend's coat, "they're saying—"

"I know, I know." We walk in a weeping group around and around the first floor halls. Bad art. Custodians, all foreign-looking, in purple pants and jackets swabbing the already shiny floors with big, gray string-mops. We're walking toward a wall that I recognize.

"This looks like a dead-end," I say. "But it isn't." Jocelyn makes a sound that's like a laugh with a moan inside, or maybe the other way around. Later, all of us will remember this moment.

After half an hour or so, some of these good people have to leave. The children's choir is done practicing; it's a school night. Jocelyn stays a bit longer, and we struggle to be practical. It's like trying to walk on sheer ice in the dark, wearing tennis shoes. That which is normally effortless has become impossible. She's asking what I need ... uh, the girls. The girls will need someone to stay with them tomorrow while I'm here. Can she do this? Yes. More friends arrive: Patricia with her famous organizational skills, Sue, calm and passive and enormously comforting, our pastor, Tony, looking shocked and distant. I find that I have nothing to say to them, but I'm intensely grateful to see their faces. My hands are crossed over my stomach, holding on to either side of my waist. I keep bending forward, bowing, then straightening up again.

Patricia goes out to get me some food; it's almost nine o'clock. She brings back a huge, dense burrito that seems to weigh five pounds. She's telling me in her clear-as-crystal voice that I have to eat. I have to get very serious about taking care of myself. She's right. I open the wrapping at one end of the burrito and smell it, then set it down.

Kris arrives. She's hurting for me, her eyes full of tears and warmth. We all sit down again on the hard chairs, and Tony says a prayer out loud. It's about Bruce and the people attending to him, and about me, Emily, and Heather. The words make me cry hard, but I'm surprised at how right it feels to be prayed over by this old friend.

An hour passes slowly by, then another. I've spoken to Paul again on Patricia's cell phone. Dave got a flight; he's on his way. Patricia and Sue will have to go soon to meet his plane. I've managed to reach my boss at school and say the words again. At 11:15 someone calls from the nurse's desk for the family of Patient Hanson.

I stand up and a tall young doctor, white coat flapping, strides toward me. He looks around at the others, then points me toward the same little private room I'd used earlier. I hesitate, then gesture for them all to join us. Everyone sits, and the doctor, who seems to be South-American, maybe Brazilian, sighs heavily. He's directly across from me, leaning forward with his elbows on his knees, long, graceful hands hanging limply down. As he speaks, his hands move. He says that Bruce's neck is broken and gestures toward his own Adam's apple to indicate the place of the fracture. He says that the damage is very bad and that the probability is that Bruce will never again have sensation or movement below—he gestures—the level of his nipples. His eyes are on mine. I don't blink or move, but I can feel Tony's hand on my right shoulder.

Patricia, ever efficient, is taking notes in a little flip notebook. Everyone else is still, except the doctor, who is saying that Bruce might have trouble breathing from now on. He says the word "ventilator." He brings both his hands up between us and lets them dangle uselessly curled from his wrists, saying that he doesn't know how much "hand function" my husband will have. Tony sighs and his hand squeezes my shoulder again.

I say that I know there is no such thing as absolute certainty in medicine, but I want to know how sure he is about what he's telling me.

Silence.

"Ninety percent?"

He shrugs. "That, at least, very likely higher." He tells me that I should not be hopeful. No other questions? No. He explains that he's just drilled two holes into Bruce's skull and inserted a pair of screws, which are being attached to a tong, which will have, initially, an eighty-pound lead weight hung from a hook at its center. This will keep the vertebrae from moving around until surgery can be done, probably tomorrow or the next day. I say that I want our kids to be able to come to see him as soon as possible and ask whether the thing he's just described looks as frightening as it sounds.

He says it depends, that I can see him as soon as they've cleaned him up, and then I can decide for myself. Anything else? No. Good luck to you, then. He leaves the room, and I ask for someone to turn off the lights, which they do. We sit together in silence, the little room lit only from a small window in the door. I say that everything that matters about him is still intact, in a fierce calm voice, as if I'm in the middle of an argument no one else can hear. I say that I want to lie down on the floor and howl, and I think Kris tells me to go ahead. Nothing happens, though. We just sit there quietly for a few more minutes, then get up and file out to the fluorescent room again.

A nurse comes out and hands me two orange plastic bags, both stamped with the Harborview Medical Center logo. One is small like a lunch sack, the other big like a shopping bag. In the big one are his fancy red ski boots, too heavy for me to hold in one hand. I set them down and look into the small bag. His wallet, brown leather with a few dollars inside. The keys to our van, still parked up at the Alpental parking lot. His wedding ring. I slide the ring onto my own thumb and tuck the rest into my purse. I pick up the bag with the ski boots and stand there holding it awkwardly. After a minute Sue offers to take the boots home with her; we can pick them up later. She and Patricia leave then to go and meet Dave's plane. It's getting on toward midnight, and the ministers are sticking with me until I am allowed to see Bruce.

Finally a nurse comes out and calls again for the family of Patient Hanson. Tony, Kris and I get up and follow her through the "No

Admittance" double doors into a wide hallway with an enormous room off its right side. Bruce is lying on his back in the very first bed, a curtain drawn three quarters of the way around him. He's too long for the bed, and the first thing I see of him is his bare feet hanging over the end. I move up to look into his face, taking in the screws and the tong as I go. He's wearing a neck brace made of stiff white plastic and navy blue pads. It pushes against his chin and jaws, making his face look round instead of long. I'm leaning over him. His eyes are open but cloudy, and he says softly that he's glad to see me. He has a nasty cut on his forehead. His hair is pretty long and mostly covers the screws, but I can see the lead weight hanging down below the top of the bed. I kiss him on the temple and tell him that I'm glad to see him, too. Tony and Kris move up from behind me and touch him through the blanket. Tony says another prayer. Bruce closes his eyes. I move down to the end of the bed and put my hands on the tops of his feet; they're ice-cold, thick, and feel as dead as a pair of steaks. His toenails are polished in an incongruous rainbow of sparkly colors, applied by Emily three weeks ago when he finished his MFA program—her graduation present.

We stand awkwardly around the bed. Bruce seems to be asleep, and suddenly I'm aware of the voices of other patients in this ER holding area. One man is carrying on a drunken conversation with his nurse. She's speaking in an exaggerated, loud voice, as if he were hard of hearing.

"Sir, we're going to have to take an x-ray."

"What?"

"You need an x-ray. We're going to take you to radiology."

"What?"

"We're going to take an x-ray, Sir."

"Oh," he slurs. "How long's it gonna take?"

"Jesus," I say. "What do you have, a date?" Tony and Kris laugh softly, and soon after that, Tony leaves, first pressing me firmly against his thick chest.

Kris and I sit on the floor against the wall outside the holding area with our arms wrapped around our knees. We are in the inner sanctum, behind the "No Admittance" doors. The lighting is softer and it's quieter than in the waiting room. I say that it would be so strange if Bruce and I could never have sex again, and then I cry for awhile. We're dropping with exhaustion, our heads back against the wall, but also somehow wide awake. She's staying until Dave gets here, so I won't have to be alone, and I'm glad.

After a half an hour or so, a few nurses in dusty blue uniforms show up wheeling a bed that seems to be constructed of thin magenta-colored pads. It's shaped like a shallow, dark box with a four-inch rim all the way around and black straps hanging down at intervals. One of the nurses tells me that this is the rotobed. She says that Bruce will be much more comfortable in it. I tell her that he has contact lenses in his eyes and ask if someone can take them out. He hates wearing them too long. He'll need them out so he can sleep; he never, ever even naps with them in. I'm very worried about this, and she tries to reassure me, but doesn't succeed.

She's in charge of getting him into the rotobed, and she wants me to move out of the way. They wheel it up next to his gurney, aligning and setting brakes as they go. There is a problem. The bed, finally in position next to him, looks not quite long enough. Because of the high rim, his feet can't just hang over the end. One of the nurses asks me how tall he is.

"Six-five," I say.

They talk among themselves. "Does anybody know the dimensions of the bed?"

"Nope."

"Does this bottom edge go down?"

"No ... just the side, I think."

"Can it be lengthened?"

"Maybe he'll just fit. He's really long."

"Is there a number we could call?"

Everyone seems dull and slow-witted. This is clearly a first, a patient too tall for their big-deal bed, and I feel crazily proud of him for thwarting them. The nurse who didn't take care of his contact lenses makes a decision.

"I think he'll just fit." She directs one helper to be in charge of the hanging lead weight, another to manage his head, and two others to help her get him across. The side of the rotobed near him is lowered, and the five of them position themselves. They're nervous and coordinated suddenly, and wide awake. One of them counts, and on three he seems to float swiftly across the distance. She was right. He just fits. He hasn't opened his eyes.

They secure him at his shoulders, chest, knees and ankles. They are relaxed and jovial again, asking me about the toenail polish. Then everyone except the nurse I've been talking with goes away. She's explaining that the rotobed will tilt from side to side up to a forty-five degree angle, that it has three vibration speeds, that it's equipped with timers so that all this can happen automatically, around the clock. She's acting as if I ought to be impressed, and I think I disappoint her. I'm still thinking about his contact lenses.

She does something at a control panel on the side of the bed, and the edge nearest us begins to rise. He is strapped in, the weight hanging free, straight to the floor like a plumber's bob, while he turns slowly like a roast on a spit, higher and higher until it looks like he'll slide into the opposite edge. Kris and I are shifting our feet. It's so smooth and quiet, turning him now slowly back the other way, facing us … he never opens his eyes. The nurse is explaining that the motion of the bed will help his lungs stay clear, but her sentences seem disjointed to me, almost nonsensical. When she's satisfied that everything works, she stops the bed and leaves us.

We wander out to the waiting area, looking for Dave, then back through the "No Admittance" doors, around and around while the night slips slowly by. We're regulars now, people who know the way.

1:30 am

We're standing in front of the nurse's station when Dave arrives, walking between Patricia and Sue with a small suitcase in his hand. He's seventy-two years old, he's just flown through two time zones, his first-born child has a broken neck—and he looks exactly like he always looks. Alert. Sharp. Completely solid. Engineer, CEO, member of the choir. Dave.

He sets his suitcase down and puts both arms around me, reliable as rock. I introduce him to Kris. He takes out a single sheet of paper from the breast pocket of his coat and carefully writes down her name and phone number and position relative to us. Minister. Looking on, I see that he already has Sue and Patricia on the page, along with their home and cell-phone numbers, along with how he met them. Driver, airport. Passenger, airport. They say goodbye and we turn away. I walk him through the "No Admittance" doors, telling him softly as we go what the Brazilian doctor said. He listens, but I can see him suspending belief. His jaw is set, mouth pursed skeptically. At the side of the bed, he leans over to look into Bruce's face.

Dave is in his engineer mode, neutral and observant. Eyes narrowed, he takes in the screws and the tong and the lead weight, examines the bed and the neck brace, then puts one hand on Bruce's shoulder.

"Hey, Buddy."

Bruce opens his eyes. Still cloudy. "Hi, Dad." He doesn't seem surprised. He doesn't seem anything.

"You're sleepy," Dave says sensibly. "Get some rest. I'll chat with you tomorrow." He actually says this. Chat. I almost smile.

"Good to see you, Dad." His eyes close again, and that's that. Dave picks up his suitcase and leads the way out into the waiting area. I tell him that they've said Bruce has to be moved to a room up in the Neurological ICU, and they've bumped out its current occupant, so now we're just waiting for the room to be cleaned. I imagine people with spray bottles and wipes at two o'clock in the morning, going over a room ... taking their time. We're staying until we see that he's settled in there, safe with the ICU people, far away from the ER holding tank.

3 am

The waiting room outside NICU is carpeted, dimly lit, and very quiet. There are couches, easy chairs, end-tables with lamps. We sit on a loveseat while a brisk, freckled nurse gives us the drill. Her speech is smooth, swift, and rehearsed, but not unkind. Harborview is a Level-I trauma center serving the whole Pacific Northwest, from Alaska to Montana. Arguably, it's the best place on the West Coast for treating someone with Bruce's particular injuries. She points to the far corners of the room we are in, and I see that small groups of people are camped out in sleeping bags on the floors. These are families, she tells us, who just live at the hospital while their loved ones are in intensive care. Sometimes it lasts for months. They have to do this because they can't afford to rent an apartment, and the hospital is fine with it.

There are no visiting rules in NICU. Family members are welcome around the clock. Nurses work in twelve-hour shifts, and each nurse is assigned to one or at most two patients. They're good, the very best. This area of the hospital also has the trauma intensive care unit, known as TICU; Bruce is a neurology patient because his injury is to the spinal

13

cord, which is part of the brain. She says this in a very matter-of-fact voice, looking at us carefully, then moves on.

Harborview is also a county hospital, which means it serves the indigent population. The neighborhood is rough, and she recommends getting security to escort us to our car when we leave, and whenever we leave after dark in the future. She also recommends that we not leave valuable or personal items in his room. Purses and wallets disappear regularly.

I start to notice something that feels odd; she is talking mostly to me. I'm the wife, the next of kin. Dave sits beside me, listening hard and asking a question here and there, but she always comes back to me. It feels almost as if she's being disrespectful. She asks if we have questions. Dave asks for her name, and the phone number of NICU, and the room number Bruce will be in. He writes all this down on his sheet of paper, then folds it back up and tucks it away. She leaves us, first promising that his room is almost ready.

4 am

He's in his room. He didn't really wake up to acknowledge us when we said goodnight. We're going home now, and he isn't with us.

If researchers tried to restore the spinal cord to precisely the way it was before the injury, the task could be declared hopeless in advance. Replacing all the dead cells, regrowing all the cut fibers, and reconnecting all the circuitry is hardly a feasible proposition; the human spinal cord contains millions of fibers, and Nature forgot to color-code them.

Luba Vikhanski

```
Neurological: Patient
arrived from ER on
rotobed. Sleepy,
oriented, knows why
he is here.
Keeps falling asleep
during exam.
Psychosocial: Wife
and father.
Appearance, behavior,
and verbalizations
appropriate to
situation.
```

TWO

Day 2: 4:30 am

The drive to our house takes fifteen minutes. A few blocks along 9th Avenue, shoot down the hill toward Elliott Bay, hop on the empty freeways, cross Lake Washington. Home. A roomy house in a neighborhood full of Douglas firs and rhododendrons, at the end of a quiet street backed by deep, wooded hills. The extravagant, thoughtless riot of vegetation—wonderfully impossible to manage, at least for me. We bought this comfortable, brick-colored house when the girls were toddlers, and it is by far the nicest house I've ever lived in, a place I couldn't have dared to dream I might own. When we moved in, I used to joke to my friends that I would be needing a new wardrobe, just to walk around in this house. It's dark now, shadowed by the weeping cherry in the front yard. All the lights are off. I park the noiseless Prius in the driveway, and we step through the front door.

Karen is lying awake on the green leather couch in our living room, a blanket pulled over her street clothes. I introduce her to Dave, and she says that she thinks Emily is still awake. Emily has been up all night long, coming downstairs at half-hour intervals. Karen's voice is fragile and weary; she must be as tired as I am. I say that I'll go up to take care of Emily, and that she should go to sleep. Dave is standing with his little suitcase outside the door of my bedroom. I tell him he should sleep in there. It has a private bathroom. It's comfortable. He starts to protest that he'd be fine down on our family room couch, but I cut him off.

"I don't want to sleep in that bed."

He looks at me. "Okay." He pats my shoulder. "Well, let's get some rest."

I climb the stairs to the top of the house, where the girls' rooms are. Emily is awake, sitting up in her bed. She says, "Mama!"—and I go to lie down with her. She's twelve, a healthy armful of ripe warmth. She wants to know everything that happened after she and Heather left the hospital. I tell her an abridged version, leaving out the parts about the no sensation and the no hand function and the screws drilled into his head. I tell her I saw him, and that he was sleepy, and that we really have to wait to see what will happen. I tell her that I talked with the nurses who are taking care of him, and they are really nice and seem very smart. I tell her that Grandpa is here, and he's going to be using my and Daddy's room.

She keeps repeating that she can't believe it. Me neither, honey. I stay there with her until she's asleep, and then it's time for me to go to the couch. Bruce has made half of our family room into a small studio. The back of the futon couch is up against his drawing table. Behind that is his desk, covered now as always with a jumble of papers, envelopes, magazines, and wires, his laptop in the place of honor in the middle. There are drawings tacked up on the walls, and paintings on unstretched canvas lying around on the carpet. I drop to the couch, close my eyes on all of it, and then I am asleep.

The light wakes me; the house is quiet. It's seven o'clock. An image rises in my head: a man strapped into a heavy black wheelchair, his hands lying useless on the armrests. He's immobile, and he's wearing my husband's face. Bruce. I pull the quilt around me and lie there crying for awhile, until I hear voices from upstairs. Emily. Heather. In the kitchen, I go to Heather and she backs her way into my hug. Her hair smells like sleep.

"You aren't going to school today."

"Good."

"I saw Daddy last night."

"Is he okay?"

I squeeze her, my arms crossed around her chest, her narrow ten-year-old shoulders tense against me. "He was really tired." She sighs and moves away. "Grandpa's here. He came on a plane last night."

Emily says, "Am I staying home, too?"

"I want to go and see Daddy." Heather is talking into the cereal cupboard.

"Grandpa and I will go to the hospital and see how it is. Later, you can both go and see him. Jocelyn will come and stay with you today while we're gone."

Heather pours milk on her Fruity Pebbles. "I dreamed there were bad guys in the front yard," she says. "And Daddy was, like, fighting them. We were inside, looking out the windows, and we were scared, but he was winning." She looks up at me. "And in the dream, you said, 'That's Daddy for you!' And then I woke up."

"He's still protecting us," I tell her, my eyes wet again. "I don't know how, but somehow he is." I touch her head. "I'll tell him about that dream. He'll like it."

Karen comes in and starts talking about the pizza the girls had for dinner last night, and then Dave appears, showered and dressed in slacks and a neatly tucked-in shirt. While he and the girls are saying their hellos, the phone rings. Our friend David. Emily called him last night. He wants to come over, and I say, yes, okay, right now. He can stay with the girls so we can leave before Jocelyn gets here; she has twin boys to get off to school, and her house is way up in north Seattle. David lives in our neighborhood. I don't even consider the possibility of leaving the girls alone, and no one suggests it.

I go up to shower in our bathroom. Bruce's clothes are lying all over the bedroom. His side of the sink is messy, cluttered with cold remedies from last winter and dusty little bottles of shaving lotions he doesn't like. With the water running, I cry again, right through my shower. When I'm finished, I stop crying. I put on some clothes and go downstairs, where Dave and David are talking in a deliberate, upbeat way about what's happened. I can see that David is taking his cues from my father-in-law … no hysteria, no panic, no tragic opera. David's daughter, Melissa, is Emily's close friend, and he's always treated Emily like family. Right now she's sitting on his lap, both his big arms wrapped around her. He winces at me over her head: Kate, I'm so sorry. I make a tiny shrug in response.

Before we leave, our phone has rung twice more, and I've quietly confirmed the news to two more horrified friends. Their tears are very hard to bear, even over the telephone, and I hang up as quickly as I can. I call Jocelyn. I send an e-mail to Bruce's friend from art school, and another to my sister across town. I remember to call one of the other carpool moms to say I won't be driving to school today; she already knows.

"God, I can't believe you're thinking about the carpool. Don't worry, okay, and I'll be in touch later to see what help you need. Tell Bruce we're praying for him." Good old Lisa. She'll do what's practical every time and not make a fuss about it. Thank God.

And then we're ready. David will stay here until Jocelyn comes, and we'll call from the hospital to give them any news. As we go out the front door, David is asking the girls if they want to go and get some videos. Sure.

The streets around Harborview are crawling with cars looking for one of the few metered spaces to park. We need to find a lot; the closest one with space is four blocks away and costs nine dollars a day. Dave pays the attendant and the two of us hike up the steep sidewalk toward the hospital. We go in through the ER entrance and follow the maze of hallways looking for the right elevator. There is an East Clinic, an East Hospital, a West Clinic, and a West Hospital. We want the West Hospital, second floor. Suddenly we're standing outside the Neuro Intensive Care Unit. There's a wide, curved desk with a phone on it, and a plastic-covered sheet instructing us to call inside before entering. I do, and the voice tells us to come through the double doors.

Bruce is in the first room, straight across from the doors. He's lying flat on his back, covered in white blankets to his chin, his hands limp on his chest. He still has the head-traction thing in place, and I try not to look at it. The rotobed is adjusted so that a person standing next to it doesn't have to bend over to touch him. I look right into his eyes and we say hello, but he is barely there; I wonder what drugs they're giving him. He wants to know how Heather is doing. I don't know what to say.

"She's okay," I finally tell him.

"Poor kid," he whispers. I don't know what he means. I haven't let myself imagine what happened on that mountain. Realizing this makes me panicky about her and ashamed of myself. After a minute Dave comes to stand next to me.

"Dad," Bruce says, his voice very weak. "So I guess I didn't dream that."

"Nope, I'm really here."

"When did you come?"

"Last night."

While they're talking, I move around to the other side of the bed. There are four tall windows looking straight down on a helicopter. As I watch, a pair of medics in bright blue jumpsuits climb in from either side, and it angles away toward the city. I'm about to ask Bruce about his helicopter ride when Dave, who has lifted the blankets from Bruce's feet, speaks.

"Can you feel this?" He's touching Bruce's left foot.

19

"Yes." I stare at Bruce, who doesn't seem excited at all.

Dave is running his fingers along the bottom of the right foot now. "You can feel this?"

"Indeed I can."

"Really?!" Relief rolls through my shoulders. I'm moving back and forth, watching Dave's fingers, looking at Bruce.

"Yeah," he says, sleepy and droll. "And this morning they stuck a suppository up my butt, and I felt that, too."

Dave and I burst out laughing, and then Dave, being Dave, immediately tries for more. "Can you move them?" A pause while Bruce concentrates and we stare at his toes. They are perfectly still. I look up at his face: eyes closed tight, big frown. On the edge of the blanket, his fingers are slowly extending and curling. His toes do nothing at all. They might as well be attached to someone else's body. Dave covers them up again and says, unperturbed, "That will come."

Soon afterwards, the doctors arrive. One is a middle-aged man with dark messy hair and a warm smile who could as easily be an artist or a musician as a neurologist. He's very relaxed and happy, as if we were all gathered to see a really good play instead of standing around the bed of my critically injured husband. I like him. The other doctor is a woman younger than me with long, ratty brown hair caught in a rubber band at the base of her neck. She conducts the neurological exam, which consists of finding out exactly what Bruce can feel and move.

She has a clipboard with a pre-printed chart on it, and she makes her way around his body asking him to perform, in what is obviously a well-rehearsed routine, a long list of tricks. "Hold your fingers out straight. Now I'm going to try to hold them together; you press against me to spread them out. Push, push, push. Good. Now I'm going to press down on your wrist. Don't let me push it into the bed. Hold it up! Hold, hold, hold. Good." After every task, she makes a little mark on her chart. She moves the parts of him that he can't move, his toes, his feet, and asks him to tell her which way things are pointing. Every answer goes on the chart.

The sensory exam is done with an ordinary safety pin. Dr. Ratty Hair sticks it into Bruce's arm where he can feel it and says, "This is sharp." Then she turns it on its rounded end and pushes that into his forearm. "And this is dull." Again. "Sharp. And dull." After covering his eyes with a cloth, she starts at his chest and pokes him, sometimes sharp and sometimes dull, all the way down his body. He never feels the sharpness, not even once. It's all dull, except for the times when he can't feel it at all.

The warm, smiling doctor takes over every once in a while, repeating something she has just done while Dr. Ratty Hair stands by, nodding respectfully. Dave and I try to stay out of the way and still see everything. Bruce is very still, but he seems to be trying hard. His nurse, dressed like all of them in dusty blue drawstring pants and matching loose shirt, sits with his back to us on a tall chair in front of a computer monitor, quietly tapping the keys, turning every once in a while to watch the proceedings.

It takes almost an hour, and when they're finished they approach Bruce at the head of the bed. The happy doctor tells him cheerfully to get some sleep now; no one will bother him for a little while. He's going to talk with me in the hall, is that okay? Bruce says, "yeah, sure," and I follow the two doctors out to the space in front of the nurse's station across from his room. Dave stays behind. Dr. Ratty Hair is looking at her chart and talking to me about what will happen next.

"Your husband will probably be spending about twelve weeks here," she begins. I don't say a word. I'm trying to imagine telling the girls Daddy will have to stay in the hospital for three months. I don't like her, and I know it's irrational, but I can't help myself. I want her to stop talking, stop saying these things, stop looking up at her boss or whoever he is for approval. He's looking at me, very kind and jovial.

She goes on. "He'll spend most of that time up on the fourth floor, in rehab, where they'll work with him on using what he has to become as independent as possible."

"They do remarkable things up there," says the man.

I'm still thinking about all that time. "Three months," I say.

"Well," she says brightly, "it could be a little less."

"I don't know," the man says, rubbing at the top of his head. "I don't know."

She gives him a questioning glance. "I was thinking he goes home a full quad in about ten, twelve weeks."

So casual. A full quad. It is Thursday, just about noon. Yesterday at this time, Bruce was picking up Heather from school with her ski gear already loaded into the van. The night before last he and I fell asleep together in our bed, his long thighs against the backs of my legs. Three weeks ago we were all in Vermont, proudly watching him cross a stage to receive a Master of Fine Arts degree he'd spent two years earning.

Now this stranger is using slang for quadriplegic to refer to him, my complicated, crazy, exasperating, beloved husband, whom she has known for all of an hour. I feel myself turn into something cold and hard-scaled, a reptile. Last night another doctor told me there would be no sensation, and today there was plenty. They're guessing, is all. They could be wrong. I want to ask if it doesn't mean something that he can feel things, but I don't trust my voice, and I will not cry in front of this woman. Quad. Fuck her. All of this goes through my head in one second, the time it takes the man to draw a breath.

"I'm not so sure," he says slowly. "I think it might be a little early to say what will happen on this one." He twinkles his eyes at me.

Yeah, I think. Yeah.

4 pm

Dave is napping in my bed. I'm downstairs where the girls are sitting with David looking at cartoons, their faces pale and tired. Emily is snuggled up tight to David, but Heather sits a little distance away by herself. She lets me hold her.

"Heather," I say after a few minutes. "What happened?"

She knows what I mean. "He fell. There was, like, a little jump, and he went over, and his tips kind of scraped, and he went upside down and hit his head and flipped over on his back." She's talking fast, looking at her lap. David and Emily are staring at us. I keep my arm around her shoulders. "I skied over to him as fast as I could. He was bleeding where he cut his face, he had blood in his teeth. He said, 'Heather, I'm hurt bad. Don't touch me. Yell for help.' I screamed as loud as I could, and I could hear him, like, trying to say help, and I was crying so hard, and I said, 'Daddy, no, I can do it." And then this dude who was at the top of the rim skied over to us, and, yeah."

"Oh, Honey." There are tears falling down onto her hands.

"It was going to be our last run," she says, and looks up at me, mouth twisted. "Just if I would have said I didn't want to go again."

"Don't you do that. Heather, don't you do that. He didn't get hurt because you wanted to go again. He was lucky you were there. What if you hadn't been there? What if he would have been all by himself? Who would have yelled for help?" I'm whispering loud into her hair because she's sobbing into my shirt. Emily reaches out and touches her arm from the safety of David's lap.

After awhile I tell her that she doesn't know how it would have turned out if they had quit earlier. I tell her they both might have got hit by a truck if they were coming down from the pass at a different time. It isn't like, oh, everything would be normal. She can't know that, she shouldn't think that way, and it's not her fault. Just the opposite. She probably helped to save his life. And he'll tell her that himself, when we go up to see him in a little while, when Grandpa wakes up.

There are street people, disheveled and blank-eyed, stationed at every intersection, and there is no place to put the car. The girls are quiet in the back seat, taking everything in, I'm sure, while I drive and their Grandpa makes conversation. Walking them into Harborview feels like forcing them to go to a really scary movie and keep their eyes open wide the whole time. And then they have to see their dad.

I haven't told them about the screws in his head or the weight hanging from his skull. I'm betting they won't look carefully now, on their first visit since the accident. The NICU halls are wide, and the four of us can walk abreast through the double doors. I'm between the girls, holding their hands tight as we step into his room.

The bed isn't rotating. He's awake, making an effort.

"Hi, Daddy ..." Emily doesn't know what to do. She isn't quite tall enough to see his face, and he can't turn his head to look at her. She stands beside him and puts one hand on his shoulder.

"Here you are," he says to the ceiling. "Hi, Sweetie."

Heather moves up next to her sister. "Daddy." I can see her forcing herself not to cry, and I have to turn away.

"Hi, Heather," he says with a voice like a sigh. His hand moves out to touch her. "How are you, Honey?"

"I'm okay." She presses her lips together and swallows. "How are you?"

I take the chair from its spot by the window and set it next to the head of his bed. One at a time, the girls climb up, but it's all wrong. When they stand on it, they're too tall, and they have to bend awkwardly over the bed rail to look down on him. It's a little spooky. What if they mess up and fall on him? They don't. They just take short turns standing on the chair while Dave and I try to say something. Has he slept? Not really. What's the rotating bed like? Torture, it makes him sick. Can he eat? No, not yet. When will the surgery be? He has to have surgery to repair the fracture in his neck. He doesn't know when they're

23

going to do it. Maybe tomorrow, Friday, or they might wait until Monday. He wants it to be soon. He's immobilized, strapped to the bed staring at the ceiling, and he has to stay that way until it's over.

The scene is unreal; all of what we aren't saying clangs so loudly in this sterile space, with the electronic beeps of the monitors as counterpoint. Daddy! Get out of that bed and take us home! Bruce! I can't do this without you, please, get up and help me. We're scared, we're so scared, tell us it will be all right, sit up and say something, just sit up! Daddy ... but we can't. We just mill around the room for half an hour, speaking in bright, false tones, until it's dinner time, and Dave starts wondering about the hospital cafeteria, and it feels like we can decently leave.

We have our food. Somehow we've managed to order it and pay for it and find a table in a spacious room with open space soaring three stories above it. On a glass wall rising high at one end are etched quotations from people who must be former patients of this hospital, in several languages, translations provided.

> *"Imaka uma diyaar ihi inaan arintan weli ...* I'm not ready to accept this yet."

> *"Soy un luchador ...* I'm a fighter."

> *"Tzi can co mot bo oc minh man va doi ban tay khoe manh boi vi doi chan cha toi se khong con lamviec cho toi duoc nua ...* I needed to strengthen my mind and my hands because my legs weren't going to work for me anymore."

Dave asks Heather about the accident. She puts down her hamburger and tries to describe it. She's using her hands to make us see how it was, but we keep asking questions. Finally, she takes the receipt for our dinner and Dave's pen and makes a sketch.

"We were in a bowl." She draws a wide circle. "And I was up here." A small stick figure along the top, with skis on its feet and poles in its hands. "And he was here, and there was this little jump." A bigger figure, also on skis, going up a tiny hill inside the bowl she's drawn. "And he went over, like this." The figure is upside down, suspended.

"And hit the snow on his forehead, and flipped over." The stick figure skier is on his back. She sets the pen down.

I want to move my hand and cover up the drawing, it hurts so much to look at it, but I don't. If she can tell it, I have to let her.

At home that night, Emily and I are in Heather's room. It's not our practice to pray together, except for the occasional grace before an important meal. We're all three sitting on the bed, surrounded by her books and clothes and soccer paraphernalia. I take their hands and try to remember what Tony said in the ER ... and then I pray out loud for us to be strong, and for Daddy to rest and know that he is safe in God's hands, and for the nurses and doctors to be smart and gentle and skilled. The girls say "Amen," and then I put them in their separate rooms, kiss them, and go downstairs.

I don't sing them their songs because that's his routine.

I don't read to them because that is also his.

I just go down to the kitchen and call the hospital. The nurse promises to tell him we said goodnight. No, there is no change.

In the morning I wake up at seven o'clock and go right upstairs to call the hospital again; this time the nurse's voice is clear and urgent. He's gone down to surgery; they've been trying to reach me so I can speak to him beforehand. She'll transfer me to pre-op. If she loses the call, I should ring right back. Waiting, I just have time to realize that her urgency comes from the fact that this kind of surgery is dangerous. The possibility that he won't survive is all at once in front of me, small but real. As I'm seeing this, he comes on the line, sounding stronger and more himself than yesterday. He says that he's ready, and that he loves me, and that he knows we can get through whatever will happen next.

I'm pulled together by his words. They're like tendons I didn't know I had, suddenly humming with strength. I tell him yes to all that, and that I'll see him later. When I tell Dave that Bruce is already in surgery, he's elated. Over breakfast, he talks to the girls about how their dad will be a lot better after this.

Heather eyes him over her cereal bowl. "But will he be able to walk?"

"We'll have to wait and see. All the surgery does is make it so his neck is stable again, and no more damage can be done." He's eating

25

granola and looking over the front page of the newspaper as he talks, as if this were an ordinary morning.

Emily wants to know what he means. I tell her about the spinal cord, how it's like a telephone line inside her backbone connected to her brain, made out of nerve cells that carry messages up and down, to and from the rest of her body all day long. Daddy's cord is damaged, like, pretty squished but not cut all the way into two pieces. Whether he can walk will depend on which ones of the nerves got hurt. The surgery is so that the tiny bones he broke in there will be sturdy, and they won't move around and push against the cord anymore.

She gets this. "That's good, then. The surgery."

Yes. But I can see that Heather is not satisfied. I tell her that the nurse told me yesterday that it will take about six weeks to know which nerves were hurt the worst. I don't tell her that it's probably most of them. She might never have to hear that, except as a scary story about what almost happened. If she gets six more weeks to be hopeful, I'm sure as hell not going to take them away.

At my desk, I discover that Emily has been emailing everybody she can about the accident. I had no idea she knew how to connect with so many of our friends. My inbox is full of puzzled messages. Is this really true?? I reply to them briskly. Yes, it's really true, and actually a lot worse than Emily knows. I'm glad she thought to write to you. I'll try to keep you posted. I'm shattered but so far also okay—surrounded with love. Soon, it's time to go downtown. We leave the girls with David again, assuring them that other friends will be stopping in. I've been on the phone for an hour; everyone wants to know how to help. The thought of all these good people ready to be in motion on our behalf is better than food, or sleep, or anything since seeing Dave walk into the ER. Driving away from our house I feel, not happy, but not quite so afraid.

We stop first at church because it's right down the hill from Harborview, because I work there, because I want to go into the sanctuary, and because Bruce won't be back in his room for another hour. This is my first time facing old friends anywhere but at home or the hospital, and I don't do well. Inside the office, the secretaries are staring, and one woman is reaching to hug me. I turn my face away and put both hands up to fend her off. I know she means to comfort me, but if I'm going to let her, I'll have to go back into the sadness first. I don't want to, I can't afford to. She backs away, looking startled. I cover by introducing Dave to everyone, and then he and I go into the sanctuary. At the door, I fish into my bag and make a joke about how it's really a useful thing to have the keys to this place.

It's a white room in the shape of an enormous ellipse with tall, narrow columns of windowpanes along the long walls. It's plain in the way that congregational churches are, but there is plenty of golden, mellow wood, and a special quality of quiet. The girls were both baptized in this space. Bruce has stood many Sundays in his choir robe right there, in the very back row on the right, facing the congregation. I've stood many times right there, in the pulpit, delivering news from the youth group or, sometimes, prayers during worship. Dave and I walk to a pew in the center section and sit down side by side without saying anything. I'm so glad to be here. I'm making a silent plea for strength when the door at the front opens, and one of the custodians comes in with a big vacuum. I quirk my mouth at Dave, who shrugs, and we leave.

Bruce's room is crowded with doctors again. He's in the bed, and now it's a regular white hospital bed with rails on either side. His neck is in a blue and white brace, and under his head is a blue piece of foam shaped like an egg crate. He's turned halfway onto one side with pillows tucked behind his back and legs. Everyone moves aside to let me say hello, but they don't leave, so I make it quick. He's pale and drowsy, and there are IV needles stuck into the backs of both his hands, their lines leading to a cart hung with plastic bags. A slender tube snakes out of one nostril and leads to the same cart; its bag is full of cream-colored liquid.

"You made it."

"I guess."

He's drugged, hardly even awake. The man standing just in front of me introduces himself as the surgeon. Dr. West. I see Dave get his sheet of paper out of the front of his jacket and start making notes. Dr. West is short, bald and very, very alert. He's giving us a recap of the procedure they just did, watching me all the time. They took a piece of bone out of Bruce's hip and used it to stabilize the vertebrae. The injury was at the sixth cervical vertebrae, and now the fifth, sixth, and seventh are fused together, with a titanium pin holding them steady while the piece of hip bone grows into place. It's all solid, clean.

The operation went well; now we'll have to wait to see what remains of the cord. Dave is asking questions. How did they get into his neck? Through the front. There's an inch-and-a-half long incision under a bandage near his Adam's apple, now covered by the neck brace. Why not go in through the back? I don't listen. I don't care. It's done, and he's here, alive. When he wakes up all the way, we'll talk, and I'll finally be sure he's still himself. Dr. West is doing a neurological exam, the very same one Dr. Ratty Hair did yesterday. We watch as he taps and pushes and pricks all the body parts, Bruce barely conscious but trying to perform. When it's finished, we leave so he can sleep.

We're sitting on one of the couches in the intensive care lounge, near the chairs where Dave and I got our orientation on the first night. The room is spacious and bright, with small clusters of people huddled together here and there. My friends are here, holding my hands and talking to Dave. I'm trying to be in the conversation, but I keep crying, undone by their kindness, by the hope that it might still turn out well, and by exhaustion. Jocelyn reminds me that this is Bad Moms Weekend.

Dave looks interested. I tell him that there's a group of a dozen or so women from Plymouth who go off together for a weekend every year. We rent a house on Whidbey Island and watch Jane Austen movies and eat a lot of chocolate. We drink wine and stay up late and have breakfast in the hot tub … we're Bad Moms, and Jocelyn's the instigator. I look at her.

"I think I'll pass this year," I say.

"Becky's not coming either. She says it's supposed to be Moms Gone Bad, not Friends Gone Bad."

This makes me cry again, which everyone cheerfully ignores.

Down the hall, halfway between the ER and NICU, there is a little espresso bar with couches and coffee tables. Sitting on high stools just outside it, I use Dave's cell phone to call home, then he uses it to call Mim, who has been Bruce's stepmother for twenty-five years. I tell him what a latte is and let him buy me one. He says that he'll probably go home on Sunday. Okay. Do we need any money? I say I don't think so. I don't say that I'm glad to be asked, but I am.

Six months ago, when Bruce was in the final push to finish his MFA program, he cashed out some stock options and set up an account to take care of our money flow while he stopped consulting. The plan was

28

for him to get the degree, then go back to doing a little technical work while he mostly practiced art. I know there's plenty of money left in that account, and I tell Dave all this—the first time, as far as I know, that he's had any idea about how our personal finances work. The only thing I'm not completely sure of is how to get the cash into our checking account, but I'm not worried. He thinks this over, then writes me a check just in case. It's another in a series of unreal moments. Dave is generous, willing to help, and has the means to do it. He's also, I can see, a little bemused to learn that his ski-bum, artist, eccentric oldest son has put together enough cash to take care of his family, even in this crisis. I take the check, with the understanding that I'll pay him back when I get the details figured out.

That night I'm alone at the hospital, hanging around in NICU when Craig stops by. Craig's an art-guy, a smooth, well-dressed character with a bizarre sense of humor; he just graduated with Bruce and he's the very first person I emailed about the accident. He's lovely. He's brought Bruce a fistful of email messages from their mutual friends at Vermont College, and he's reading these out loud with plenty of editorial comment and inside jokes about the writers, most of whom I know only by name. Bruce is enjoying it, smiling above his stiff neck brace and rolling his eyes. Craig touches him gently, leaning over the bed rail as calm and casual as if he were sitting on a couch chatting over drinks. He wants to know what Bruce did today.

"I brushed my teeth."

Raised eyebrows, mouth turned down ironically. "Very impressive! Major surgery to personal hygiene, all in the same day!"

"Fuck you."

"If you could, pal … no, seriously, that's excellent. Tomorrow you'll be washing your own socks, or something."

"Right. I'll make it a performance piece."

Craig has a perfect smile, generous and open. He flashes it at Bruce, then looks around. "There's a hell of a lot of white space in here, man. You could do some very cool projections." Video projection is Bruce's current art passion; it involves sending images through a laptop computer hooked to a video projector. He likes to do it on public spaces, like the sides of buildings. It's guerrilla art.

Craig leaves after promising to be back soon and often, and then the nurse named Karen brings in a little tray with a plastic cup of butterscotch pudding. I open this and give him a few bites.

"You're eating," I say. "Your first meal." I look at the pudding. "Pretty sad."

"And you're feeding it to me." His eyes are on me for a second too long. Does he want to talk about his hands? Do his hands work? Watching the doctors do their neurological tests, I couldn't quite tell. The fingers all moved in the usual way, but maybe they aren't strong. Is that what the ER doctor meant when he was talking about "hand function," that Bruce's hands would be weak? I have no idea. My whole knowledge about the spinal cord is contained in the two-minute lecture I gave to Emily at breakfast. About that time, Karen the nurse leaves her chair by the monitor, and we are actually alone. He wastes no time.

"So what are they saying?"

"They aren't sure." I'm not going to tell him about that ER meeting.

"Will I walk?"

"Maybe." I say it very quietly.

He sighs.

"They say it will take about six weeks to know what you've got left."

"Jesus."

"I know." I lean close to his ear and whisper. "I haven't said it, but this really sucks."

I feel his hand on my back. "Yeah," he says. "But here we are."

We've been together for eighteen years. Some things don't take a lot of words.

When the spinal cord is partially damaged, the injury is referred to as incomplete and the person has limited sensation and movement in the lower body. The proportion of people with incomplete injuries, who sometimes recover substantially, is on the increase and, in the United States, now stands at some 60 percent, probably thanks to improving post-injury care.

Luba Vikhanski

```
Pulmonary:
Progressive inability
to clear secretions
despite frequent
assisting with quad
coughing. Oxygen
saturation drop to
low 80s requiring
treatment with 100%
oxygen and NT
suctioning.
```

$$\boxed{\text{THREE}}$$

Day 3

Heather has a soccer game this morning at an indoor arena in Redmond, a twenty-minute drive from our house. I send Emily to her friend Melissa's for the day, then suddenly I'm standing with Dave inside Arena Sports Center in my long wool coat, hands in my pockets, shivering under harsh lights and trying not to flinch at the sound of the soccer ball slamming into the sideboards. There are two soccer fields and a hockey rink in here; it's always chilly and very loud. Heather is playing right forward. Her main advantage over the opposition is speed; she has Bruce's long legs and athleticism, and it's good to see her racing full out.

I tell her coach about the accident. His face makes what has become a familiar look: eyebrows pulled in hard, lips drawn open in a gasp, then released, oh, no. Oh, yes. Heather scores one, two, three goals in this game. Afterward I arrange for her to spend the day with a friend while her grandpa and I go to the hospital. Someone will bring her up to meet us later; she asks me not to tell Dad about the hat trick, and I promise I won't.

I'm not as frightened on the way into Harborview as I was yesterday. The operation is done, last night Bruce and I managed to exchange a couple of private sentences, the injury might not be as bad as they originally said, and I just went to a soccer game. Okay. In his room, though, something is wrong. He's got a mask over part of his face, a blue plastic cone that covers his nose and mouth, and it's blowing mist on him. He pulls it away to croak hello at us, then pushes it right back.

The nurse—a young guy with a solid build and intelligent gray eyes—explains that Bruce has been having some trouble breathing. He points me toward one of the computer monitors perched on a shelf behind the bed. It's small, with just one display, a green number that reads 95, then 96, then 95 as we watch. The nurse's name is Larry. He tells us the number is a measurement of Bruce's oxygen saturation—his "SAT." He says that 95 is okay, but they're watching it because it's been falling below 90. He adjusts the mask over Bruce's face as he speaks, then gives a little shake to a thick blue accordion tube that leads from the mask to a green tank mounted behind the bed.

Bruce's eyes are frightened. He's pale and pinched, looking much sicker than when I left him last night. I smile at him, trying to project confidence.

"We went to Heather's game."

He tips the mask away, rasps, "How'd she do?" then pulls it quickly back.

"They won," I say. "She wants to tell you about it herself."

He nods ever-so-slightly and closes his eyes. I let him rest and try to glean information from Larry. No, Bruce didn't get much sleep last night. The medication they gave him wasn't helpful; they're going to try a different drug tonight. Does he need anything? Uh, maybe some lip balm. As we're talking, I'm watching the green number, and sure enough, it drops to 93, 92, at which point Larry walks over and touches the oxygen mask.

"Bruce," he says, enunciating. "How are you doing?"

Suddenly my husband is choking. He says in a whisper, "I don't know ..."

"I'm going to get a respiratory therapist in here to work with you." Larry's voice is all business. He picks up a phone, speaks for five seconds, then turns to me, explaining that it's very common for high spinal cord injuries to cause respiratory problems. I feel the word, ventilator, rising up like a black shadow just behind me. Dave is in my field of vision somewhere to the side, looking out the window. He walks up and takes over the conversation while I struggle to regulate my own breathing.

After a few minutes, a small man with a crew cut and a bristly salt-and-pepper mustache strides into the room. His presence changes the atmosphere instantly. He has the intensity and physique of a gymnast about to perform: controlled, relaxed, and confident. He introduces himself to Bruce.

"Hi, I'm Rich Garcia. I'm a respiratory therapist. I'm going to see if I can help you get your lungs working."

Bruce says his own name in a whisper, one hand clinging to the oxygen mask. Rich takes the mask from him and sets it aside. He's working so smoothly and gently, and he seems so familiar and at ease with this scene, that I almost relax.

He listens with the stethoscope, then produces an odd-looking contraption made of molded plastic. It's about eight inches high, with a handle on one side, a graded tube in the center, and a flat piece sticking out on the other side. It has a flexible tube attached to its base, at the end of which is a white spout. He sets the spout between Bruce's lips. Sucking on this thing, Rich explains, will loosen the gunk that's collected in Bruce's lungs. His difficulty breathing is nothing to be nervous about, just a result of having been flat on his back for a few days, as well as having a weak cough. The tube is called an incentive spirometer. Using it will really help. Is Bruce willing to try?

Of course. He takes the spout between his teeth and sucks with all his strength. Inside the flat part, a tiny yellow disc lifts into an area I see is marked with a frowning face. Rich puts a hand on Bruce's chest to stop him. He explains, pointing, that the idea is to keep this disc hovering here, where the smiley face is. Too hard a draw will lift it too high; too weak a draw will not get it there. Okay, try again. Bruce watches the disc intently as he pulls. Rich is murmuring encouragement, and the little disc stays right in the center of the stupid smiley face. Inside the graded tube, another yellow disc, this one shaped like a giant pill, is rising straight up. Now both Rich and Larry are saying. "Good! Keep going, that's great, a little more ... good, fantastic!"

Bruce lets the spout fall out of his mouth, and then, for the first time, I hear him try to cough. It's pitiful. His face is drawn with effort, and nothing is happening. Rich gives him back the oxygen mask while he describes what's next. It's called a quad-cough, and it's really just the Heimlich Maneuver. Rich is going to put both his hands here, just on Bruce's diaphragm, and together they're going to get that stuff out of his lungs. He'll push, and Bruce will cough as hard as he possibly can, and together they'll get it done. He turns to me.

"Some people don't like to watch this."

I say that if Bruce can do it, I guess I can stand to see it. Rich smiles at me. Right answer. It doesn't look like the Heimlich Maneuver. It looks like violence. He puts the heel of one hand up under Bruce's rib cage and the heel of the other hand on top of that. He braces himself, feet apart, knees flexed, and they do a series of three breaths. When Bruce is breathing out, Rich is pushing on his diaphragm, progressively harder, until, on the third breath, he shoves his hands with all his strength into that diaphragm, using the muscles of his back and legs to make it work. It does. The sound of thick phlegm coming up is disgusting, and also wonderful. Larry hands Bruce a long, clear plastic wand, which turns out to be attached to a vacuum pump. Bruce slips it into his mouth, and then I do turn away, not to see the gunk sliding safely out of him.

Everyone pauses. "Think you can do that again?" says Rich. The quad-cough is with us. It becomes the chief activity for the rest of the day. Same routine every time: oxygen SATs drop, nurse pages a respiratory therapist, Bruce sucks on the spirometer, hands on the belly, one, two, shove. Nasty, filthy retching sounds, followed by the vacuumed wetness, followed by doing it all again, until Bruce is limp and wan on his blue egg-crate pillow, and able to breathe for awhile.

In the meantime, a steady stream of people tiptoes in to say hello to him and offer whatever help they can think of to me. Sue has brought strawberries and bottled water, cheese and crackers. There are magazines, books, tapes, flowers, cards, and a stuffed animal. Larry is watching to make sure there aren't too many people in the room at once; when it gets overwhelming, he sends us all out—and Rich is right. No one really wants to be present for the quad-cough. Around dinner time, the girls show up. They've spent the day with their friends, and this is their first chance to see him since the surgery. They're expecting him to be better. They're expecting him to be sitting up in bed, like in the movies, and no one has prepared them.

He looks terrible. The accident was Wednesday afternoon. It's Saturday night, and. he's been sleeping in one-hour snatches for all that time. He's had major surgery, he can't move, can't sit up, can't roll over, can't even lift his head off the egg crate. He can hardly breathe, but here are the girls, needing their dad. This bed is at least better than the rotating one. It can be lowered so that his face is near theirs … this also means they get a close view of the nose tube, the oxygen mask, the IV needles, his barely-conscious eyes. Emily is brave and game, determined to be a good daughter. She tells him a little about being with Melissa all day.

He tries. He only has a whisper, but he asks how she is, tells her thanks for coming to see him. She takes this as permission to get away, and does, out into the hall with Dave. He asks Heather about her soccer game, and she tells him she got three goals.

"The hat trick. I'm proud of you."

"Yeah."

There is nothing to say, except I love you, and I'll come back soon, and I hope you're feeling better. It is not allowed to say, I can't stand this another second. It is not permitted to ask why this happened. No one has told either of them these rules; I only have enough energy to see what is happening, not enough to figure out what it means or whether I ought to try to change it.

Day 4

When we wake up in the morning there is no hot water. I don't know what's wrong; there seems to be a small leak because the floor around the heater is damp. Ten days ago, a week before the accident, we had a strong-but-deep earthquake. It seemed not to have done any damage at the time, but maybe something went wrong in the plumbing. Who knows. I give Dave some phone numbers of friends who live nearby. One of them knows a plumbing contractor. Between them, they arrange to get us a new hot water tank installed the next day. All of this is taken care of while I go to the neighbor's house and ask if Dave and I can use her shower. I have to tell her about the accident, the reason Dave is here, the reason Bruce is not. I sit there numbly while she makes the usual response: shocked face, hands touching mine, anything I can do ... thanks, just your shower for now.

We decide to take Emily back to Melissa's for the day. She wants to be with them, and they want to have her, so I'm not going to argue. Heather will come with us to the early church service, then go off with other friends until the evening. Dave is leaving for Minnesota just after lunch; some church friends will come by the hospital to take him to the airport. The early church service starts at nine. We sit in the front, close to the door, Heather on one side of me and Dave on the other. There is a moment in the service when Tony and Kris stand at the front of the sanctuary, and people are invited to come forward and ask for private prayers. This is risky business for us liberal Christian types; it looks like an altar call. We tend to be service-oriented, politically active, and intellectual. We don't do prayer especially well, and I've been part of the move to figure out how to change this. Now I don't want to walk up to Tony and have him put a hand on my shoulder because I know it will be shattering.

Heather surprises me by standing up and moving to the back of the little line that has formed in front of Kris. Kris looks over at me over her head, her eyes speaking so clearly I can almost hear her voice. Oh, God, how can I do this? Kris has sons the same ages as our girls. Their family skis together all the time. Heather stands before her and says something, then Kris closes her eyes and puts her hands on Heather's two shoulders. The two of them bow their heads, and I get up and go to Tony's line. I stand there crying while he whispers urgently. He leans over and hugs me, says, "We're with you."

After the service, the three of us walk across the street to the downtown Hilton. At the very top, with a grand view of Puget Sound and the Olympic Mountains, is a four-star restaurant. We sit in soft leather chairs at a linen-draped table for an hour, watching the ferries run back and forth between downtown and the islands while we slowly eat expensive, delicious food. I have a latte that seems to be made with pure cream. I linger over it, taking great pleasure in watching Heather stuff herself with pancakes and bacon. We're removed from the horror, lifted right out of it for this one hour, surrounded by crystal and light. Every sense is indulged. Then we take the elevator back down to the street, and I deliver Heather to the people in the church who'll be taking care of her. Dave and I drive up to the hospital, park the car, and go back in. He's got his suitcase because he's flying back to Minnesota this afternoon.

Larry is working again today. He meets us outside the room and says that last night was pretty hard; they had to do the quad-cough almost every hour, so Bruce is really tired and won't be up to much by way of visitors. Okay. That sucks. Dave and I go in very quietly, but he isn't asleep. The skin on his face is slack and has almost no color. I kiss him and he whispers, "Bad night."
"I heard." I touch his hair, the only part of him that looks normal.
"We'll keep it quiet today."
"It doesn't matter. Where are the girls?"
"Emily's at Melissa's, Heather's with Victoria. They'll be here later."
"How are you?"
"A mess, basically. But I can sleep." I'm touched that he asks me, and suddenly guilty because I can not only sleep, I can walk the hell out of here anytime I want. I tell him about the water heater, about the church service, about the breakfast at the top of the Hilton.

"Don't talk about food."

"Are they giving you anything?"

"They want to be sure I can swallow. Fuck, I can't even breathe."

Sure enough, the green numbers on the small monitor are saying 91, 92, 91 … when it says 90, a little alarm begins to beep, and Larry is right there. He adjusts the oxygen mask, checks the sensor attached to Bruce's right index finger, and calls for a respiratory therapist. This time it isn't Rich, but a kind-faced woman who introduces herself as Karen and goes right to work. The incentive spirometer comes out, and I realize what it reminds me of. It's a bong—a water pipe—the thing people used to smoke pot with. There is even the familiar sound of hard sucking, and the little cough afterwards. While Bruce is using it, the phone rings at Larry's workstation, and he tells me I have a call at the desk.

It's Jon Huseby, the man who was with Bruce and Heather at the scene of the accident. He tells me who he is and asks how it's going; he says he's a doctor. This news gives me an odd sensation inside, like a tiny bell has been rung somewhere behind my rib cage. A doctor? The man who came when Heather screamed was a doctor? I tell him about the breathing troubles, and he responds with very pointed questions. He seems to know everything about this, and when I comment on that, he says that he's the chief of pulmonary intensive care at Providence, a hospital just up the street from Harborview. Again, the little ting inside.

"Listen," he says. "I see this stuff all the time, these injuries, and I don't—something about your husband, I just—I never do this, but this morning I talked about him at my church."

He pauses. I have time to say thank you, and then he goes on.

"It's just—your husband, you have to imagine it. He was lying in the snow, and he knew what had happened. He knew he'd broken his neck, and what it meant. He couldn't feel anything … and he was worried about your daughter. I just—it was—he just got to me. And I—I see this stuff every day, but—"

"It's okay," I say, trying to control my voice. "I know what you mean. You'd have to know them. I'd be surprised if it was any other way. But thanks so much for saying that. I'm really glad you were there."

He sighs. "I'm glad I was, too. It was incredible. I have a ten-year-old daughter myself, and I just—" he cuts himself off, and we are both silent. Finally, he goes on. "Listen, if you need to talk with anyone, if you think they're telling you stuff that doesn't make sense, call me." He gives me his pager number, which I write on my hand. I tell him more about the breathing problems, and he says not to worry, that it sounds like the respiratory therapists are doing exactly what they ought to be, and that these problems are probably temporary.

"Probably?"

"Spinal injuries are hard to predict, but at your husband's level they don't usually involve long-term respiratory issues." He tells me again not to worry. Right.

Back in the room, the RT is lunging at Bruce's chest with full strength while Dave sits calmly in the chair by the window, his packed suitcase at his side. We watch in silence as Bruce manages, with huge effort, a tiny, delicate cough. I cringe at the sound of thick mucus coming up. He clears his throat like an old, old man, and even worse is the wet rattle of the vacuum wand that follows. The RT makes some notes on her chart and promises to come back and check on him in an hour. All of us thank her, and then it's time for Dave to say goodbye. He tells us both that he'll be back out soon, and to hang in there. I walk him to the hospital front doors where some friends are waiting to give him a ride. The only surprise is how bereft I feel, watching the car with him inside drive up Ninth Avenue.

By the time I get back upstairs, a respiratory therapist is working on Bruce again. He tries so hard to cooperate and cough, but even I can see that it isn't working. Watching, I find myself breathing and making a little cough on his cue. I put my hand on myself where the therapist is touching him; my diaphragm muscles move effortlessly under my fingers. His muscles are apparently not doing anything. They'll have to run a tube down into his lungs and suction out whatever is in there. They ask me to leave the room while they do it, and this is how I know it must be painful. I go out and sit on the floor of the hallway, my back against the wall of his room, my knees up against my chest. Twenty minutes go by. The respiratory therapist comes out, closes the door behind her, and walks off up the hall. A nurse appears and I stand up. She closes his door and walks me away from it.

"I'm going to suggest that he not have visitors now. He's asking for you, but what he really needs is rest, and I think you do, too. You should go home."

She has a good face, lined and intelligent, and her eyes are all kindness. I shake my head. "If he's asking for me, I should stay here."

"No. He has to rest."

I realize this is a call she gets to make, that I can't go in there unless she lets me, and that she isn't going to let me. I ask her about the breathing problems. "Is this how it usually goes?"

She shrugs. "Every case is different. Some people sail through this acute phase, some people have a harder time." She's walking me out of the ward as we talk. We go through one set of double doors and are almost to the entrance to the lounge. I stop.

"But the trouble is from the surgery, right? Not from the injury?" This is my way of asking her if it is temporary. If he can't breathe properly because of the surgery, then he'll recover from that, and it will be okay. If he can't breathe from the injury, he could be like this forever. She doesn't read this into my question.

"Well, it could be either, really."

For the first time in my life, I feel faint. She doesn't notice, though, because she's already saying goodbye, patting my shoulder and telling me to go home and get some rest. She walks away, and I lean against the wall to keep from falling. I sink down and put my head between my knees until there are no black spots in my vision, and then I go into the lounge where families and friends of people in intensive care are sitting around in little groups. They're holding their heads in their hands, leaning into each other, staring out the windows, talking in low voices, crying, waiting.

I don't know what to do now.

After a little while, I decide to go and find the chapel. This hospital must have some kind of chapel, and it might be good to go in there. I'm picking up the phone at the self-help information desk when my boss and her husband appear at my side. She is Edith, director of the school where I've taught math for the last ten years. She's a brilliant person, warm, original, and always flustered—one of those people who seems not quite made for this time and place, not quite able to comprehend how things actually work. She dresses in flowing clothes and Birkenstocks, and she's never cut her hair in her life. I'm so glad to see her. Her husband, Don, is a medical doctor who teaches and does research. She takes both my hands and I tell them what's been going on. Don is looking at me carefully.

"Have you eaten anything today?"

"This morning." People keep asking me this, and I keep telling them I'm eating, which I am, whenever I'm near food. It must not be very often. I must look hungry. Don suggests that we go down to the cafeteria and get some soup or whatever they have. For the next hour, the two of them feed me and talk with me. She says that I shouldn't worry about my classes; they have it all arranged to cover me as long as I need them to. I thank her. Inside, I am almost smiling at the idea of worrying about my classes. Don tells me that Bruce is in spinal shock, which means that the tissues around his cord are swollen from the trauma. It's like a bruise anywhere on the body. Things swell, and then the swelling goes down. The swelling can interfere with signals moving through the cord, even if the cord isn't damaged.

"Really," he says. "It's way too early to know what you're looking at, long term."

"How long does it take for the swelling to go down?"

"Six weeks. About six weeks, then you'll have a better idea what he's got left." Don has a bristly gray beard and sharp brown eyes. He's watching me closely as we talk. Whenever I stop eating, his eyes go to the bowl of lentil soup, and he doesn't say anything until I take another bite. I ask him about the breathing. I still want someone to say it went bad because of the surgery. This time I don't mask the question, and he reassures me, just as the doctor from the mountain did earlier. We unload our trays, and then they take me to a bookstore so I can help them buy some books for Bruce. While we're there, I choose for myself a small, blank-paged journal. Buying it feels like the bravest thing I have ever done—a promise to keep a record of what happens, no matter how this all turns out.

Late that afternoon, I give up and go home. I'm sitting up in our bed. My sister has come over to help me figure out what to do next. Sue is going to help me. It's bizarre. All our lives, I've been the one who helps Sue. Now she's got a pencil and paper and she's taking notes from the family calendar because I can't seem to get control of the information in my head. Holding my pillow against my stomach, I start saying random things that I know aren't on the calendar.

"I have to drive Emily's carpool to school every day."

"Okay, what time is that?"

"We leave at 8:40. Heather catches her bus at 7:40, so it works. What else? The soccer season starts this week. They have practices, I can't remember when. And games." She makes a note. "They have choir on Wednesday nights."

She's peering at the calendar. "It says there's a soccer practice on Thursday. Is that for both of 'em?"

I glance at the calendar. It hurts me. It's marked up in our four separate handwritings. Emily has used her gold gel-pen to note the dog's birthday. In my writing is a reminder that the children's choir sang on March 4th. Bruce has scribbled in an appointment next week with the guy who manages our finances. The days leading up to last Wednesday are right there, and I can't stand to look at them, to think of our family moving carelessly, innocently toward this moment. I turn away. Focus.

"I think that's Heather's practice. I'll have to call somebody and find out where it is." Sue makes another note. I tell her about the music lessons. Piano, cello. Two different teachers in two different neighborhoods, both on Tuesday afternoon. She writes it down.

"What else?"

"I don't know. The soccer. I'll have to find the paperwork, or call them, or something." She makes another note and then waits. I have my knees drawn up, both arms wrapped around my pillow. She's at the edge of the bed with one leg curled underneath her. Always between me and Sue is an odd, cool space. Even now, when my insides are all in shreds and I'm unable to look at my own calendar, I can feel myself holding her at some kind of distance, and I can feel her searching carefully for the boundaries she shouldn't cross. She doesn't touch me. She doesn't suggest that she'd be glad to stay with me now that Bruce's dad is gone. She's here, though, trying her best to be useful without getting in my way. That's how it's been with us forever, since I was her fifteen-year-old idol and she was an eight-year-old suddenly not welcome in my room anymore.

Before I go back to the hospital that night, I get both girls safely home. The three of us have dinner, a meal of lasagna and salad with brownies for dessert. This is from Lisa, my carpool mom friend; she's already organized dinners for us for the next two weeks. In the morning, I'll get up with the girls, see Heather off to her bus, drive Emily and two other kids up to school, then go to the hospital. While I'm there, another friend will come over here and stay so the men Dave hired can install our new water heater. I'm describing all this to them as we eat. I tell them that what they have to do now is just what they've always done: go to school, live their lives, be kids. I'll be here every day when they get up, and every day when they come from school, I promise. I'll make sure they get to all the places they usually go. They look at me seriously.

"When is Daddy coming home?"

I haven't wanted to answer this question. "A long time. Maybe twelve weeks."

They stop eating. I see them calculating, and I let them. "June?"

"He can't stay in the hospital until June." Heather's voice is small. "Mama!"

I don't want them to be crying. I don't want to be crying. I'm standing up, doing the mother thing, stroking their hair and making my noises, like when they're sick or having a bad dream. The dog is on his feet, pushing his way in between us the way he always does when we're hugging. Over their heads, I'm looking numbly around the kitchen. Mail all over the countertop. Flowers someone sent next to the sink. Photos on the refrigerator: Bruce and Heather and our old friend, John, in Virginia; they look brisk and happy, dressed for cold weather with a waterfall in the background. The picture isn't yet three weeks old.

"Why is this happening?"

"I don't know. There isn't a reason. Shhhhhh."

After awhile we put the food away; there is way too much lasagna. I'm not going back to the hospital tonight. I'm going to load the dishwasher and wash some clothes for the girls. I'm going to send some email and thank the people who've been taking care of them, and the people who drove up to the mountains to rescue our car, and the people who helped Dave figure out the water heater problem. I spend some time on the phone working out the soccer schedule. Every conversation requires me to repeat the latest news about Bruce. People ask how he is, and I say he can't breathe well, hasn't slept in four days. I'm talking with my friend Sue, who was with me at the hospital the first night. She's volunteered to be here tomorrow when the workmen come. She says she can't just sit here, do I need anything done? I'm standing in front of my open refrigerator. It's a mess. I say without planning to that she can clean my fridge.

"Okay. I can do that."

I've been to her house. Sue has the kind of house where a stray piece of paper stands out like a yard sign. Her drawers, closets, garage, and basement are all meticulously ordered. Her sewing room is legendary among our friends; dozens of spools of thread and yarn are arranged by color. In her house, dust and cobwebs simply do not exist. I tell her I'm sure she can handle my fridge. "I won't even bother being embarrassed about it."

"Good."

"Yeah. It's very freeing, this hospital thing." I'm trying to be light, but my voice is kind of bitter. "I can get away with all kinds of stuff."

"You go right ahead, Kate. Get away with everything you can."

"Sure. Next I'll have some of you come over and clean my garage."

"We'd do that. That would be no problem."

"Have you seen my garage?"

"It would be no problem. Go to sleep. I'll be over in the morning."

"I'll be gone before you get here, but the door will be unlocked."

I call the hospital. The nurse tells me that they got him up in a wheelchair for a little while today, and that it went well. She says that he had some company earlier, and that he's resting right now. I ask her to tell him goodnight for me. I say she should call if he needs me for anything at all, and she tells me to get some rest. I climb alone into our bed and fall asleep quickly, before I have time to feel anything.

Hope is a potentially important coping strategy for both the person and the family with spinal cord injury ...

Dr. Wise Young

```
Assessment:
Respiratory status of
a significant medical
concern at this time.
His cough is
inadequate at this
time to protect his
airway; not ready to
begin PO [food by
mouth]...
```

FOUR

Day 5: 7:40 am

Before Heather leaves for school, I take her aside and give her an old ID card with a photo of her healthy, smiling dad. I tell her to keep it with her and hold on to it when she gets scared. She tucks it into her backpack, accepts a quick hug, and marches off to get her bus. Watching her turn the corner by the juniper hedge, I'm afraid of her stoicism, relieved that she's able to manage herself, and ashamed of my relief. I go upstairs to wake up Emily and find her sitting up in her bed with bluish circles around her eyes. She says she woke up in the night again.

"What time?"

"I don't know." This is an old dance. She knows I get anxious about her not sleeping, so she tries to minimize the hours she spends sleepless in her room.

"Approximately," I say, giving her a you-can-tell-me-I-won't-be-mad look.

"I think I woke up at four." I know this means two-thirty.

"When did you go back to sleep?"

"Six. About six." This means she didn't go back to sleep. I feel guilty for my own sleeping, guilty that she thinks she can't disturb me, guilty that part of me is glad she didn't. She looks fragile, and when I give her a picture of Bruce, she cries hard and I join her. An hour later, I'm driving her up to the school where she's a seventh-grader and I'm the high school math department, on leave until further notice.

Hillside Student Community is a funky, homemade place with five or six dozen students and a faculty of family members plus a few select outsiders, of which I am one. The buildings are hidden in a forested, suburban neighborhood of showy houses. Here and there, boats are parked in roomy driveways next to expensive cars. I've always loved the contrast; driving into Hillside is like finding a paper kite shop fancifully tucked in next door to Boeing. Getting out of the Prius, I take Emily's hand, and together we walk quickly past the kids milling around the driveway and into the main classroom building. She started here as a sixth-grader last year and liked it fine, but this year she's had trouble connecting with any of her classmates.

In spite of that, I'm glad she's here now, where the adults at least know her well and can be trusted to take care of her. Heather has the opposite situation. She's tight with her friends, but the adults at her public school can't possibly look out for her in the same way these people will shelter Emily. One of my students is coming toward us with her arms outstretched, and I walk past her with my head down, one elbow up as if to fend off a punch. I can't bear sympathy. I can hardly hold myself together as it is. I take Emily into her classroom at the back of the building and hug her hard. Her teacher gives me a look that says, I'm so sorry. I nod at her and almost run back to my car.

At the hospital, nothing has changed, unless it's for the worse. Another rough night, worse than the one before. Respiratory therapists here hour after hour, all night long. His eyes are red-rimmed and lightless. I sit beside the bed and take out my new journal. Blank page. I start with date and time, and then:

"Beside me is the bed with its head angled up and its pedals and levers. Hill-Rom is the maker. In the corner above him a color monitor recording the inside struggles. The narrow tube going into his nose is attached with white tape. Behind his wheeled bed is an upright cart thing made of aluminum rails and pipes. It holds the hissing equipment to which nine fat cords are attached: four black, two green, one yellow, and two white. He makes the nasty cough-up sound, suctions out the stuff, then lets his hands lie. He's so tired. He's just so tired."

This entry is interrupted twice. The first time, he needs someone to adjust the hoses to his oxygen tank. The mist has collected in one of the curves, and it makes a rattling sound until his nurse comes to give it a shake. I stand up and watch carefully so I'll be able to do this for him myself. The second time, he needs antacid and eye drops. Karen dumps some antacid into his feed bag: I make a note in the journal to get Visine. And this is the way the morning goes by. I write a few phrases, try to watch and learn, and offer help where I can. He lies very still, trying to breathe, not sleeping. How could he sleep? He has a hose going into his nose and down into his stomach. He has another one going into his penis all the way to his bladder; there's a circular plastic bag hanging from the side of his bed two feet from my knees, slowly filling with pale amber liquid. He has an IV needle stuck into the back of his right hand, and he's wearing a big collar made of white plastic that doesn't look comfortable.

At home, he always went to sleep with one pillow underneath his head and another one on top of it. He liked to have only a sheet over him. He liked to sleep on his side with a blanket between his knees. I'm anxious because I'm thinking that he can't even start to get better until he can rest and eat, but he can't rest and eat until he starts to get better. I make an effort to calm myself down, to project confidence at him. It won't help him to have me sitting here despairing and terrified. Breathe. Okay.

Around one o'clock a woman shows up and asks to talk with me. Her name is Norma; she's a social worker and her job today is to help me figure out how the hospital is going to get paid. She's been in touch with Premera Blue Cross; he has good coverage for everything except rehab. They'll pay for the helicopter ride, the ER services, the surgery, intensive care, anything that isn't rehabilitation. For rehab, they'll give him thirty days.

"The doctor said he'd need two or three months."

She nods, not unkindly. "I know. And it costs $1,500 a day. Most policies don't have nearly enough coverage. Will he be doing rehab here at Harborview?"

"Is there an option?"

"It's here or the UW. No one else has the right equipment or physical therapists for his kind of injury. Where do you guys live?"

"Bellevue. It's probably easier to get here from our house." Getting to the University of Washington usually means snarled traffic for about four different reasons. It's not something I'd want to have to do a couple of times a day if I didn't have to.

"The programs are the same. Harborview and the UW are part of the same organization. They even share staff, so it wouldn't make any difference which one he went to."

"Then I guess he'll stay here." And in this casual way, having consulted no one and explored no other options, I am led to make a decision that I don't even know is important.

She asks if I've seen the rehab floor yet, and when I tell her no, she suggests we go up right now. "It's in this same part of the hospital, two floors directly overhead." She wants to hear about our kids. "Boys or girls?"

"Girls." We're on the elevator heading up to the fourth floor. "They're ten and twelve."

"Hard on them."

I just lift my eyebrows. What does she think I should say? If it were any harder on them, they'd be clawing their own faces off, okay? We step into a wide hall and turn left, toward 4-West, the inpatient rehab unit at Harborview. It's painted pink, with lavender trim. There is a nurse's station with a u-shaped hallway around it; this is lined with doors opening to what must be the patients' rooms. Parked outside nearly every door is a wheelchair, and sometimes other wheeled equipment I don't recognize. A black man dressed in striped hospital pajamas strolls by. He's wearing a blue crash helmet and he looks stoned. Norma sees me glance at him.

"This is rehab for all the neurological patients, including the people with head injuries."

I'm trying to take it in. Bruce is going to live here for months. I'm going to bring the girls here to see him. While he's here, the six weeks that Don mentioned yesterday are going to pass, and when that time is over, we're all going to know what our future will look like. I follow Norma past the nurse's station, through a room with a row of computer monitors, and on into the gym. It's wide open and full of light, surrounded on two sides by a bank of floor-to-ceiling windows.

"This is where the real work gets done," she says. I don't like the way she keeps watching me, as if I ought to be talking more, or asking questions, or crying. Something seems to be required of me, but I don't know what it is, and I don't want to. She lets me wander around, but she is always just behind my elbow. I keep my face turned away from her and don't speak. The more she looks, the more I shut down.

Harborview. I am looking west at the city and Puget Sound, at skyscrapers and freeway traffic, buses, ferry boats, the shipping docks where boats loaded with Japanese cars wait to be emptied. All the people in Seattle are going about their lives. In the distance straight ahead are the Olympic Mountains. Automatically, I scan them to locate the pair of matching snowy points that are called The Brothers, where Bruce and I hiked on our honeymoon in 1986. When we came out of the forest after ten days of climbing, the ranger gave us tea and, smiling, wondered out loud what the marriage would be like, after such a beginning. We didn't imagine this.

The gym has four enormous raised platforms covered in blue exercise mats. There is a set of parallel bars, a row of weight machines, a table, an exercise bike, and a set of four steps going nowhere. Brightly colored exercise balls stand unused in one corner where a young Black Labrador sleeps. No one is exercising, though, or at least no one is doing anything I would recognize as exercising. A tall man in khakis and a white tee shirt is walking very slowly next to an elderly Asian woman in hospital pajamas. She has a wide blue belt looped around her stomach; he holds fast to the belt where it rides against her lower back.

On one of the mats a couple of young women are trying to teach a man with one leg and one arm how to get himself rolled over from his back to his stomach. He lies between them, the stump of his arm across his chest, and struggles to follow their instructions. I think again of bringing the girls up here, and look away. Norma walks me back through the computer room, talking calmly about all the kinds of therapies Bruce will be getting. She wants to know when he might be moving out of NICU.

"They said maybe Friday." I picture him, immobile and gasping in his bed, and try to believe he will be well enough in four days to come and do "occupational" therapy. I haven't even seen him with the head of his bed raised, much less able to sit up. "I don't see how, though."

She smiles at me. "Oh, you'll be surprised how fast he'll start feeling better. I'm going to tell the people at Health Coverage Services to come and talk with you about your rehab benefits. Will you be here for a little while?"

"I have to leave by two. Our younger daughter will be coming home from school." She says she'll send someone right up, and I go into Bruce's room to wait. He's awake. He's staring at the ceiling with one hand suspending the oxygen mask just above his mouth and the other gripping the slender suction wand. I tell him a little about the rehab floor, glad to see interest flicker in his eyes.

"Also, I got an email from Keith this morning. Turns out he knows a woman who has a spinal cord injury. She broke her back about a year ago, I think he said in a climbing accident down by Mt. Rainier." Keith is Bruce's younger brother. For years the two of them lived and worked at Snowbird, skiing 300 days a year and not living up to their potential. Now Keith has a family of his own, and a respectable job, but he's still in Utah near the good snow.

"How's she doing?"

"Walking, with crutches. She was never supposed to get better." I am so glad to be able to tell him this. I am so glad to see him narrow his eyes at the thought that someone else made it, so glad to recognize the old him in that tiny, defiant gesture. But I've saved the best part for last. "And, she did her rehab here."

"Really."

"Yeah. Keith gave me her email address. I'll write her tonight and ask who you should look out for."

"That's good. Did you see a computer in rehab?"

"There's a room with four or five of them. Beside the gym." Karen the nurse comes in and says that someone is here to talk with me. I kiss him and say I have to go talk about money, and that I'll be back later tonight.

"When?"

"After the girls get ready for bed. Probably nine."

A pause. "See you then. Tell them hello."

"I will." I take my bag and head into the hall. A woman with white hair is waiting beside the first set of double doors. She invites me into a side room I haven't even noticed before. It has a couch, a coffee table with a box of Kleenex, and a telephone. This must be where they take people after someone dies, so they can make their phone calls and get themselves together before walking out into the world. I don't want to be in here, and I don't sit down.

She says what I already know. Our insurance is only good for thirty days of rehab. He'll probably be there for another six or eight weeks after that, which means the bill not covered by insurance will be around $70,000. She says this very casually, as if she's telling me that the library book I put on hold hasn't come in yet.

I don't say anything. I'm having another of those moments when I feel myself turning into a reptile. My skin seems to harden, and inside me things become cool and slow.

"There's Medicaid, of course. But you have to meet certain requirements."

"Yes?"

"Well, you can't have more than $2,000 in cash or assets."

I try to make a joke. "Hopefully they won't make us sell our house."

"Oh no, they let you keep your house," she says, looking into my eyes. "And one car."

Her bluntness takes my breath away. Before I can say anything else, she asks if we might have any other resources. I pull my coat around me and open the door. "We have resources," I say to the air over her shoulder. "I have to go. My daughter's on her way home from school."

She follows me to the elevators. "It was nice to meet you. We'll be in touch."

At home, the water heater guys have come and gone. My friend Sue is sitting at my kitchen table doing needlepoint. She greets me with her wide, calm smile, ready for anything. I don't want to talk about the hospital. I ask her if she really cleaned my fridge.

"Well, I did," she says. She has a light, easy voice, full of good will, ready to be merry. She opens the refrigerator door. It's dazzling in there. Every shelf is perfectly clean, every condiment bottle polished. The remainders of last night's lasagna are centered on the top shelf next to a full jug of milk.

"Wow."

"I wasn't sure what to do with some things, so I left them."

"It didn't even look like this when it was new." She's going over the contents of all the containers that looked marginal when Heather comes through the front door. She walks in the kitchen, looks quickly at the two of us, and sets her backpack on the table. Sue takes this as her cue to leave. I walk her out, give her a quick hug, and come back in to face Heather.

"How was school?"

She's pulling a big envelope out of her backpack. "They gave me this." The envelope is stuffed with notes her friends made for her—construction paper cards with stars and flowers and hearts, telling her they're sure her dad will get well. Among them is a full-sized sheet of white paper with a long passage from Isaiah carefully copied out in her friend Marie's hand:

"... even young men stumble and fall, but those who trust in the Lord shall renew their strength ..."

"Marie said her family knelt right down and prayed, all of them, when they heard."

"That's good." I picture Marie and her two pretty little sisters and her two beautiful-people parents on their knees. I've been so wary of Marie's family. Her parents are Young Life leaders, the kind of conservative Christians I least understand. But Heather loves Marie, who is bright and funny and the only girl she knows who can beat her in a foot race. "That was really kind of them."

She's looking through the pile of cards. "Can we go see Daddy tonight?"

"I think tomorrow would be better. He's really tired today, it's hard for him to sleep. I'll go back up, though, and bring him this." I take the card from Marie. "Maybe you could make him one."

She gets to work on a pencil drawing of some flowers someone has sent. Our kitchen is filling up with flowers, potted plants, and piles of cards, every one of which says the same thing: "We were so sorry to hear ... you're all in our thoughts and prayers."

Emily comes in a few minutes later. She also has a backpack full of handmade cards, including a huge one for me from my students.

"How is Daddy doing?"

"The same. Tired." I talk a little about the rehab floor he'll be going to next, about the gym and the people I saw there.

Emily has a direct, tell-me-now approach to any crisis in her world. When she was nine and her cat was killed by a car, she marched right down to look at its body and touch its fur. She was sobbing the whole time, but she knew what to do, and she wasn't scared. She watches me carefully, a twelve-year-old ready to be crushed. "Mama, what's going to happen?"

"I don't know." I put one hand into her blonde hair. "They say it will take six weeks to find out how bad his spinal cord was hurt, so we just have to wait." She gets out the calendar and counts out the weeks.

"Starting now or when he got hurt?"

Dear God. "I don't think it's that exact, but let's start counting now."

While she's doing this, the doorbell rings. I answer it with Rocky doing his joyful, clumsy dance around my legs—a friend stands on my porch, her arms loaded with our dinner, another bunch of flowers, and a card. I take the bags, say my thank yous and offer what little news there is. The flowers are lilies; the card says, "We were so sorry to hear ... you're all in our thoughts and prayers." The dinner is lasagna.

That night at the hospital, I get to hear about how they sat him up again in the wheelchair. This is how he puts it: "They sat me up," as if he were a doll to be propped into position by a special team of doll-handlers. His voice is still a whisper, and his breath is very short. I want to hear about the sitting up, but I don't want to make him try to talk. I show him the sketch Heather made.

He's lying on his side, pillows stuffed in a line behind his back to hold him up, one hand holding the oxygen mist tent over his mouth.

He motions me to bring the drawing closer, then asks me to get his glasses from the nurse's desk so he can see it better. It's a complicated drawing, three-dimensional, detailed, and properly scaled, not like anything she's ever produced before. In one corner is her signature and the date, just in the place he used to sign and date his own work. He looks at it a long time. While I'm taping it to the wall beside his bed, I tell him that Jocelyn is going to set up a visitors schedule so he always has company.

"That's so nice of her."

"She says people are clamoring for something to do. I don't know how she got the job of coordinating them, but she's on it. She's asking people to fill in the hours I'm not here, in two-hour slots. You're all set up through Friday already." I pull out the card Emily made for him, which is not a card but a giant purple-ink message on butcher paper. She's written, in her curling seventh-grade-girl script, that she has good confidence in the doctors and nurses who are taking care of him, and that she loves him and misses him.

He looks at it and sighs a tiny, weak sigh. "Emily. I miss them so much."

I can't speak. At home, his presence is in every room. He's hurrying through the front door, moving around the kitchen eating and talking on the phone, bending over the computer and making rude comments about Microsoft ... we are, all three of us, hollow with longing to have him back. I hang his ski pass on the IV pole next to his bed. He eyes it.

"Good idea."

"I thought so. Plus this." It's Heather's school picture from last September, a 3x5 head and shoulders shot in which she looks radiant with smarts and goodness. He closes his eyes as if it's too bright, which, in a way, it is.

Around 10 o'clock, Larry offers to wash his hair for him.

Bruce, still lying prone and propped on one side, looks at him wearily. "Do you have to?"

"I could cut it instead. It wouldn't be stylish, but it would be out of the way."

"Fine." He cuts me a glance, whispers louder. "Do you mind?"

"If you cut your hair? It's your hair. Go ahead."

"It's just such a hassle."

Larry describes the hair-washing process to me. He will lay Bruce out flat, slide some towels under his head, put a plastic bag over his hair, squirt some water into the bag, add soap, rub it in through the bag, then somehow rinse and dry it. He's standing at the head of the bed, one muscular arm leaning on the head of Bruce's bed. "I could buzz it all off in two minutes."

"Do it."

I watch, then, as Larry efficiently turns my husband into someone I've never seen before. When he's finished I ask for the hair; there is enough to fill up a large Ziploc plastic bag, the kind I use at home for everything from leftover pasta to loose crayons. I stash the bag in my purse, thinking of the time when we first became a couple. We were both seeing the same hairdresser then, a bubbly, cheerful woman who told me one afternoon that if he and I ever had kids—not to get ahead of things, sorry!—but really, if the two of us ever had kids and they didn't have great hair, it would make no sense. I have good hair, but his is even better: richly colored, thick, curling, and right now it's in a bag in my lap. He suddenly looks thin and young. I'm furtively examining the red puckered scabs where the bolts were screwed into his skull; they're almost healed over already. Larry holds up a mirror.

"Wild!" Bruce is pleased with himself. A new person. "Hey," he whispers to me. "I could get in free on Buhner Buzzcut Night."

"Good idea." Jay Buhner is a bald guy who plays right field for the Seattle Mariners. One night every summer the Mariners let everybody in free who agrees to get a buzzcut at the stadium gates. "Little early, though. They're still in spring training."

"We'll do it again later." He's still holding the mirror, looking at himself in amazement. "Wild."

Just before I have to leave, another respiratory therapist shows up to do the cough. He's a dark-haired body-builder type I haven't met named Jon. I watch Bruce sucking on the bong, but go out to sit with my back against the wall when it's time for the counting and retching. It lasts a long time, maybe fifteen minutes, and when I go back in, I hardly recognize Bruce. I stand next to the bed and look down at him.

"That was so incredible!" His eyes are absolutely stoned, wide and excited, almost holy.

I can't help smiling. "You look so weird. What was incredible?"

He smiles back, a loopy grin that almost makes me wish I'd known him in the days before he got clean and sober. He whispers urgently. "This guy, Jon, he was like—like a bear! Like, right through the ceiling, hovering over me, and coming down for me, and then we were—finding it, we were going for it! Raaaaarrrrhhhh!"

I have no idea what he means, but obviously he liked whatever just happened. "You're really loaded," I tell him. "What did they give you?"

"I don't know. Oh my God, that was so amazing."

"Honey, I have to go, it's late." I lean over to kiss him, careful of the neck brace, careful of the nose tube. "Get some sleep tonight, okay? Just for a change. I'll come back in the morning after I take Emily to school." I hesitate, looking at his blissed-out, naked face. For days, I've wanted so much to sit and talk with him, to have just five minutes of that mutual cozy, comfortable privacy we've learned to share so well. I am realizing now, though, that I might survive without it. "We're morphing into something different here, our family," I tell him. "We're not just the old four of us. We're larger than we used to be." I get close to his ear and lower my voice. "I'm game. I think I'm game."

At home, my friend Anne is sitting at my table correcting her students' English papers. She talks calmly and gently with me for half an hour, as if putting my kids to bed while I hang out in intensive care is our usual routine. After she drives away, I feed the cats and put them downstairs. I take Rocky up with me and let him sleep on the carpeted floor of our bedroom. I leave my door open in case the girls wake up and want to come in. I climb into our bed alight with grace and gratitude, and sleep all night.

Day 6

When the sun wakes me up at 6:30, I reach for the phone and call the hospital. The nurse named Vicky tells me that he had kind of an exciting night. He thought he felt his left quadriceps muscle move, and he was awake a lot, trying to make it happen again, but couldn't do it while she was there.

"That's so great," I say, trying and failing to match her cautious tone.

"Well, yeah. But I didn't see it, and he didn't get any sleep to speak of."

"How's his breathing?"

"The same. He works really hard, maybe too hard. The RTs had to come every hour."

Shit. I tell her I'll see her in a few hours and put the phone in its cradle. Something good to tell the girls, finally.

Heather isn't impressed. "He moved his leg?"

"Well, no, he just felt like this muscle—" I show her with my hand—"this muscle right here, could move."

"One muscle?"

"It's a start."

She looks away. "I just want him to come home."

"Me too." I want to tell her about spinal shock and the swelling again; I want her to be hopeful. I want her old, self-confident, jubilant, thoughtful self. I miss that Heather almost as much as I miss her dad. I wonder what I must seem like to her.

Emily's reaction is just the opposite. "He's going to get better," she declares. "He is so going to get better. Can we go and see him tonight?"

"Sure. He really misses you guys."

She looks at me. "I miss him so bad I can't even stand it. Remember how I always used to fight with him?"

I nod. Emily and Bruce could get each other into a spitting rage in nothing flat.

Someone has left a big paperback book on the night table by the visitor's side of Bruce's bed. I've spent the morning sitting by the window reading it while he tries to rest and one helicopter after another lands, unloads, and takes off just outside. He can't breathe, can't speak, can't swallow, and still can't sleep. There's nothing to do or say to make this bearable, though every wall and surface is now covered with my attempts. His CD player is here, with half a dozen discs set neatly beside it. Flowery cards are taped and pinned up everywhere, and real flowers fill the window ledge. I've brought his magazines: Scientific American, Wired, Harper's, The Atlantic, and people have dropped off books by the armful.

The book in my hands, though, came from someone official, someone in the hospital. It's called *Yes, You Can! A Guide to Self-Care for Persons with Spinal Cord Injury.* On the cover is a collage of photographs in blue-gray tones, dominated by an image of an athletic-looking man in a wheelchair. His muscular arms are raised up in celebration. He wears a white sleeveless shirt, a white baseball hat, and stylish sunglasses. His expression is triumphant, as if he's just crossed some kind of finish-line.

The table of contents almost does me in. Topics include "Bladder Management," "Pressure Sores," "Bowel Management Program," and "Sexuality."

I turn to the pages on "Sexuality." There are the familiar diagrams of male and female organs, just as I remember them from junior high school. Ovaries, fallopian tubes, scrotum, seminal vesicles … so far, okay. There is a sub-heading called "Changes After SCI." I read about the two kinds of erections he might be able to get. The pronunciations are helpfully included. In a psychogenic (SIGH-ko-JENN-ick) situation, the good old things work: fantasy, seeing hot-looking women, reading explicit material. The book says he "may" be able to achieve this kind of erection if his injury is in the lower lumbar or sacral area, which I know is down in the lower back … or, if his injury is higher and incomplete, he may still be able to achieve it.

He's lying beside me, utterly vulnerable, with his high injury which may or may not be incomplete enough to allow him to have a sigh-ko-jenn-ick experience ever again. The other kind of erection is called reflexogenic (re-FLEX-o-JENN-ick), which is, according to the book, triggered by any kind of physical stimulation to his genitals. The writers advise that he may have already noticed this happening when he washes or applies his condom catheter. I decide that I'm not ready to read about this and close the book. I hide it under some magazines on the lower shelf of the night table, where he won't be able to see it.

That morning a couple of friends from church stop in; they're not part of the scheduled visitors, just guys who want to say hello. One of them takes me into the little room where the Medicare woman talked to me yesterday. We sit down on the couch and he talks me through a process he uses with his clients, people who've hired him to serve as a "personal coach." He draws a bicycle wheel with my name at the center; along each spoke is a concern I must figure out how to attend to. He pencils in the words as I say them. The girls. Bruce. The house. Paperwork for the hospital. Bills. Myself, my own health. This exercise makes me feel weak and besieged, and I'm glad when it's done.

In the afternoon, I take the girls to their music lessons. Heather's piano teacher is a neat, methodical person. She hears our news quietly, takes her place next to the bench, and conducts the session as if nothing's changed. I fall asleep on her couch listening to Heather struggle through the piece I know she hasn't thought of since last Tuesday.

Emily takes cello from a gifted Korean woman who lives in a fabulously decorated house with a grand, open view. When I tell Fay that we've had some trouble in our family, she takes both my hands in hers and questions me carefully. I leave Emily with her so I can take Heather to her soccer practice, and when Emily comes out to the car an hour later, she says she didn't even play.

"Fay just wanted to talk about Dad."

"Was that okay?"

"Yeah. No. She said next week we'd have a regular lesson."

"You didn't practice anyway."

"I know. I will this week. Are we still going to the hospital tonight?"

"Someone's bringing us dinner. We'll go after that."

The dinner is, again, lasagna. We're so disoriented we don't even laugh. In the refrigerator there are two Tupperware containers full of enough lasagna to feed the three of us for days. I set out plates and ask what they hate the most so far.

"Lasagna." Heather is trying to be funny so we won't have this conversation.

"I don't like it when kids at school ask me how he is." Emily says this with no hesitation. "And then they don't listen when I tell them."

"I hate that," Heather says. She pushes the food with her fork, frowning. "Or like, if they start talking about something else before I get finished."

I force myself to take a bite. "I hate it—I really hate it!—when people are so nice all the time. It makes me feel like I'm wearing a sign that says 'I'm pitiful!' I hate it."

They both nod firmly. Emily tries the salad.

"I'm going to start asking people to say something mean to me, just so I can feel normal."

Heather says, deadpan, "God, Mom, where did you get those ugly earrings?" It's my first truly happy moment of the day.

As we cross the bridge over Lake Washington that night, I tell them about the haircut.

"What!"

"No, I like his hair, Mama, no!"

"You guys, it's okay. He looks fine." I didn't know it would be this big a deal. They sweat it all the way into the city, bugging me for details and talking about how I shouldn't have let them do that, should have made them leave his hair alone. We park illegally and get out of the car. I hold their hands, keeping them close on the dirty sidewalk, and march them resolutely into the building, down the hall to the elevators, and into NICU. I can feel their panic in my palms and fingertips, but there is nothing to do except go forward. His room is dimly lit, the sky dark beyond his window. Computer monitors glow; lights blink. His SAT is hovering in the low 90's—bad. His cheeks sag.

"Hi, Daddy." Emily's voice is the one she used when she was four years old, high and uncertain. There is scary stuff everywhere: needles, hoses, bad smells, and the person in a neck brace lying on his side with a buzzcut, his mouth partly open, isn't anybody she knows.

"Emily."

While they try to talk, Heather takes questions from the current scheduled visitor, who happens to be my friend Sue, the same woman who cleaned our refrigerator. I quiz the nurse about how the afternoon went, listening with part of me to each of the girls and to Bruce.

Emily: "How are you feeling, Daddy?"

Sue: "Have you started soccer yet?"

Nurse: "I just wish we could get the pulmonary status under control."

Heather: "I had practice today."

Emily: "Daddy?"

Nurse: "He's really a fighter."

Bruce is trying to cough up something thick, and the gurgling, desperate sound of his failure sends the girls skittering toward the door.

"I have to go to the bathroom."

"Me, too."

I walk them out of his room and down the long hall to the public restroom. Inside, they are both shaking, and Heather is crying hard.

"I thought he was going to be better," she manages to say.

I can't witness their sadness without falling into it myself. The three of us stay in the bathroom until it feels like we can breathe normally, and then we go back down to his room. The respiratory therapist is just finishing a session, which means Bruce is producing what seems to be a quart of wet mucus for the vacuum wand. Heather puts both hands over her ears and says, "LA LA LA LA LA ..." until the sound stops.

They can talk for a few minutes after that. We all kiss him goodnight, and say thank you to Sue, who will be staying with him until I get back. On the way out of the hospital, I buy the girls Italian sodas and cookies at the Bistro. I play their favorite Dixie Chicks songs as we cross the I-90 bridge. I sit with them in their rooms for as long as they want me to. I brush their hair like I did when they were small, and they let me. We are like three people crawling around in pitch darkness, clutching a plug, desperate to find an outlet that must, must be around here somewhere. We have discovered that there is broken glass beneath our knees, and that sometimes the room spins crazily. We have to hold on tightly to each other. Downstairs, our friend David is waiting so that I can go back up to see Bruce once more tonight.

At three a.m., I wake up in our bed, panicky and alert. Something bad has happened. I reach for the set of glass and mahogany prayer beads someone gave me a few days ago. It's under my pillow. I hold onto the beads, breathe through the sense of terror, and fall asleep. When I wake up at six-thirty, I pick up the phone and call NICU. The nurse says he was moved in the night. Someone needed his bed, someone with a new injury. She connects me to the place where he is, and I wait while they get a phone to him.

"Kate!" His whisper is loud and urgent.

"Where are you?"

"I'm in the basement, in some kind of holding room." He has to pause for breath every couple of words.

"What? I thought they were moving you to rehab."

"They don't," he gasps. "Have a room."

I think of the night he got hurt, when he spent hours and hours lying like a slab of meat in the ER holding area while they got him a room in NICU. They must have done this to someone else that night. "Oh, shit."

"This is fucked, oh, my God. They just caught somebody smoking in the bathroom. This is insane."

"Smoking?" I picture the oxygen tanks. "Okay. I'll call somebody. I'll find somebody to come and stay with you until I get there." I hang up and lie straight, thinking, running the prayer beads between my fingers, wondering who I can ask.

An architect has designed a three-room studio for me. It has a grand entrance to the first room, an airy, modernist creation with open white walls, high windows, and, in the center, an easel and a cart with art supplies. Off to the side is a door to the second room. Entering it, you find clutter … at the far end is a door to the third room. Opening this door, you are faced with a dark, slimy, organic mess … it is difficult to know where you are going … the room doesn't seem to be bounded; any direction is similar to any other. The architect … tells me that, while the first two rooms are where I would like to work, it is in the third room where my true work lies.

Bruce Hanson

```
Assessment: Patient
motivated to get up
but exhausted. Short
term goals: to
require moderate
assistance with bed
mobility, to transfer
from bed to
wheelchair with
moderate assistance,
to self-propel
wheelchair one
hundred feet.
```

FIVE

Day 7: 9:30 am

He's in his Hill-Rom bed with his oxygen mist blowing, his blue and white neck brace, his feeding tube, his IV drip, and all his belongings in bright orange bags stuffed onto a shelf beneath him. I'm next to him in a folding chair that touches the striped curtain swung closed around us. After the serene, controlled air of NICU, it's like we've been thrust into the street. The little machine that monitors his oxygen SATs is still on its cart right at the head of his bed ... the green numbers hover in the mid-nineties. My friend Nancy is pulling on her coat. She's old enough to be our mother, and right now I wish she were our mother. She's telling me how the morning went.

"They don't really have the staff to take care of him here; I had to make them chase down the respiratory therapist twice."

"When are they saying he'll get a room in rehab?"

"They keep saying, 'soon', but they don't really know. I think they have to wait for the custodial people." She says she has to get to a meeting and goes up to touch his hand and tell him to hang in there. Nancy is smart and used to taking on authority; she's been a professional advocate for homeless people for twenty-five years. She has a pleasant, firm voice and a way of looking people right in the eye. If anybody could get action on behalf of Bruce, it would be Nancy, but here he still is.

After she leaves, I go up to ask him if there's anything I can do.

"Comfort me," he whispers. "This kind of took the wind out of my sails."

If he's ever asked me for emotional support in all the years of our marriage, I don't remember it. He is the original ultra-low-maintenance, self-contained man. I squeeze myself up behind the top of his bed, my back against the wall, and put my two hands on his head. I lean over and whisper, very deliberate. "You can coast. It's like you had to run a hundred miles in a year, and you ran ten in the first week. You can rest, you can coast, just for awhile." I want so much to put my arms around

64

him, but I can't get that close with all the equipment in the way. So I just stand there with my palms against his stubbly hair and keep murmuring about how well he's done, how he can rest now. All around us, just outside the curtains, is noise and movement, but we are utterly alone.

The transport people are dressed in bright purple, the color of Virginia Avenue on the Monopoly Board. They have a fat metallic clipboard stuffed with paper, which turns out to be his chart, and they seem to know how to manage his machinery. They swing his bed around corners alarmingly fast. I walk along behind them to the elevators reserved for patients, and we ride without speaking up to the fourth floor and through the entrance to the rehab unit I visited a few days ago. They push him into a long, narrow room with space for two patients; he's going to be in the spot near the door. The bed near the window is occupied by the double-amputee Indonesian man I saw in the gym. He's watching television and, aside from a single glance, doesn't react to our presence. A nurse comes in and invites me to unpack Bruce's things into a small closet at the left side of his bed. While I'm doing this, she pulls the curtains around us and tries to talk to Bruce.

"Mr. Hanson? I heard you had kind of a rough night, huh?"

He can barely open his eyes. "Yeah," he whispers.

She raises her voice, as if her volume will compensate for his lack of it.

"We're just going to get you comfortable and then your doctor will be in to have a look at you."

His doctor is hugely pregnant, blonde and short. She takes one look, then makes the comment they all make: "You are so long!"

"Tall," I say automatically. "He's tall."

At home that afternoon, I have a list of things to bring to the hospital. Pull-on pants, the looser the better. Tee shirts, sweatshirts. Shoes a couple of sizes too big. The special juice and cloth to clean his glasses. His guitar. Emily is helping me pack his bag; she's very excited. These are his clothes. When he's wearing them, he'll be back to being her dad, and she wants that to happen right now. She keeps finding things she wants to see him wear—his Mariners' shirt from the 1995 season, his green camp sweatshirt with the picture of a loon, his tie-dyed tee shirt that he used to paint in.

I leave her stuffing everything into an overnight bag and go to the computer. There's a message from our friend Mike, who has just spent a two-hour shift with Bruce. He writes that while he was there, Bruce moved the toes of his left foot. Twice.

I reply: "much jumping and screaming at that news ... I think Emily just choked the dog. These guys don't know who they're dealing with"

Mike has heard that I can't bear kindness. He answers: "do you have to bother me with this shit at work?" The sound of my own laughter surprised me.

That night, before I leave for the hospital, I take Heather up to her room and sit with her. I've brought her a shirt from our dirty laundry. She takes it in her slim hands and puts her face into the folds. The smell of his skin, his deodorant, his lively self, is right there between us, and for a long time we just indulge ourselves in it, nearly groaning with pleasure. She tucks it under her pillow, and I allow myself to hope she'll sleep well.

Day 8

It's 10 am, cool and rainy. I've parked the car in the lot four blocks away from the hospital and marched up the steep sidewalk. I've bought a latte in the Bistro on my way to the 4-West elevators. I approach his room hopefully, but when I get there I see right away that it was another bad night. He opens his eyes, but he isn't in them; he looks blind.

"Hey." I take his fingertips in mine, careful not to disturb the IV needle.

"Not a great night," he whispers.

"What happened?"

"I ripped the fucking nose tube out." His hand moves up to touch it. "They just put a new one in."

Part of me is pleased. This is him, this is just what he would do. He would never put up with anything touching his face when he was trying to sleep. I've seen him spend five minutes trying to track down a stray cat hair that had found its way to his nose. But this is also Thursday morning, which makes it eight nights in a row that he hasn't slept. I ask if they're going to let him rest now.

"No. They said I have until ten or so, and then something else happens." He flicks his eyes across the room. "I think I messed up that other guy's night."

I look over at the other bed. The Indonesian man is lying on his side, facing away from us. "You couldn't help it."

"No shit. Who is he?"

"I don't know his name. He's missing an arm and a leg. Someone told me he was on a cruise ship when an oxygen tank exploded."

"God."

"He seems pretty healthy, though." In contrast to Bruce, who seems very sick. "What did they say is happening at ten?"

"PT."

"Physical therapy? After you were awake all night again?"

"It's their job." His eyes close, and he drifts off.

By one o'clock, I've met a whole team of people, all of whom have come to the bed, introduced themselves, waked him up, and described their plans for his stay at rehab. There is a woman named Cecille, heavy-set and dark-eyed, who will be teaching him how to dress himself and brush his teeth. Josh, who has a serious expression and the build of a jockey, will be working on wheelchair skills. A young woman named Fleur will monitor his swallowing abilities and decide when he gets cleared to eat; she takes me aside and asks if I've noticed any cognitive changes.

"He's tired," I say.

"You know that he had a small fracture in his skull?"

A shiver travels up my arms. "I didn't know that."

She shrugs. "It wasn't enough to require any special procedures, but we'll be watching him for signs of traumatic brain injury."

"He's fine. He just needs to sleep. And eat." I can tell she's trying to decide if I'm in denial. "He hasn't slept for more than an hour or two at a time since the accident," I tell her. "He doesn't have a brain injury."

"Well, just keep an eye on him, and let us know if you see anything unusual."

Right. Like, what would constitute unusual behavior in this situation? I say that I will, and then I ask if there's a chance he could get moved into a private room.

"They're already working on that. I heard it will happen later today."

She doesn't bring up the fact that he can move his toes, and neither does anyone else. I keep saying it, but their faces are always neutral. Don't be hopeful, that's the message.

As it happens, I'm there when they move him to Room 464. Jocelyn has organized a gang of women to clean my house. Some of them will still be there when school gets out, so I can stay all through this day. I need to get a sense of what it will be like for him. I need to tell everybody who'll be taking care of him that he's going to be their favorite patient. I need to be able to describe all this to everyone who keeps asking for news. I take his things back out of the closet in the first room and hang them up in the new one. I do everything as silently as possible, but it doesn't matter.

Every time he starts to fall asleep, his oxygen SATS go down, which sets off an alarm, which eventually brings a nurse. The nurse always talks with him, then picks up the phone above his bed to call for an RT. Then the RT comes, but not right away, like when he was in intensive care. They do the bong, and he blows into a little plastic thing that looks like a hash pipe, and then the quad-cough. After four or five rounds of that, he suctions out whatever is in his mouth, and then drifts off again, until the next time.

I can tell it's dinner time by the smell. No one brings him a tray because he can't cough well enough to clear his airway if he swallowed something wrong, which he probably would. I close the door so we won't have to smell the food. It's an enormous door, three feet wide and heavy. When it's closed, the sounds from the rest of the hospital vanish. I'm telling him that I won't be coming back up tonight, that I've promised the girls to do something with them. One of the vigilantes will be in, though.

"That's okay."

"Fred called me." I hate Fred. A couple of years ago we were clients at his marriage-counseling practice—I spent almost every session feeling patronized and unable to make myself understood. We stopped going as a couple; now he's just Bruce's therapist. "He says there's a men's group tomorrow, and he wants me to tell them something about what's going on." I can't read any reaction to this, except Bruce does open his eyes, and it looks like he might be thinking it over.

"Tomorrow's Friday," he says finally. The men's group meets every other Friday.

"Yeah. I could send him an email tonight if you want to say something to the guys." I'm trying to be neutral. I think the men's group is just a way for Fred and his partner, Joe, to get more money out of their clients. It's one of those places in our marriage where we aren't in sync, but I have been deliberate about keeping my hands off. Now I have to deal with Fred's solicitous phone calls.

"Okay. Do you have something to write on?"

I get out my journal. "Shoot."

He whispers to me for ten minutes while the light from the window fades. No one disturbs us. His breath doesn't fail him. This is what he says:

> ...I knew when I landed exactly what had happened to me ... my body was numb—in fact it felt like I was lying on the snow with my feet in an impossible position, in the air. It was the position they must have been in when the fracture happened, like a switch was flipped off ... I saw Heather being safely skied away by a patroller, so I moved my energy and focus to my neck ... I'm now, after six days in intensive care, in the rehab facility preparing to get down to the hardest work of my life, and ready to do it ... I have my hands, lots of wild feelings in my legs, and yesterday I moved my toes for the first time. I also learned that I can squeeze my anus—priceless information, I'm sure! ... I've got enough to make a good life. It's actually my belief, though, that I will be back in Edelweiss Bowl at Alpental with Heather. We'll ski to that spot. We'll sit there and have a picnic.

I write it all down as fast as I can, and we are both kind of high by the time he's finished. He says that other people will be seeing this besides the men's group, and I say, yes, I'll send it out like a broadcast. I leave with the journal in my bag and run to the car. I drive fast across the bridge and up into our neighborhood, and when I get home it looks warm and inviting. I call the girls and sit with them on the carpeted steps to the living room, my hands on their knees. They look lonely and scared. I tell them that he's going to be okay, not right away, but definitely okay. I tell them to get ready to go out to eat and do a little shopping.

I'm on a fuchsia-colored couch in Limited Too, waiting outside the changing rooms while Emily checks out one more outfit possibility. Heather is beside me with her smooth head against my shoulder, talking about the way her fifth grade teacher sings their spelling words to them during quizzes. The store is full of preteens moving through racks of clothes designed to make them look like Britney Spears before she hit puberty. The speakers are playing her voice singing a sultry version of "Satisfaction." I see my own face in the mirror; I look as if someone has turned the gravity way up.

That night, I sit down at the computer and type Bruce's words into an email, which I send, not just to Fred, but to everybody in my address book.

Day 9

I am sitting on a narrow couch in a little alcove just outside Bruce's room. With me is the psychologist assigned to us. He's tall and elegantly dressed, and he's asking how I am doing. I think this over.

"I think," I say slowly, "that we are almost obscenely well-equipped to survive this crisis."

"How so?"

"We have all the right resources." I'm staring at the wall across from us. "We've both spent years in twelve-step programs learning how to live one day at a time. We have enough money. We have family willing to help us, and we're on good terms with them. Our kids don't act out in any scary ways, and they have friends. We have a whole church full of people right down the hill from this hospital ready to march up here whenever we ask them. We're educated, we know how to access information, and we're capable of advocating for ourselves."

I have a low voice, and he is bending his head to hear me, but not too close. I feel grateful to him for giving me a little space, for not touching me in any way, for not insisting that I look into his eyes. "We both have brothers who know construction and can help with whatever we have to do to our house." I shrug. "We have all the right resources ... and we live fifteen minutes from here." Then I do look at him. "I've seen the families camped out in the intensive care lobby. I've seen the patients on this floor who don't have any visitors. I can't imagine how they cope." He agrees that it's very hard, and then I ask whether he can put me in touch with a family support group for people in our situation.

To my surprise, he says he doesn't know of any. I think he must be mistaken—all these social workers and psychologists would certainly have set up some kind of program for families. "It would help my kids to talk with other kids," I say. "Our friends are amazing, but they don't know what it's like." Maybe he didn't understand what I was asking. He says again that he doesn't know of any family programs, but that he will check. And then he asks me whether I think Bruce is depressed.

I look away again. Stupid. "He's tired," I say. "He's trying to breathe so he can sleep so he can do his rehab and get out of here. He's probably scared, but he doesn't have time to be depressed."

Back in the room, the woman named Fleur is standing by his bed with a little cart. She's describing her plans to measure his lung capacity, but Bruce is so out of it he can't even whisper a complete sentence in response. She's pretty and polite, with straight black hair and a good smile; I see her trying to decide how much she should push him. I want to tell her to leave him alone, that if he could cooperate, he would. I want her to know that he's completely determined to get well, and that he's not being lazy or self-indulgent or cloudy from a brain injury.

"Mr. Hanson? This will only take a few minutes. Are you able to work with me?"

His eyelids move enough to show his pupils, then close again. His breath is coming in tiny little gasps, spaced at intervals that seem way too long.

"Mr. Hanson?"

He tries to answer her, but it's as if he's underwater. She makes some notes on the clipboard, checks her watch, and tells us both she'll be back on Monday. Have a nice weekend. On the whiteboard across from his bed, his schedule is marked, so I know that what just happened was "Speech Therapy." Now he gets to rest for an hour, when it will be time for "Occupational Therapy." I'm glad I'll be able to stay for the first part of this because the plan is to get him into a wheelchair, something I haven't yet seen.

First, a red-haired nurse named Jean comes in to drop something into his IV drip. She says it's ephedrine, and that it will raise his blood pressure so he doesn't get dizzy when he sits up. Cecille the OT arrives next, pushing a black wheelchair in front of her. She arranges it next to his bed, locks it into place, and lowers the armrest closest to him. Jean adjusts the height of the bed so that it's level with the seat of the chair, and then the two of them get into position to help him sit. Jean is half-facing him on the far side, one knee on the bed and an arm around the middle of his back. Cecille is holding his drawn-up knees in the circle of her arms; her feet are planted wide, hips low. They count, and on three, they shift him smoothly so that his upper body rises and his legs swing gently down. He's sitting up in bed.

He's slumped backwards against Jean, who has slipped behind him and wrapped both her arms around his chest. The nose tube dangles across his face, and I have to stop myself from holding it still. Cecille has his two legs firmly in her hands, her own knees making a brace against his. They have wrapped his legs from his toes to the tops of his long thighs in ace bandages, and there is a rectangular bag made of clear plastic strapped to his left shin, with a tube leading up beneath his hospital gown. Cecille glances at the contents of the bag.

"You want me to get that?" she says to Jean.

Jean tells her to go ahead, then speaks to Bruce from behind him. "Bruce? How are you feeling?"

He seems to be experimenting with keeping his eyes open. "I think I'm okay," he whispers. "Kind of woozy." He looks like a sack of disorganized skin.

Cecille has unfastened a clasp on the leg bag and is watching pee run out a little hose into a jug she's taken from beneath the sink behind her. "That's normal," she says. "It will take a few minutes for your body to adjust. Take your time." She's got one arm across his thighs and is using the other hand to close the clasp again. We all wait. After five minutes pass, I'm getting anxious about having to leave. Cecille and Jean are chatting quietly about scheduling; someone is having a baby, and there are not enough nurses. "Bruce? Do you want to lie down again?"

He opens his eyes, focusing on something low in the corner of the room. "No."

"Good. I need to get you up because you're going to get measured for your permanent wheelchair today." At the words, permanent wheelchair, my eyes go to the floor. Goddamn her. "We're going to move you now," she goes on. "You tell us if anything hurts or if you start to feel dizzy." Cecille leans toward him, locking his knees together between her own. "I'm going to have your head over my shoulder," she tells him. "And my hands underneath you." She demonstrates. His arms are hanging limp, his chest pressed against hers. She braces herself, then tilts his flaccid weight toward her body and slips both hands under his bottom. His face is toward me, but he's looking at the wall. She goes on. "Now, I'm going to rock you, like this." Her upper body sways forward and back, and he sways with her. "Good. Now. I'm going to count to three, and on the third count, I'm going to swing you this way and right into the chair."

"Okay."

"Jean," she says. "Can you get the tubes?"

Jean comes around the bed and wriggles into the space just behind the wheelchair. She has the IV line and the feeding tube loose in her hands, like reins.

"Ready?" I don't let myself look away. "One, two, three." She pivots, the bulk of his weight against her chest, and guides him securely across and into the wheelchair. Jean arranges the lines while Cecille holds him upright, facing him with both hands on his shoulders. His nose-tube drips from his face until one of them secures it against his cheek with a piece of tape. They decide to bring along his oxygen tank in case he "de-SATs." Cecille goes off to find a cart for the tank after helping Jean strap him into the chair, one belt across his lap and another around his chest. She gets a blood pressure cuff from the rack above his bed; he is still okay. Sitting up and getting safely into the chair has taken almost an hour. Before I leave, he gives me a single glance that is nine parts exhausted and one part rueful.

I am almost guilty at how easily I slip away from the hospital, its power vanishing as I drive swiftly across Lake Washington. The house, thanks to my friends' efforts, is vacuumed, dusted, orderly. Flowers stand in vases all over the kitchen, mail is neatly stacked, and the newspaper sits unopened on the table. The dog is thrilled to see me, whining with pleasure at the sight of his leash in my hands. I have forgotten that it's Friday. Heather will be at a girl scout meeting after school, so I have an extra hour, plenty of time to take Rocky out. I walk him briskly through the hills of our neighborhood, aware of my hamstring muscles, my straight back, my breath. In this familiar neighborhood, I feel vaguely false, like a returned exile, or a foreigner trying to pass as a local. Back in the dining room, dog panting happily at my feet, I turn on the computer. Keith has sent his flight number and arrival time—tomorrow evening, thank God. I get out my journal and write them down, knowing the details will slide away unless I make an effort.

By a quarter to five I have seen both the girls off to their friends' houses for the night. Heather is still too quiet, and it hurts me how willingly she goes away to be with another family; this is unfair and a little crazy, since it's exactly what I require from her. Emily's blue eyes look tired and sad. When she hugs me, neither of us wants to let go, but we do. I promise to tell Bruce she'll be up to see him tomorrow, and then I am alone again. Jocelyn has scheduled someone to be with Bruce until eight, which means there will be time to answer email and pay bills, maybe even time to soak in the bath before I go back up.

The phone rings. I am standing in the corner of our kitchen, my back against the wall. His latest doctor, a woman with dark curly hair and an oily voice, is telling me something has happened. I should not be alarmed, but something has happened.

"What?"

"Well, his occupational therapist noticed this afternoon that he seemed to be losing function in his right hand."

I'm suddenly bent over, half-crouching.

"Kate?"

"Yes."

"We're not really sure what's going on, but I wanted you to know that I ordered a CAT scan, which he's just finishing, and another MRI."

"What do you think it is?" Racing thoughts. Is his spine still unstable? I thought the surgery would make it stable. Why would his hand not work, unless something new was wrong with the cord? What could be wrong today that wasn't wrong yesterday? The yellow kitchen walls seem to be breathing. I close my eyes to shut out the image.

"It's best not to speculate," she says in a pleasant, firm voice.

What if he loses it all. What if everything goes back to what they said in the ER. The word, ventilator rises like a snake into my throat.

"Kate?"

"I just don't understand what could cause this." Unless it's something really bad.

"We should know more after the MRI. I've asked them to call me with the results tonight, no matter what time it is."

How generous. I'm moving to find my bag now. "I'll be there," I tell her. "You call me in his room after you get the results."

"Try not to worry," she says.

On the bridge, halfway across the lake, I suddenly have an image of myself driving along with a bad guy sitting next to me, there, right in the passenger seat. He has a long, sharp knife with a shining blade pressed hard against my throat. This is how frightened I am: Ted Bundy, knife at throat, driving into danger. I could not be more frightened than this. I hold the steering wheel with both hands, keeping in my lane, and head straight into the dark circle of the Mt. Baker tunnel.

In his room, the lights are dim. My sister Sue is there, along with Patricia and Christine. Christine is one of those middle-aged women who looks striking and original in bold make-up. She wears whatever she wants—red cowboy boots, silk jackets, hats. Half the guys I know are secretly in love with her, including Bruce, probably. I don't care. She's also a nurse. I walk into her round arms and whisper that I am scared, I am so scared. She murmurs into my ear, one hand drawing slow circles in the center of my back.

The SAT monitor starts to beep. I turn away and stand at the edge of his bed. He's holding the oxygen mask over his nose and mouth.

"Sucks," he gasps.

"I'll get them." He closes his eyes and I go to the desk, the lights too bright after his dim room. They don't want to see me. I am too much trouble. It's seven o'clock on Friday night, the middle of the shift, and people are trying to get their breaks in. I tell them he needs a respiratory therapist, his numbers are low, can they please call?

One of the women behind the wide desk asks if he needs a nurse, too. I hesitate, trying to calibrate whether she'll be offended if I seem to think a nurse couldn't help, or relieved that she doesn't have to find two people. "He just can't get any air," I say finally.

She picks up the phone. "I'll call RT, then."

In the room, we wait for ten minutes. Fifteen. Twenty. The monitor is beeping non-stop, and his grip on the oxygen mask is rigid. My sister is shaking, trying not to cry. "He's drowning," she says. "Where are they?"

At that moment, a woman I haven't met strides in. She ignores us, flips on a light, and walks up to his bed. "Mr. Hanson? Are you having some trouble?" Her voice is loud and a little annoyed.

He nods once behind the mask.

She strolls away from the bed, looking around the room at the cards and pictures we've pasted to the walls. It's too much. Christine, Patricia, Sue and I all speak at once, hesitantly, trying to be respectful.

"He's been waiting a long time."

"Could you please hurry?"

"He just needs help to cough."

"We called at seven …"

She's made her way, finally, to the sink beside his bathroom. She stops dead and looks over at us, huddled nervously beside his bed. "Do you mind if I wash my hands?"

Then we are all apologizing. It's the only thing to do. If she leaves, who knows when somebody else will come? She takes her time cleaning her hands and drying them, then goes to help him breathe. I leave the room, closing the door behind me, and wait in the hall for it to be over. When she comes out, I say again that I'm sorry, we're all sorry.

She shrugs, ready to be mollified. "What was all that?"

"We're just scared," I say. "He's not getting better. He's getting worse. I'm sorry we yelled at you." I feel craven and defeated, watching her walk away.

Six hours later, everyone else is gone. It's two o'clock in the morning, and I'm standing again at the end of his bed in dim yellow light, watching while yet another RT tries to help get air into his lungs. The MRI is finished; he had to endure forty minutes with a rigid piece of molded plastic clamped like a bridge over his mouth from ear to ear. He had to lie alone in a dark, roaring tube, waiting for it to be over so he could find out why his right hand—his drawing hand, his painting hand—has gone still. The answer is that they don't know why. The tissues around his cord are swollen, like flesh that has been bruised, but the vertebrae are stable. They've given him a massive dose of steroids to control the swelling because the millions of neurons that make up the cord are a fabric of gossamer, so fragile that even a little swelling will destroy them. This seems to be what happened earlier today, though no one can say why, or whether it will happen again.

A side effect of the steroid is that it inhibits sleep. He's like a man being tortured for information about something he used to know, something he forgot years ago. He's like someone kept brutally awake for so many days and nights that he has lost everything except the need to rest. After the respiratory therapist leaves and we are alone, he seems to be breathing evenly. I am standing at the far corner of the bed, empty and exhausted.

Gradually then, so slowly that I'm not sure when it begins, I notice a warmth growing in the room, like a low musical tone—a cello, maybe, or a distant, deep timpani. I do not move or turn my eyes away from his white shape on the bed, but I have the feeling that if I did, someone enormously comforting would be standing just behind me.

Tension drains away from my face; muscles I hadn't known were clenched relax. I'm having a sensation precisely the opposite of what happened in the car earlier, and just as real. I could not feel safer than this. I have an utter conviction of personal security, and more—the knowledge that something very much larger and lovelier than what I can see is, in fact, happening. In church sometimes, Tony talks about the "love that will not let us go." He talks about being broken open so that the spirit can enter. Maybe that's what this is. Maybe I am having sleep-deprivation psychosis. Maybe this is why there had to be a Jesus—so that people experiencing this particular feeling would have a name to hang on the sensation. I don't know, or care. I close my eyes and let myself rest in it for as long as it lasts.

Day 10: 5:50 am

I'm finding my shoes and making sure my keys are somewhere in my bag. In ten minutes, someone Jocelyn has lined up will be here to take my place in this room. I've been sitting in the chair beside Bruce all night. The feeling of safety, which I have decided to think of as "having Jesus with me," is still there, right behind my exhaustion and despair. Bruce has been waking me up from a half-sleep every hour or so, anxious about his SATs, needing me to get a nurse or an RT. Why do his goddamn lungs not stay clear? What is all this gunk they keep sucking out of him?

The desk nurses are sick of me. The one I have privately decided is in the wrong line of work keeps saying, with false concern, that I should go home and get some sleep. I want to do just that, but I can't. I don't trust them to take care of him. He's defenseless, immobile, could not be more vulnerable. He can't yell or make any kind of noise. He can't reach anything except his call button, which is permanently clutched in his working left hand, but they don't always come when he presses it; this is why he's had to keep waking me up. As I lean over to kiss him goodbye, he takes my hand and slips it under the white blankets to rest on his left thigh. Beneath my fingers, the quadriceps muscle moves. We're both silent, but I'm crying again. Flex, relax, flex, relax. He's been lying here trying to get his leg to move, and I've been wishing I could go home.

I should not be driving, but I am. Most of the traffic is against me at this hour—cars full of people going to work early. My eyes feel like they're full of sand beneath my lenses, but it's good because the irritation keeps me awake. At last, the exit. Coal Creek. I start to relax. Wind up the hill. The bank, the grocery store. Our street, less than a mile to go now ... I wake up with a jerk, the wheel in my hands, the car heading directly at a row of mailboxes. Adrenaline. Brake! Open the window. Okay, keep going. The driveway, at last.

I decided not to think of myself as cord-damaged, and chose to be just another athlete trying to make a comeback from a serious injury.

Words to Bruce from Cate Casson, who broke her back in 2000 and eventually left her wheelchair behind.

```
Family is making
treatments difficult.
Patient is getting
only 2-3 hours of
sleep each night.
```

```
┌─────┐
│ SIX │
└─────┘
```

Day 10: 6 pm

I'm in SeaTac airport, waiting at the gate for Keith's airplane to land and making notes in my journal about how it feels to be terrified. Until yesterday, I hadn't known that fear is physical, hadn't understood about the vertigo, or the limpness between the shoulder blades, or the slow wave of adrenaline-blood with its sickening, cold momentum. I have an image of myself riding in a little roller-coaster car, up and down as Bruce's condition changes. I'm thinking that I ought to find a way to be more level, to be less at the mercy of whatever is happening at the hospital. I'm imagining my little car traveling along with Bruce, only along much gentler curves than the ones he must ride, the two of us in sync, but not bolted together. This is when I look up to see Keith walking toward me down the gateway.

He's a Harrison Ford kind of guy: tall, fit and capable in the way I grew up thinking men are supposed to be capable. He knows how things work, things like plumbing and engines, things with moving parts that have to fit together.

He gives me a hard, quick hug, and then I surprise myself by taking his hand as we walk through the airport. Keith and I get along; I've always liked his gross guy jokes and the way he's hard to impress. I also know he likes me, but holding hands in public would be out of the question under any other circumstances. We find the car, and I fill him on last night's fiasco while I drive to the hospital.

"So, what the hell ... his hand was working and now it's not?"

"They don't know why."

"Christ." We're driving through downtown, and he's staring out the window without seeming to see the city. It's a pretty evening, with bright clouds reflected in the office buildings against a clear sky. "What about the rest of it? How's his breathing?"

I'm so glad not to be asked whether he's able to move. His lungs are all I can think about, that and his lack of sleep. "Not terrible, not good. He's kind of caught in this spin cycle. He needs to get up in the wheelchair—supposedly every day for a couple of hours—or else stuff pools in his lungs. But the stuff in his lungs is so bad that he can't get any rest—which means he's too tired to get up. Which means more stuff pooling in lungs. He tries, though. He tries so hard. He was supposed to get physical therapy today, but he couldn't because they don't want to even sit him up until they've figured out what happened to his hand."

"What's their theory?"

"I don't know. If they have a clue, I can't tell what it is. They ordered another CT scan today—I think they're just trying to cover their asses." I frown at the car in front of me. "No, they want to figure it out. Some of them do."

"It's their job."

I give him a look. "That's exactly what Bruce says. It's their job. What I hate is how fucking much hassle it is to get anything done. Today, for a stupid X-ray, they hauled him out of bed and made him wait for an hour in this noisy hallway. It's too bright, and there are people hanging around talking about what to order for dinner and where they're going after work. He can't breathe, can't even swallow his own spit, hasn't slept in a week, and here's this fat guy running his mouth about moo-shoo pork—and I'm watching the gauge on his oxygen tank because I'm worried it will run out before these people get the X-ray done."

"Why can't he swallow?" Keith is looking puzzled and suspicious.

I shrug. "They don't know that either. They're going to try again on Monday. He literally can't swallow his own spit—he has to use this nasty little vacuum to suck it out of his mouth." I pull off the freeway and onto the James Street exit. "They aren't saying, but I think it's connected to his voice. He still just has a whisper."

Keith shakes his head. "Shit."

"That captures it."

"What about the kids?"

"Crazy scared." I look over at him. "It'll be really good for them to see you." I don't have the strength to tell him how desperately they want their dad back.

"They're still kids," he says roughly. "They still get to be kids." How, I think. How can they?

"Heather's got her soccer tryouts this weekend. It's this big competitive thing—everybody hoping their kid turns into Mia Hamm. I don't get how she's able to do it. Plus she has a cold."

"Today she did this? The soccer?"

"This morning, and again tomorrow. If it's okay, you can stay at the hospital tonight and then go to our house and sleep in. Somebody from church will show up at six to relieve you." I drive slowly past the hospital, looking for a parking place on the street to save the $7.00 lot fee.

"Sure, whatever you want. I'm only here to see the Bruiser and do what you want."

"We'll do that, then. We'll hang out here for awhile, then I'll take you to our place so you can get the other car." I pause. I'm feeling kind of stupid to be stressing over soccer. "In the morning I have to go to the tryout. She told me on the phone that she looked out today and saw all the other kids' parents in the stands, and—" A car parked along the curb starts up, and I move into position behind it.

"Shit." He runs one hand through his hair. "What a shitfest."

I park the car and when we get out, I take his hand again. We walk into the hospital this way; I can feel through his fingers that he's a little afraid. Keith is the most macho of the three brothers, the one who races cars, ski-jumps, works part-time as an emergency medical technician. Every time I've been to his house in Salt Lake City, he's been doing eight things at once, and none of them have to do with sitting down. I know that Bruce—my introspective, complicated, thoughtful husband—spent his childhood in competition with this man, and that they grew up into a mutual respect neither of them would have predicted.

In the room, Keith walks right up to the bed and looks down into his brother's face. He has one long arm braced against the wall, the other hand on his hip. He's wearing straight-legged jeans and a tucked-in plaid cotton shirt; he looks western, a little like a cowboy. When he talks, his voice is a drawl, but still seems loud and shocking in this quiet room.

"Hey, Bruce. You awake in there?"

"More or less." The whisper. Bruce moves his hand across the blanket toward Keith. "Good to see you."

"You look good. You look a hell of a lot better than I expected." I'm wondering if this is true, or if Keith had decided ahead of time to say it no matter what. Bruce looks horrible: bald, drawn, barely conscious. The three of us talk for awhile. Bruce wants to know where Emily is. I tell him she's spending the night with David's family, and that all of them are going to the coffeehouse.

He looks at me with his pale, vacant eyes, slowly focusing on my face. I wait. "The coffeehouse," he says finally. "That's tonight."

"St. Patrick's day."

"Already," he whispers.

"Don't think you're going to make your gig there."

"No, probably not." I explain to Keith that my youth group at church is having their big fundraiser, a kind of cheesy talent show with really expensive desserts. Bruce was supposed to be one of the acts—he and a couple of guys playing the blues.

Keith nods. "That's right, you got that harmonica thing. I forgot about that." He's been roaming around the room, inspecting the view, reading the nurse's whiteboard notes, keeping both arms folded across his chest. He looks over at the bed. "I'm going to be here all night," he says. "You up for that? I came here to hang out with you, Buddy. You're stuck with my ass for a few days."

"You can whip me into shape."

"Damn right. I got till Wednesday. Think we can get it done by then?"

"No problem."

Day 11: 9 am

The soccer tryouts are at one of the local high schools, on the football field. It's been raining. The stands are full of parents with their hands in their pockets, all hunched under umbrellas, watching their ten-year-old daughters playing what seems to be an endless game of keep-away. I spot Heather, gamely chasing balls around while grown-ups with clipboards ignore her. Look at that one, I want to say. Look at her.

Late that afternoon she and Emily get their first look at Room 464 in rehab—their dad's home for the next few months. They're sitting on the couches across the hall from his door while I check to make sure this is a good time. As if there is such a thing. His breathing sounds wet and rattly, which means it won't be long before someone has to come and make him do the lung-clearing routine. I look at the SAT monitor. 96.

"Can you manage ten minutes?"

"I'll try."

They tiptoe in. This is better than NICU, where they saw him last, because the bed is low enough for them to sit down next to him. I can see that they don't want to, but after a minute, Emily makes herself. He whispers a question about the coffeehouse, and she starts to tell him who sang what, and what was the funniest skit.

"Stan and Julia sang a song for you."

"What song?"

"All Across the Universe. It was pretty, but people were crying."

"Were you crying?"

"Like, yeah." She looks at him solemnly. "Of course I was."

"I'm sorry this is hard for you." His words are coming out with gurgles deep in his chest as counterpoint. He makes a weak effort to cough, then slips the suction wand into his mouth and lets it vacuum up the mess. Emily cringes at the sound, but she doesn't pull away.

"Oh, Daddy." She's rubbing one hand against his shoulder. She has wonderful hands—smooth and strong, plump and pink. "I just miss you."

Heather comes out of his bathroom, and Emily takes this as her exit cue. She kisses him and tells him to get some rest. Heather walks around to take her place, acting like I've never seen her act in her life. She can't fling herself down beside him, can't tease him, can't make jokes, can't bait him to tickle her, can't seem to think of anything to say. She stands a couple of feet away from the bed, talking at the air over his head, and then moves quickly away.

I know how hard this is for her by the set of her small shoulders and the line of her jaw. She's trying—it's painful how hard she's trying—to keep him from knowing that she's in trouble. I turn away and see that she's drawn something on one of the whiteboards. It's a graph of her feelings since the accident. It starts off in the center of the board on the left side, with a point marked "accident." The line dips swiftly all the way to the bottom, reaching a moment she's called "thought he'd die." It rises about halfway to the height of the starting point; this is "driving home with Jill." Then it crashes again to the bottom: "thought he'd never walk."

The next high point is "toe feeling;" there is a dip to "same old same old," and then the line rises to "toe wiggling," way up near the top, and falls slightly from there to float off the right side of the board at "now." She's left her name and the date in one corner. I label it at the top and write, as I used to at school, "DO NOT ERASE." She's trying to communicate, I guess, that she's been sad but is now doing okay, and I want her to see that someone has heard.

"Hi, Heather, hi Emily. Come here, you little dweebs." Keith gets to his feet from his place at the kitchen table, where he's been eating our latest donated meal and talking on his cell phone. He hugs both the girls, one at a time, and smiles down at them. "You guys are looking good. You been at the hospital?"

"Yeah."

"Your dad's doing good," he says. He looks at me for emphasis. "He really is. I stayed there with him last night, and he was sleeping pretty good." They help themselves to chicken and mashed potatoes. "Course, tonight, I plan to go up there and kick his butt, so he might not feel so good tomorrow ..."

Emily is across from him, trying to tell if it's okay to laugh. Heather just rolls her eyes. We're talking about the schedule for tomorrow afternoon; he's planning to take charge of the girls. "So which one of you has soccer tomorrow?"

"I do," Emily tells him. "Hers is on Thursday."

"Soccer," he says scornfully. "Girls soccer." He rolls his eyes.

"What about it?"

He makes a little noise with his mouth, like spitting out a gnat. Pteh. "You mean, besides that it's not actually a sport?"

"Oh, sure, like you've ever played it." Emily pretends to be deeply offended, even though she doesn't much care about soccer.

"I suppose car-racing is?" Heather does not have to pretend.

"Car-racing," he says, "is fun. It's loud. And you can get dirty. And you have to get your knuckles bloody a lot. And it's really expensive. Definitely a sport."

"Right. For guys."

I move around the three of them while this mock argument unfolds, picking up their empty plates and rinsing their milk glasses in the sink. He's messing with them, making them laugh. This is how they get to be kids; a grownup who loves them shows up and helps them remember how to play. Thank God.

After Keith leaves, the phone rings. It's the soccer people, telling Heather that she didn't get on the club team she was trying out for all weekend. She knew it was a long shot; last year she missed it by a hair, but this time she was competing against kids with a full year of club play up on her. She comes into the dining room where Emily and I have been sorting family pictures, looking for good ones to take to the hospital. I've had the notion that it would be good for all those people in and out of his room all day to get a better sense of who he is.

I look at Heather's face and see that we have to be alone. Can Emily do this for awhile so Heather and I can walk Rocky? Emily, seeing what the deal is, nods. She's sitting on the carpet, surrounded by photographs of the four of us, years and years worth of them, in all seasons and ages, blithely enjoying our still-innocent lives.

"Everything's ruined," Heather says, looking away so we won't see her cry.

I put Rocky's lead on him and hurry her out. It's dark and cool but not raining. We walk slowly up the street, heading for the grocery store and the Dairy Queen. I let her talk, safely covered by the darkness. It's not just the soccer, she says. It's not just the accident. It's like— everything is—ruined. We had it perfect, and now it's ruined.

I'm still thinking about those photographs. I tell her that I look at them and hope I was never stupid enough to take any of it for granted. I turn around to look at our house. Framed by giant trees. Curving driveway. Lights on in the kitchen. I ask her if she remembers how I used to say, "gosh, what lucky family lives here," when we were coming home. I say that we are still that family. Even if it doesn't seem like it, we are still who we've always been, only more.

She is silent, and then: "At school last week we had DARE, and you know, it isn't just about not doing drugs. It's about other stuff—and don't get worried because I'm not thinking about this—but it's about suicide and stuff like that, too. And Officer Bob told us that, you know, when it seems like things are really hard, one thing to do is, like, think of something you really, really like."

My bright, strong, original, beautiful ten-year-old daughter has just said the word suicide to me. All else falls away. I listen with all my senses, searching around inside for the Jesus-is-with-me feeling. It's there. She goes on.

"And I was thinking that someone should tell him that there are things that won't change by thinking about ice cream."

"Maybe you should." I've got Rocky on his extra-long lead, and he runs back and forth around us, sniffing at all the usual bushes and making us pay attention to which side of his lead we are on. "Kids do that kind of stuff, right? Come into your classes and talk about stuff that's happened to them? Maybe when you're older you could do that. You could probably help somebody."

"There was a guy last year in a wheelchair who came to talk to us."

"I remember you told me that ... last spring, right?"

"And I'm not saying Daddy won't get better, but—I was thinking about that guy, like, just if he didn't get better, what it might be like—" She stops, afraid that I'll think she's being disloyal.

"It's okay. What about the guy?"

"He was cool. He was funny, and like, really strong in his arms and shoulders."

"How did he get hurt?"

"Diving. He told us all about being careful with diving."

"That was good advice." We're making the turn toward the store. We talk the rest of the way about times we remember people telling us things that have happened to them. She's still thinking this over on the way home. I'm trying to figure out an image to give her, some small picture to hold onto when it all feels ruined. It's there, but I can't quite get it right, so I decide to wait. Heather has a million-dollar bullshit detector. She wouldn't put up with anything half-assed right now. It's all right anyway; as our house comes into sight again, she tells me that she feels completely different from how she did when we left. That she is surprised by this, that she is not yet aware of how much comfort power is in the raw exchange of honest words, reminds me how young she is.

Day 12: 7 am

Keith is laughing and talking about the goofed up time they had in Bruce's room last night. I'm organizing lunch for the girls and getting ready to drive the carpool and go to the hospital myself. The plan today is for Keith to sleep now, then be here when the girls get home, then spend another night with Bruce.

"Some big guy was there, some friend of yours—Doug?"

"Doug Stultz."

"Yeah, we were rockin' out. Bruce had us find some radio thing ... blues music."

"KPLU All Blues. Sunday night. That's something, he knows what day it is."

"Shit, yeah. Kate, he's doing good. His head's in a good place, he's still getting stuff back. The general trend is up." He laughs again. "I think we pissed off some nurses, though. We were partyin' in there."

"Is he breathing?"

He waggles his fingers. "That's up and down."

When I get to the hospital that morning, it's all down. Rich, our favorite RT, spends an hour with Bruce in the morning and still can't get his lungs clear. In the end he has to send a hose all the way down into both lungs—which is not only painful, but somehow humiliating, as if they've together failed at a task they should have been able to do. Then the pretty speech therapist named Fleur arrives with her devices for measuring his swallow and voice. He can't even sit up long enough to do the test, which it is obvious he wouldn't pass anyway. While she's there, his unctuous doctor comes by to tell him she thinks he ought to consider a stomach tube because that will be more comfortable and he'll probably also have less nausea.

He doesn't want a stomach tube. He wants to eat. I ask what's going on that he can't swallow, and Fleur says that she's scheduled him to go down on Wednesday and see an ear-nose-and throat specialist to find out. I ask why he can't have it done today, and Dr. Smooth Eyes replies that the hospital is really full, and almost everyone's schedule is packed. Then she asks if she can talk with us privately.

"Sure."

Fleur pushes her cart out and closes the door behind her.

Dr. Smooth Eyes hugs her clipboard to her chest. She's a good-looking woman with thick, dark curly hair cut stylishly, and she's used to people who don't talk back. "I'm going to suggest that you may want to think about how many visitors you're allowing to come in here."

The snotty teenager in me wants to say, okay, you suggest it, and then I'll tell you to fuck off. "They were noisy last night," I say. "I heard. Sorry."

She nods. "The staff is concerned that all this activity is keeping him from getting any rest."

Oh, Jesus. "He's not getting any rest because he can't get any oxygen," I tell her.

"Well, it's just something you both should think about."

"Thanks, we will."

She asks me to step out while she does an exam and moves past me to draw the curtain around the bed. I go into the hall and find Fleur waiting there with her cart and her clipboard.

"Kate, I forgot to ask if you've noticed any communication or cognitive problems."

I want to kill these people. Why are they all so determined to try to fix what isn't broken while dragging out the effort to take care of what matters? "He doesn't have a brain injury, " I say. "Earlier today he reminded me that our car is due for its oil change. He gave me detailed instructions for how to get into our online banking program and use it to pay the bills. He's fine, or he would be if he could sleep and eat, preferably sometime this month." I sound angry.

"I know it's hard," she says.

"What will the test on Wednesday tell us?"

"Probably it will show whether or not his vocal cords are moving when he tries to speak or swallow."

"Why wouldn't they be?"

"Sometimes they get damaged by the surgery." She shrugs and puts one slim hand on my upper arm, a mixed message. "We'll know on Wednesday. Try to hang in there."

Before I leave that afternoon, I have seen him up in his chair again. The process of getting him out of bed is excruciating to witness. A nurse arrives with medication delivered to the hanging bag that drains into his nose tube. This is ephedrine, prescribed to keep his blood pressure up. She lifts his blankets and hospital gown and slides a wide girdle beneath him, then pulls it tightly around his stomach, so that he is cinched from navel to nipples—another measure to keep his blood pressure from falling. He is already wearing ace bandages from his toes to the tops of thighs for the same purpose.

Josh arrives: a jockey, small and finely made, sturdy and fast in his every movement. He goes through a ritual bending and stretching of Bruce's long legs, showing me as he moves each dead limb how much range of motion to shoot for. When he presses on the ball of Bruce's right foot, it suddenly jerks to life in his hands. Josh calmly presses hard into it, stretching the heel cords and explaining to me that this movement is involuntary, a spasm caused by incomplete signals to the brain. He lifts each leg straight up, marveling as they all do about how long these legs are. He bends the knees all the way to the chest, showing me how to do it, firmly and smoothly. Bruce is passive for now, holding his suction wand loosely and staring at the ceiling

We will have to do this every day, Josh says, or the joints will lose their lubrication and become rigid. He has dirty blond hair and a short beard, and he is a very intense guy, in the way that people with too much to do in too little time are intense. When he helps Bruce to sit up, he's talking the whole time. "Okay, now when my arm goes around your back, I want you to put your arm down on the bed. No, further back. Good, now don't push until I say … okay, now I'm going to get you started, and let's see how much you got." Together, they slowly, slowly get him to a more or less sitting position, but I see clearly that my husband has no stomach muscles at all. If Josh doesn't hold him firmly, he collapses into a bundle of limbs, wrapped and strung with tubes.

In the gym, though, once he is on the wide blue exercise mat, he is able to semi-sit with legs dangling, hands on the mat for balance, for a few seconds. I steady him from behind while Josh wheels a full-length mirror over and sets it right in front of Bruce, who looks ironically at his own image for the first time, me kneeling behind him with my hands on his shoulders.

"That's a sight," he says. He's wearing his fancy designer glasses. They have a narrow rectangular shape with interesting shades of brown and gold along the tops and earpieces, and I think that if not for these glasses, he would be hard to recognize. The best moment of the day happens soon after this, when Josh encourages him to try to move his feet, and his left leg swings slowly forward and back. He is not paralyzed. He is ill and weak and there are still many weeks to go before we will have to face whatever this turns out to be. For now, I think of how it would feel to look on and wait while nothing moved at all, and I allow myself to be hopeful, a little bit hopeful.

Evening, and I'm at home alone, wondering where Keith and the girls are. It's an hour or so past when I expected them, and I am panicky. My fingers are twisting at my clothes, pulling on my lips, pinching at each other. I can't figure out where I have his cell phone number written down. Feeling stupid, I call his wife in Salt Lake City and get the number from her; I simply cannot pace around my house any longer hoping they'll show up soon. When I get him on the phone, they're in the middle of some joke, all laughing, and I'm evenly divided between relief and embarrassment.

I do the email. There are a dozen messages of "thoughts and prayers," which I don't reply to. There is a note from my blessed mother-in-law to say that she's decided she has to see Bruce now, that she has booked herself a flight and will arrive late tonight, that she's also arranged her transportation and a hotel room close to Harborview, that she wants nothing from me—except possibly instructions about what time of the day or night I need her to be at the hospital. She's been married to Bruce's dad for twenty-some years—the world's most diplomatic, organized, intelligent, helpful stepmother. Dear Mim. I write quickly back to say that the hardest hours to cover are just before dawn, and that if she can plan to show up around four a.m. and stay until someone else arrives at seven, that would be perfect.

It's shocking how shameless I've become about asking for this kind of favor, and even more shocking how readily people continue to agree to whatever outrageous task I drop in their laps. The next message is from Eileen, an old friend now living in San Francisco; she's going to come and stay with me and help with everything. She's been trying to get me to give her some idea of how long this will last so she can buy her return ticket, but I don't know, and I haven't answered her.

Her email is funny: "Well, since you haven't had the courtesy to reply to me, I'm just going to leave the return open! I may never go home." Her arrival is perfectly timed—within an hour on Wednesday morning of Keith's departure. I answer that I'll be at the airport, and to stop being such a bitch.

Best of all is a message from Cate Casson, the friend of Keith's who broke her back on Mount Rainier a year ago. She was also flown to Harborview, she was also told that she would spend her life in a wheelchair, and she is currently getting around with crutches. I had sent her a note a few days ago, begging for whatever insight she might have to offer to Bruce. Her reply is long and detailed; some of the advice definitely applies to me. "Do you lose your mind and embrace despondency, bitterness, and anger … or do you keep your sense of humor and love of life and face this new 'challenge' as you've faced all challenges. Fully armed."

I read it quickly, print a copy to bring to the hospital, and write those words on my hand to remind me. Fully armed.

Day 13: 11 am

Bruce is having a blood transfusion. No one knows what happened, but the routine tests they do to him every damn morning showed a low red-blood cell count, and so now he's having somebody else's blood pumped into him. It's odd. He used to be a regular blood donor, though a squeamish one, always requiring the extra few minutes of lying down, and the cookies. Maybe he's getting his own blood back. Dr. Smooth Eyes is trying to convince me this transfusion is a good thing because he'll get a boost of energy from it. She frowns, though, when she says she'd like to know where that blood went. It's a mildly puzzled frown, as if she's misplaced a magazine. She's thinking of ordering an X-ray to make sure the blood isn't in his stomach. Maybe, she speculates, that's what's making him feel so sick. I want to rip the room apart, but I just stand there with my hands in my pockets, waiting for this useless conversation to be over.

We're in the gym, and Josh is showing me how to do a pressure release. This is a maneuver that has to be performed every fifteen minutes whenever Bruce is up in the wheelchair. He's in it now, his feet resting on their little trays, encased in brand new white tennis shoes two sizes too big, meant to go on easily when his feet swell. The size doesn't matter anyway; these shoes aren't for walking. He needs them to protect his toes in case whoever is pushing his chair drives it into something. Josh shows me how to lock the wheels: a flip of a narrow metal pin on either side near the front of the chair seat. He positions himself behind the backrest and stretches one leg behind him, the other knee forward in a kind of lunge position, grabbing firm hold of the chair's handles. He pushes with his knee, the wheels roll back, and the chair tilts easily to rest against his thigh. Bruce is suddenly leaning back and looking up at the edge of the ceiling. Josh is calm, moving the chair up and down a little against his leg, describing the way to find the balance point so that it doesn't feel heavy.

I have to do it now. I lock the brakes, which takes more effort than it appeared to. I find the metal pins and push them until they dig hard into the gray tubes of the chair's tires. I get into place, arrange my legs, heave back hard on the handles, and suddenly the weight of Bruce's body and chair is against me. It isn't hard to hold him there; I look down and smile.

"How's it goin'?"

"I need to spit."

"That's so romantic."

Josh walks over to get a paper towel and holds it under Bruce's lips while he tries to spit. When he's finished, Josh wipes his lips and chin and tosses the towel into a wastebasket. I'm looking at the paper-towel-holder, wondering if it's there for just this purpose. A minute has passed, which means I have to get him safely back to the floor. Josh watches while I slowly, slowly, ever-so-gently lower him back to an upright position. He nods in approval.

"How's your back?"

"Mine? Fine."

"You don't want to strain your back. Just always be sure your legs are doing the work, and you'll be fine."

Then he's moving off with Bruce in front of him, and I'm standing there thinking of doing pressure releases every fifteen minutes for the foreseeable future, so that the skin on my husband's ass doesn't come apart under the weight of his bones. Okay.

Soon after that, he crashes again. Too woozy to deal with being up. Too full of lung sludge. Too exhausted. Too nauseated. Back to bed in a black fit of rage and frustration.

11 pm

The girls are asleep, and I'm waiting for Keith to come here so I can go do my turn at the hospital. I am more or less rested because I slept through both of their music lessons this afternoon, first on the wide couch in Heather's piano teacher's living room, then later in the leather chair in Emily's cello teacher's beautiful conservatory. It isn't too embarrassing; Bruce used to fall asleep in that chair all the time when he brought Emily there. It's a delicious chair, the kind that holds you no matter what your shape, and the sound of two deep-voiced cellos is resonantly soporific.

I sweep my kitchen floor and imagine paying Fay to bring her cello up and play for Bruce so he can sleep. Our van pulls into the driveway—and for a moment I actually think it's Bruce, driving home at last from wherever he has been.

Day 14: 3 am

I've decided that I hate this hospital and everybody in it, but especially the Nurse-Who-Is-In-The-Wrong-Line-Of-Work, the one who insists on calling Bruce "Mr. Hanson," no matter how many times we both tell her that he'd prefer she use his first name. She also calls me "Mrs. Hanson," a name I've never used. She also comes to help him only when I physically go to the desk and insist, and she knows that I know she sometimes naps there, ignoring the patients' call lights blinking at her.

She thinks Bruce is too sick to be in rehab, and she's right, goddamn her, but while he's here it's still her job to take care of him. Maybe if she put her heart into it, he'd actually improve enough to start getting better. When his SATs fall, she taps the monitor with one finger and says that sometimes it doesn't read accurately. This makes Bruce and me both panicky; he's not getting any air! It's not the machine, stupid! He needs a respiratory therapist! Her solution is more medication, none of which has done anything except make him dizzy, depress his "pulmonary status," and get him even more agitated than he was before she dumped it into his feeding tube. Her latest idea is wrist restraints, to keep him from messing with his oxygen mask. I want to come after her with a sharp weapon for thinking such a thing. He's almost completely paralyzed, you dunce! His arms and one hand are all he can get to move, and you want to strap them down? She desperately wants me to get the hell out of here and leave her alone, which, of course, I will not do.

10 am

In the waiting room outside the office of the ear-nose-throat specialist. Bruce is inside with Fleur, getting examined. Keith is with me, his suitcase packed. Our friend Dan is here, wearing business clothes and looking very uneasy. This morning happened to be his first shift as a vigilante. Spending last night in battle with the Nurse Who Is In The Wrong Line Of Work is providing me with a steady supply of adrenaline. I'm not even tired. I could keep pushing these people all day. Keith is talking about how pissed off Bruce got yesterday after I left, during the meeting called "Rounds," which they had to hold right in his room because after they dosed him with Benadryl he was too dizzy to make it to the conference room.

"It was fucking ridiculous. He was hanging in that goddamn Hoyer lift deal with his gonads exposed and his room full of doctors—"

"Wait, they tried to make him get up?"

"No, he wanted to get up. He just about killed himself to get up, but his blood pressure was off ... so they were putting him back to bed, and that's when everybody came in the room." Keith snorts. "I gotta hand it to him. Even in the shape he's in, he was sticking up for himself."

He says that there were like, nine people in the room—besides the doctors. All the therapists came, including some he hasn't even used yet, people from social services, probably a couple of janitors, God knows who all. He says that Bruce—unable to sit up without keeling over and barfing, with a white hose dangling out of his nose and a bag of piss hanging off his bed—Bruce, whispering, told them all where to shove it and got himself heard. What they're doing isn't working, and he wants to know what the hell else they have to offer.

Keith sounds mildly surprised at all this, and impressed. Good. He says Bruce is thinking about finding someplace better to get rehabbed. I give him a sharp look.

"Like where?"

"I don't know. I don't think it's really going to happen, but he's going over it in his head, I'll tell you. He was working out what it would take to move him by car ..."

A door opens and a movie-set doctor comes out of the exam room. He has styled, wavy hair and the look of someone who spends many hours at the gym. Everything about him is striking, even in these circumstances. He waves all three of us into the room where Bruce and Fleur are, and says without introductions or preamble that he's done the exam, and Bruce's vocal cords are paralyzed. He says that this is why he has no voice, and why it's so dangerous for him to swallow—he can't feel things as they pass through his esophagus, and he's in danger of aspirating anything he tries to eat or drink. His weak cough could make this fatal.

I'm so stunned I just stare at him, then find my own voice. "Why would his vocal cords be affected? Aren't they above the level of the injury?"

Movie doctor nods. "They are. But it wasn't the injury that damaged them, it was the surgery." He uses his hands to show how it happened. "The surgeon opened Bruce's throat at the front, here." He puts his thumb and one finger around his own Adam's apple. "Then he reached in and took hold of vocal cords, esophagus, everything, and pulled it aside." His fingers make a loop in front of his own throat, and he makes a gesture like someone gathering a curtain to fasten it behind a hook. We all stare at him, and he drops his hands. "They're very gentle, of course, but the vocal cords are fragile, and this isn't an uncommon outcome."

"Will they get better?" I can hardly believe he's saying this. Why didn't Fleur give us some idea this might have been the deal? She must have known.

"In most case, given enough time, yes."

In most cases? "How much time?"

Shrug of made-for-big-screen shoulders. "It varies."

"It always varies," I say, wanting to stick pins in him. "What's the range of possibilities?"

He purses his lips, thinking. "A good outcome might be as soon as twelve weeks, bad as long as a year—you could probably reasonably expect about six or eight months."

It's still March. Bruce might not eat or speak until Thanksgiving? He might have to leave the hospital with a tube in his stomach, and a hanging bag of baby food beside our bed every night? What the hell?

"How long is he scheduled to be here?"

"Until June."

"Well, we'll be checking him a couple of times between now and then. In the meantime, he should get that"—he points at the nose tube—"replaced with a stomach tube right away. It'll work a lot better."

An hour later, Keith and I are going back to SeaTac. I'm trying to thank him, trying to find a way to say that his presence—his particular self, and no other—has been exactly what we all needed. He is not, however, the sort of man you can say such words to without making him squirm. He's done enough for me; he doesn't have to squirm, too. I do tell him, though, that I've been thinking of what happened to him and Bruce and Paul when they were kids in a completely new way.

Their mother got cancer when the boys were five, seven, and nine. She was told to expect only one more year, and this prognosis was given to the boys. (Your mother has cancer. She only has two or three months to live.) She lived for ten years, but the threat of her death was always there, and the knowledge of her illness was the invisible air they all breathed. She kept every aspect of her struggles private, though, once the first announcement had been made. Bruce has spent years of his life with therapists clearing away the wreckage created by that silence; I have no idea what it was like for Keith.

"I've heard Bruce talking for so long about how it was when your mom was sick," I say. "I look at the girls now, and I know I didn't have the slightest clue."

He stares at me, eyes changing from startled to focused in an instant. He shifts in his seat, shakes his head a little, and looks away. After a minute he says, "I can't go there."

"Sorry."

"No, it's okay. Your kids are great. They're going to be okay."

"If they are, it's partly thanks to you." That's the best he will let me do.

When we get into the terminal, I check the United monitor to see if Eileen will be on time. She's on the ground, almost an hour early! His flight isn't going to board for forty-five minutes; I tell him I'm going to get her, and we'll come see him off at his gate. I have this insane idea that they have to meet each other. I race off to the other end of the terminal, but when I get to her gate, it's already empty, everyone is gone. Sweating, I run to her baggage claim, but no dice, no Eileen. I go to have her paged and wait where I am, watching the clock while it gets closer and closer to his departure time.

Finally, it's too late. I think she must have taken a cab into town, thinking I couldn't get here to pick her up. My adrenaline-fed body is shutting down. I kneel where I am, right in the middle of the empty baggage claim, and pull out my phone to call the hospital. The only thing I can think of to do is call the rehab floor and ask the desk nurse to watch for my friend. I'm trying to find the number in my journal, and I can't. I can't remember if I have her cell phone number. I missed saying goodbye to Keith. I can't seem to do anything at all. I'm sitting back on my heels, crying and trying to pull it together when suddenly there she is, kneeling in front of me.

"Oh, Honey," she says. "What are you doing?"

"Trying to find you," I say, and when she laughs, it is okay again.

When I saw my dad fall, I thought he'd be okay, but then he screamed. I asked, "Are you okay?" He said these exact words: "Heather, I'm hurt bad. Call for help."

People said it'd be okay. It wasn't okay. I miss him. Daddy, I love you.

Notes in the hospital journal from
Heather and Emily, March 21, 2001.

```
Patient is exhausted.
Family awakens him at
every change in
breathing or drop in
SAT.
```

SEVEN

Day 14: 11:45 am

Back at the hospital, I lead Eileen quickly up to the fourth floor, answering her questions and talking all the way. She's one of those warm, brainy women who process information at warp speed, and she has a gift for getting people to bend the rules when the cause is just. We met twenty-five years ago, when we found ourselves serving as the two-woman support team for a mutual friend who was dying of brain cancer. We were barely in our twenties. Since then, she's become a nationally known advocate for HIV/AIDS issues. She's savvy to every system, not afraid of anybody, and she's just dropped whatever important job she was doing to come and help me for an indefinite time. I pause in my race to bring her up to date and look at her. Stylish, short hair. Designer glasses. Perfectly fitting clothes that manage to be beautiful without screaming to be noticed. Slender face, subtle jewelry, eyes radiating competence. Old friend.

"What?" she says. "What's wrong?" One fine-boned hand on my forearm.

"It's good to see you," I say. "You look great."

"Well, you don't. Are you eating anything at all?" She tugs at my jeans, which are indeed sagging on my suddenly narrow hips. Now we are outside Bruce's closed door, and there is Mim, standing with a few of our friends in her elegant coat, her face calm and ready to be useful. It's the first time I've seen her here; I'd forgotten that she was here. She takes my hands in hers and gives me a look warm enough to wear.

I nod at the door. "What's going on?"

"The respiratory guy is working him over," my friend Becky says, raising her eyebrows. "It looks so painful."

"How's Bruce doing?"

Mim answers. "He seems very tired, but okay."

"Be right back." I step into his room, closing the heavy door behind me. They're doing the bong. I watch the little yellow disk ride up the tube ... not good. 1500 cc's, which is less than he could get last week in

100

NICU. He stops, sets it aside, and nods to indicate he's ready to cough. The RT is a woman I don't know. She braces herself, plants her palm under his rib cage, and they count. Again and again. Finally, he coughs up a mess of grey-yellow stuff so thick it clogs the suction wand. I wait. When they're finished, the SAT monitor reads 95. Not bad, but after all that it should be higher.

I go to the side of his bed and kiss his cheek. Slack, dry skin. "Eileen's here."

His eyes flutter. "Cool. Bring her in. Wait. Give me a minute, I think I gotta cough again."

Back in the hall, I'm in the middle of introducing everybody to Eileen when I remember all at once that it's Wednesday, and Heather's school has half-days on Wednesdays, and she'll be on her way home right now, with nobody there to meet her. I say all this quickly, give both Mim and Eileen a fast hug, then hurry away, promising over my shoulder that I'll be back with both the girls later.

6 pm

Heather wants to talk. We're in the family room, hanging out on the futon. Outside it's raining, but still light. The days are getting longer.

"I don't like all these people in our house at night."

She isn't suggesting she doesn't like the people, only that she liked it better when the four of us could just be. When we didn't need any help. "I know," I say. "Sometimes I don't, either. But you have to admit, most of them are pretty nice."

Lame. Except when she's been on an overnight at a friend's house, either her dad or I always put her and Emily to bed. Every night of her life. We read the parenting manuals and followed the advice. Establish a routine and stick with it. We did, and it worked. First a snack, then go upstairs and brush your teeth.

Then a story, then the Cowboy Song, the Train Song, then goodnight, Sweetie. Safe and loved, everything predictable and clear. Now, she gets a quick kiss from me, followed by the sound of my car backing out of the driveway, and then she's alone in her bed. Emily is close by in her room, but downstairs is somebody who is not us. No matter how nice they are, their presence hurts.

I'm making myself sad. I tell her that it's harder for me if I think about how it was before. "It won't be like this forever, you know."

"I know. I just get tired of it."

"What else?"

She's quiet. "You don't want me to ask you this, but I can't help it." She's not looking at me. I know what she's going to say.

"Oh, that one. You mean the why-did-this-happen-to-us question?" She nods, says again, "I can't help it."

"I'd kind of like to have an answer to that, myself, you know." I have my arm around her, and I can't believe how comforting it is to touch her, to function as her mother. "Here's a story I think about sometimes. There was a family. A mother and a father and their one child, a son. In their village, the most important thing was to have a son, and they were, like, crazy about their boy, who was smart and strong. It was the kind of village where the job of the daughters was to marry, and the job of the sons was to take care of their parents when they got old. It was a big deal to have a healthy son.

"So, one day this precious boy was out on his horse, and the horse got scared by a black bird flying into its face. The horse took off too fast, and the boy fell." She moves under my arm. I give her a little squeeze. "The boy was hurt. He couldn't walk. He was alive, but he would never be able to take care of them when they got old.

"They were sad for a long time. For years, they went around feeling as if they'd been chosen for the worst punishment in the world. Everyone else's sons were fine; theirs wasn't. Why did they deserve this? Why them?

"Then the generals came to the village. The generals said that there was a war to fight. They needed men to fight it, and all the young men had to go, every last one—except this couple's injured son. He stayed behind because he couldn't fight.

"In the end, none of those other young men made it back. Every other family had lost its sons, except for them. Their son was alive, and he was with them." We're both quiet, watching the rain dripping from the jungle of rhododendrons in our back yard.

"So ... there was a reason?"

"I don't know. I think the story means that, you know, everyone's heart breaks sometime, somehow. If you love somebody, it's guaranteed, sooner or later, something sad is going to happen. Which is why I try not to ask, why us? Why did this happen to us? Because I know that something's going to happen to everybody, and the more they know how to love, the more it's going to suck."

"It does suck."

"Yes, it does."

Day 15

I've spent all night at the hospital again. At three, when I thought it might be safe to go home, Bruce was lying awake. His tingling legs were driving him crazy; we discovered that if I rubbed them hard, it shut them up and he could get a little rest. I set up a chair at the foot of his bed and did them in one minute sets, counting slowly to sixty again and again. At four, I couldn't do it anymore.

"Are you crying?" he whispered.

"Yes."

"You should go."

"No."

Now it's morning, and I have to get myself back home, but I'm afraid to drive. Remember the mailboxes, last week? Don't drive, Kate. Too late to make it home before the kids get up, but that's okay. Eileen is there. Sit on the couch outside his room and try to think how to do it. Who can help me? Okay. My friend Sue. Sue lives in Bellevue. Maybe she can come here and get me and drive me in my car to our house. Eileen can use it to drive her back here to get her own car. I picture this again and again, hoping that it's logical. What's Sue's number? I feel drunk, but somehow I find it. My phone has juice. Good. When Sue answers, I manage to explain what I want her to do.

Can she? She repeats it all back to me, my plan. She says no problem. Okay, see you in half an hour. It's 6:45 am. On the way home, she doesn't make me talk. Thank you. When I think I can pull it off, I call the girls, using a strange, bright voice. I lie to them. Say that I fell asleep in Daddy's room, but I'm coming home right now. Are they getting breakfast? Good. Can I talk to Eileen? Bye, Honey. Eileen gets on. I give her a collapsed version of the plan. She's cool. Whatever, she'll do it. I hang up and close my eyes. Sue drives. Good.

Day 16

During daytime hours, Eileen and I settle speedily into a two-woman, two-daughter household. When we ought to be sleeping, we morph into support team, with Eileen on one of the three-hour late-night shifts, and me on the other. She copes with our suburban life as best she can. I smile at the idea of her—world citizen, political activist, lesbian, executive director—playing at being a housewife in my upscale, all too Republican neighborhood.

This morning she notes undiplomatically that this life is, uh, really kind of boring.

"Well, yeah. But it has some good features."

"Uh, huh. Like what?"

Pause. "I'll think of one, give me time."

"Uh, huh. What am I doing today?"

I'm about to drive the carpool and go to the hospital. Nights there have been hell, daytimes only a little better. High point yesterday: sitting on the edge of the exercise mat with feet dangling, Bruce lifted his left thigh an inch off the mat. Low point last night: multiple. Hourly visits to the desk, begging for someone to come help him get some air. Minutes crawling by while he lay awake, struggling not to feel like he's choking. He's getting the stomach tube today; it's what the hospital people call a "minor procedure."

Normal people call it surgery. In his stomach, a few inches above his navel, some doctor is going to make a hole wide enough for a thick tube. This tube will go all the way into his gut. If it works out right, he'll have less nausea and be able to stay alive until his vocal cords wake up. And the nasty nose tube will be history.

"The bills."

"Oh, my favorite."

I show her how to get into our online banking account, how to find the regular payment list, and hand her a fat stack of unopened mail. "Now you're a secretary, too. Cool. I always wanted a personal secretary."

"I also do laundry."

"Oh, good, I forgot to mention that." I'm kidding, but she assures me earnestly that it's no problem, just show her where the girls keep their hampers.

"Maybe later," I say. "If you prove yourself with the dishes."

"Bitch."

"Bye."

10 am

The post-op waiting room is way down in the basement. There must be thirty people in here, lined up in plastic chairs listening to a loud television program in which a pair of women are pulling one

104

another's hair while a studio audience howls and whistles. There's no way to know where Bruce is or how the "procedure" went, or even if he's had it yet. I just have to stand around in here in case someone remembers to come and get me. Some friends walk in, one of them a woman currently on staff at Harborview as a hospital chaplain while she's preparing for her ordination. It's the first time I've seen her since the accident. She comes toward me with tears all over her face, a sight that instantly revs up my own emotions. No.

"No crying," I say loudly. "No crying, dammit! C'mon, you're supposed to be the professional here."

She says it's different when it's someone you know, but she wipes her eyes and shakes it off. I'm glad because I don't have the energy to explain how hard it is to keep doing what I must if I let myself be sad. I hadn't even known that being sad was something you get a choice about. It is. There are moments, usually alone in the car, when I feel myself about to give way, and I just choose not to. Boom, like that. Not doing that now, maybe later. Boom, gone. Keep driving.

So we visit without crying, and after a little time, a nurse does come to find me. All is well. He's going back up to his room, where he'll be sleepy for awhile. Probably tomorrow they'll try the new hookup to be sure it works, and then they'll take out the nasty nose tube. At last.

1 pm

Do they let him rest? After his sixteenth consecutive night of wakefulness, with his drastically reduced diet, his mind-blowing prognosis, his drugged, numb, dead-weight body unable even to remember how to breathe? Now, after his "procedure," which involved a general anesthetic, an incision, and a foreign object inserted into his flesh—does he get to rest quietly for a single afternoon?

Of course not. Cecille is here with his new plastic splint, specially molded in the shape of his resting right hand. It comes equipped with wide Velcro straps, three of them. One covers his fingers, one is just above his wrist, and the last is in the middle of his forearm. She sets his hand into it, fastens the straps, adjusts them, checks the fit, and pronounces it good. Now he must learn to take it off and put it on again by himself. The Velcro is strong; it makes a loud tearing noise when he pulls.

I hate the look of this thing. It turns his hand into a useless club. Cecille has explained why it's necessary. Because he's lost mobility in these fingers, they will curl tightly and permanently unless he's vigilant about moving them, and about allowing them to be at rest in a natural position. He has to wear this whenever he goes to sleep. Fine. We get the point. He's got the splint. Now, please leave so he can rest. These bitter thoughts are only mine. He's resigned, not happy, but silently cooperative. I have to force myself to be civil. I know it isn't her fault. Cecille is one of the most thoughtful, cheerful people here. But I still hate the splint.

She passes Josh on her way out. He's all excited; he's got a new wheelchair for Bruce to try, a new model 9000 XT that is light and should be easier for Bruce to move by himself. I can't believe they're going to make him get up, but he's willing, so I keep quiet. His legs are already wrapped. The nurse comes in to drop the ephedrine into his feedbag and cinch him up in the belly binder. She takes the cuff down from where it always hangs above his bed and does a blood pressure check. Better wait for the ephedrine to kick in. Josh, who is always trying to manage a few patients at once, glances at his watch and hurries away. We wait. Bruce falls asleep the second it is quiet, his lungs gurgling faintly.

In fifteen minutes the nurse comes back in, wakes him up, straps on the cuff again, and says it's a go. She hustles off to find Josh, and Bruce goes back to sleep. Five minutes pass, and then they come back in together and wake him up again. They take a long time sitting him up, trying all the way to get him to help them, but I can see that it isn't working. When it's time to move him into the chair, Josh has me stand where I can see how it works. He's an expert. He plants his feet on either side of Bruce's, locks Bruce's knees between his own, puts his head under Bruce's right arm, puts his hands under Bruce's butt, rocks back and forth a few times so Bruce can get the feel of letting his upper body rest against Josh's shoulder, then suddenly counts to three and pivots Bruce across the space and into the chair. The whole thing takes about ten seconds.

It's hard to believe that little Josh can so easily move my super-tall husband all by himself, and I say so. He shoots me a quick smile. "It's all in finding the balance point," he says. "You'll be able to do it, too."

Before I leave, I get to see Bruce gamely pushing himself down the rehab hallway under his own power. A nurse follows with the oxygen cart, and Josh is everywhere at once, checking for ways the chair might be adjusted to make it fit him better, watching his posture as he tries to push the wheels, narrowing his eyes at the fit of Bruce's hips in the chair seat. He decides it's too wide, and makes himself a note to call the company and ask for a leaner model.

Oh, one more thing. Josh wants me to learn the forward pressure release. Okay. Just when I was getting so expert at the tilt-back one, too. We both stand facing Bruce in his chair, and Josh tells him to put his hands flat on his knees, then lower himself so that his chest touches his thighs.

"Try it," Josh says to me, pointing at a chair. I do. I sit down, lean forward, and sure enough, I can feel that there is no pressure on my butt. Cool. "Now try it without using anything but your arm muscles." Okay. It's very hard not to cheat; my abs just kick in automatically. When I can make them relax even a little, I get a sense of how much strength he has to have in his arms, just for this simple maneuver.

Bruce lowers himself ceremoniously down and stays there for twenty seconds, then Josh, kneeling in front of him, puts his two hands flat on the broad part of Bruce's chest and helps him rise slowly upright again. Then he has me get into position, and I try it. Up he goes and I'm kneeling in front of him, looking up at him for the first time in weeks.

"Hi, there."

He makes a face. "This is hard, fuck."

"But you're doing it. I like looking up at you."

"It'll get easier," says Josh breezily. "You'll be surprised."

Bruce lifts his left hand to touch my hair, and it's enough. It's more than enough.

10 pm

Dark. I'm in the chair between his bed and the window, and he is sound asleep. Sound asleep, with the oxygen cannula stuck between his lips instead of into his nose. Why? Because he's a mouth-breather! He's been asleep for an hour—a blessed, uninterrupted hour. Emily has left for a weekend visit to Orcas Island with David and his family, Heather is doing yet another round of soccer tryouts this weekend, and Eileen is at home catching up via the internet on whatever it is she was doing to make the world a better place before I asked her to come here. I'm content to sit and read, or I would be if my so-called friend Eileen hadn't made off with the little flashlight I gave her just for occasions like this one.

I take the hospital journal and lie down on the floor under his bed, where there is a tiny light. Eileen made an entry when she was here on the first shift last night: "We're creeping toward midnight together, both anticipating the magic moment when we get to turn you so you'll be more comfortable and get rid of the noise created by the oxygen mask you thought you'd try and which turned out to be quite a misery … this must be a constant for you, always waiting for something or someone, the fifteen minute intervals creeping by."

I'm thinking that this is one of those nights he and I would have gone to take a sauna. A sauna that lasted for an hour, with many trips out to sit steaming in the cool night between periods of baking ourselves like potatoes. Then home to bed, together, to take advantage of a kid-free house and no worries.

Day 17: 12:45 am

Only three hours later. The RT named Shannon, the one Keith called "that body-builder chick," is here giving him the workout. His SATs were in the high 80s, which woke him up in a hot hurry. I try to imagine how scary this must be, like waking up with a pillow held firmly over your face. Shannon does it all three times, the bong, then the violent, murderous quad-cough, then again, and yet again. He produces gobs of sticky sludge every time, and still the machine stubbornly reads 93. She gets him all arranged. Blue egg crate pillow under his head. Three soft pillows stuffed hard behind his back. One medium pillow between his knees. Sheet all the way up, blanket folded at his waist.

The tube feeding thing is running. It makes a constant, soft, whirring noise like a fan. She checks to make sure it's not clogged, tells him to call if he needs her again, and turns the lights back out as she goes. Me, she mostly ignores. I know she thinks I should go home and let the nurses take care of him. Tough.

1:15 am

After half an hour of leaning against his bedrail, hoping to hear his breath even out and watching the numbers sink again, I'm back at the desk. Not panicked, but close. Oh, shit. It's the Nurse-Who-Is-In-The-Wrong-Line-Of-Work.

"Hi, Mrs. Hanson."

"The monitor says 83. Can you page Shannon?"

She stands up. "I think she's still on the floor."

I take a breath. "He's been dropping since she left. Can you please find her?" It's all I can do not to yell.

She walks toward his room, slowly. "Let me come and talk to him."

I pass her on the way, turn on the lights that bother him least. He looks so frightened, I feel the skin on my arms start to crawl. This should not be happening after the stuff Shannon just did. Not so soon. The Nurse-Who-Is-In-The-Wrong-Line-Of-Work moseys in and turns on the most brutal light, directly over his face. She glances at the monitor, gives it a tap, and checks to make sure the lead is securely attached to his finger. All this before she speaks to him.

"Mr. Hanson? You having some trouble?"

He nods miserably, gripping the oxygen cannula between his teeth.

Finally, finally she picks up the phone on the wall behind his bed and says, "Respiratory to 464 STAT, please."

Five minutes later, Shannon comes in and starts all over again. This time he gets a nebulizer first, a sprayed-in medication delivered through a little canister that he has to hold in his mouth and suck on. She does the quad-cough, putting all her strength into forcing whatever is in his lungs to pop out, but the numbers still won't move. 84.

"Sorry, buddy," she says. "I gotta suction you."

He endures this slow and painful process with his eyes closed and his good hand clenched, but when she's finished, the monitor still reads only 88. She adjusts the flow of oxygen to its maximum output, 5 liters. No change. The Nurse-Who-Is-In-The-Wrong-Line-Of-Work is standing at the end of the bed. Shannon looks up and tells her to call the resident.

Bruce's eyes are open, the question in them obvious. I say it for him. "What's going on?"

Shannon's on one side of him and I'm on the other. She gives me a look across his body that says, don't talk in front of him, you'll scare him, and shrugs. "I don't know. He's not crashing."

I'll take that as a good thing, I guess. In a few minutes, the Nurse-Who-Is-In-The-Wrong-Line-Of-Work comes back with orders from the doctor. Bruce is going to get an X-ray, right here and now, along with blood gases. This might be pneumonia. They've switched the oxygen delivery system again, so that now he's got a mask strapped tightly over his face. He's breathing 70% pure oxygen, and still the monitor reads only 93. The doctor will be here in a few minutes to talk with us. Okay. The skin all along my arms is prickling now, cool and crawly, and my fingertips are icy wet.

After another ten minutes, the doctor walks in. I recognize her—it's Dr. Ratty Hair, the woman who once predicted that he would go home a "full quad." Any other doctor in this hospital, I would be overjoyed to see, but even in these extremities, I can't be more than neutral about her. She's obviously been sleeping. Too fucking bad.

It takes the rest of the night for everything to fall completely apart. The chest X-ray is duly given, by a burly woman with a portable machine and a rough bedside manner. I restrain myself from slapping her when she yanks the metal sheet out from beneath him, making him wince. The results are inconclusive. The blood is drawn, the tests done. The results are inconclusive. Dr. Ratty Hair tells me that probably Bruce will have to be transferred two floors down, to respiratory intensive care. I become irrationally concerned that he will be shoved out right now, stuck somewhere waiting for a bed. I imagine him going through the whole crazy ordeal of getting moved again, twice, with the waiting in the basement, and the days slipping by while he can't get well. I am quite crazy, imagining that we will have to take this whole room apart and pack it up right now. The problem, of course, is that I have no confidence in this doctor.

I'm being a terrible advocate. I'm letting Bruce down. She's trying to convince me that he'll get better care in RICU, to which I want to reply that they could hardly do worse. I say only that I don't want him to get jerked around. She tells me that rehab is very expensive, and that if he uses up his insured days here being sick, we'll have to pay ourselves for him to be here later, when he's well enough to take advantage of the therapies. I tell her that money is the last thing I'm worried about. She says that the hospital could start making my family pay cash, $1,500 per day, the minute the insurance runs out. I tell her, through my teeth, that I don't care.

She says that the nurses here have been complaining about how hard it is to take care of him, which infuriates me so thoroughly that I walk away and close the door to his room in her face, then open it right up again to tell her that it wasn't our idea to move him here. It was perfectly obvious, I say bitterly, that he wasn't well enough to do rehab. Somebody else made that decision. I close the door again and turn around, breathing hard. He's fallen asleep, but the monitor is reading 87, so I know he will wake up in a moment and start the process all over again.

7 am

I'm stumbling down the steps of the main hospital entrance. I have to get to my car. Eileen has been with us for the last few hours, and she's up there still. They're going to move him back to intensive care today because they think he has pneumonia (in spite of the inconclusive X-ray), or maybe a pulmonary embolism. People with spinal cord injuries can die of pneumonia—and pulmonary embolism is even more lethal. So it's a good thing, going to intensive care. I know this. It's morning, Saturday morning, before most people are up, but there is a lot of traffic around the hospital. I'm walking up the street to my car, listing a little, when suddenly Jocelyn's face appears in the window of a dark green minivan.

Like a drunk, I start to sob at the sight of her. I am humiliated and helpless, breaking down right on the sidewalk, clinging to a mailbox. She pulls over and I tell her what's happened. She was just showing up to cover somebody's shift; she'll go in and try to get some more information and let everybody know what's happened. Okay.

10 am

The phone rings. It's Dr. Smooth Eyes, and she wants to go over the plans to move Bruce down to respiratory intensive care sometime today. Dull and beaten, I say I think it's a good idea. She tells me that she had a talk with Dr. Ratty Hair.

"She shouldn't have said that to you about having to pay cash at the hospital."

"No."

"The hospital wouldn't do that. I've talked to her about this. She shouldn't have said that the nurses have been complaining, either. Everyone likes your husband very much."

Even in my ragged state, this strikes me as hilarious. This insufferable, oily person is telling me that I'm married to a popular guy. Hot damn. I can't say anything without laughing, so I just keep quiet. The silence drags.

"He's a very nice man, and everyone on the floor will be anxious to see him come back, as soon as he's feeling better. We'll hold his room just as it is."

This is news. This is the best thing I've heard in so many hours. They're going to leave his room just as it is, and when the lung thing is cleared up, he'll cruise right back in, no starting over. Okay. I manage to tell her that sounds fine.

11 am

For the first time since he offered me his number, I call Jon Huseby, the doctor who happened to be skiing in Edelweiss Bowl when Heather screamed for help. He questions me closely about last night, and I do my best to describe what I think happened. He reassures me, saying clearly and in few words that this kind of complication is common, temporary and treatable. He says it's good that they didn't have to intubate Bruce; this means he didn't quite get to the high danger zone. I think of Shannon saying he's not crashing, and of the Nurse-Who-Is-In-The-Wrong-Line-Of-Work tapping the monitor as if it were the problem. My skin prickles. We were close to a disaster. I ask, amazed at my own gall, if he would go and see Bruce in respiratory intensive care. There is a pause.

"I'm sorry if I'm being out of line," I say. "It's just that I know what it would mean to him to lay eyes on you, and have you tell him what you just said to me."

He says his schedule today is full, but that he'll try. And then, the head of pulmonary ICU at Virginia Mason hospital says he's glad I called him. He says that he's been thinking of Bruce, and that in spite of this setback, it's really, really good news that he's already getting so much return in his legs. I hang up the phone, put my hands over my face, and pray words of gratitude.

Bruce, my first impression is how much respect the folks who are on this unit have for you. These, the guys with you hour in and hour out, have great admiration.

Note in the hospital journal from a visitor to respiratory intensive care, March 25, 2001.

Patient very pleasant
and cooperative …
sitter at bedside
throughout the night
… large support group
of friends and family
…

EIGHT

Day 17: 4 pm

Respiratory intensive care is on the second floor, in the old part of the hospital. The waiting room is tiny, with one couch, two chairs, a telephone and, of course, a TV set. Everything is shabby, as if it came from a Goodwill store. Inside, where the patients are, there are no private rooms. There are only beds, ranged against the walls of an open space, with privacy curtains pulled between them. Equipment is everywhere: machinery with thick cords and mysterious purpose, an abundance of computer monitors, Hoyer lifts, and wheelchairs.

To get to Bruce, I have to walk past three or four other patients, lying exposed on their beds in hospital gowns. All of them have ventilators. They've crashed, to use Shannon's word, and now they're hooked to these breathing machines. So far, Bruce is not.

His nurse is named Cheryl. She's moving around the cramped space with absolute composure, smiling easily at us both, asking questions about our family, our dog, where we live. She's generously made in every sense—her body is generous and soft, her face is broad and friendly; her every gesture speaks of something abundant and good inside. Best of all, she is his nurse, the one who will be spending the most time with him.

I'm asking if it would be okay for our friend Darrell to come in and do some hypnosis with Bruce, to help him sleep. Darrel is out in the waiting room now. Cheryl is leaning over Bruce, adjusting his egg crate, and she looks over her shoulder at me.

"Sure," she says. "That's a great idea." She turns back to Bruce. "Have you done this before?"

He gives his little nod, pressing his chin into the neck brace. "Yesterday," he whispers.

"It seemed to help," I say. "At least, you were sleeping for awhile, before all this bullshit."

"It did help."

"Well, bring him in, I think it's a fab idea. Just give me five minutes, and I'll be out of your way."

6 pm

I'm with Heather, explaining that Daddy has had to go to a different part of the hospital because they think he has pneumonia. She's quiet, in the way that means there is far too much to say. Finally she says simply, "I miss him." I tell her she might feel better if she wrote him a note; I could bring it to the hospital and write down for him what he wants to say back. She sighs. I think of the two of them, all the years of their special let's-go-do-something bond, built like a platform on which she now sits, alone. What good is a stupid note, when what she wants is to have him chase her around the front yard until they both fall down like puppies in the wet grass?

I stop, seeing suddenly that I am doing to her what I've noticed others doing to me: imagining how wretched I am, then pitying me for it. We sit quietly, her head in my lap. She takes my hand and puts it to the side of her head, which is her signal that she wants me to move my finger around and around in the sweet curling spaces of her ear, something we started doing before she could talk. When I finish one ear, she turns over so I can do the other. Then she stands up and gets paper and pencil, and writes him a note. The next day, I show her my journal:

> Dear Heather, Thank you for your note. I miss you so much! It was very good to have your note so I could hear you. Heather, some of these questions are too big to answer, or too big to answer in a note. Right now for me to think about why this happened isn't very helpful. What can I do about it is helpful, and that's where my energies are. What can you do about it? You can continue sending me notes that say how much you love me. One of the really painful things about this is that we don't get to share all the little day to day stuff together, like, you know, how school went, and kicking the soccer ball in front of the house, and talking about some question that comes up, and watching the Wild Thornberrys. As I get better, we'll have time to do some of this, and things will feel a lot better. Until then we have to do the best we can. Love, Daddy

115

Day 18: 9:30 am

I walk into RICU unprepared. Our favorite respiratory therapist, Rich, is there in his white jacket, arms folded, talking energetically to a small, well-dressed man who is listening with great intensity. Cheryl smiles at me from her perch at the computer, and our friend Jim is sitting comfortably in the visitor's chair, just finishing his shift. The visitor's chair has been occupied every second since Bruce was moved in here yesterday; Jocelyn told me that people have been wrangling over the privilege of being assigned this duty.

Bruce himself looks—dare I think it? Rested. Yes. And pleased. Automatically, I check the SAT monitor. 98. Wow. He's got a kind of funnel blowing moist oxygen into his face, but he isn't gripping it, and—dear God—they've taken out the nose tube, which means it's possible to see all of his face. I smile at him.

"You look great."

"So do you," he whispers. "Kate, this is Dr. Huseby."

The small man takes my outstretched hand. He has a good face, with clean lines and intelligent eyes; I laugh out of sheer happiness. "You came up," I say. "I'm so glad to meet you."

"I'm so glad you called me," he says. "You're absolutely right. This should not be happening."

And then he and Rich are off on a long exchange, discussing all the possible reasons and remedies for Bruce's current troubles. Rich glances over at me in the middle of this and says, "Kate, this guy is the best. He is just the very best."

I'm standing next to Bruce, enjoying the sight of his tube-free nose. I ask him if there are any other angels he needs called to his bed. He says that's okay, these will do fine for now.

Day 19: 2 pm

I stand up to stretch, and suddenly Stan is there in front of me. "Stan!" He's tall, as tall as Bruce, which means that when he puts his arms around me I get a powerful reminder of what used to be an everyday event. Ah. I don't want him to let go, but I pull away and smile at him. We talk for a few minutes, and then I say that I have to take off … he says that's fine. He has a book with him. I suddenly get it.

"You're the two o'clock person."

"Yeah, is that okay?"

"Of course. I just—it's so odd how people from all these parts of our lives just appear ..."

"Yeah, well, from what I hear his dance card fills up pretty fast."

"A popular guy." The popular guy is currently sound asleep, not even appreciating what a giant fan club he has.

We see Stan maybe once or twice a year, when we have a singing party. This is a kind of whoever-shows-up event that always ends up with a dozen or so people in our living room, doing old rock and roll in harmony, laughing and trying to remember how the words go. Stan has a charming way of sitting bent over his twelve-string, eyes squeezed shut, fingers feeling around for the chords that lead him into a song. "It's in there somewhere," he will say. We know enough to wait. After a moment or two, the familiar bars of some tune by the Beatles or Simon and Garfunkel fill up the room, and we're off.

I'm in the car again, hurrying to get home before Heather, and I'm trying to squeeze in a phone call to Jill. A friend with connections at Alpental did some digging, and reported that Bruce is famous up there—the guy who crashed and got lifted out. She had no trouble finding out the last name of the patroller who was first at the scene, and now I am crossing the bridge and punching Jill's number into my phone. When she answers, I tell her who I am.

"Oh, my God, I am so glad you called. I have wanted so much to talk to you."

I can see her standing in our driveway, looking at me over Heather's head. "I just wanted to thank you for taking care of Heather," I say.

"Heather—she is a great kid. I was glad to do it. How's she doing?"

"It's hard," I say. And then I thank her for not telling me what had actually happened.

"Oh, man." She blows out air into my ear. "Thanks for saying that. I really worried about it because I kind of lied to you—but I thought, this woman has to drive—"

"Right. You were right, you did the right thing."

"I'm so glad to hear you say that, you have no idea. And Bruce, I hear such good things about him, how's all that going?"

I tell her about his lung problems, and then about him having sensation over most of his body, and finally about him getting a little return in his left leg and toes. She probably knows all this already, but she's very enthusiastic and encouraging anyway. She gives me her e-mail address and asks to be included in the Great Big List. Before we hang up, I ask if she'd be willing to take Heather skiing sometime. I say that I'd do it myself, except I can't keep up with her. That was Bruce's job. Jill is quiet, then says of course. It would be a privilege.

That night, I send an e-mail to David's Great Big List. "I want you to know that sometimes I just scan through your names, so I can remember that I'm not even close to being in this alone. Your presence out there is a comfort past even MY descriptive powers, and your presence at the hospital is what gets us both through. Thank you."

Day 20: 7:30 am

I'm in the kitchen, looking for something to put in Emily's lunch when the phone rings. It's Bruce, talking in a loud whisper, very proud of himself. He called home, and it's a huge deal, to have enough breath to make a telephone call. I am absurdly excited; an ordinary thing is happening. Bruce, away, is calling us to say hello. How fantastically, outlandishly normal. He asks me to put the girls on. Heather takes the phone, looking confused. "Daddy?" She lights up. They talk for a few minutes. Emily jumps around the table, demanding her turn. Her round face is a picture of delight when he says her name, and then, being Emily, she launches immediately into a detailed monologue about her Northwest History assignment, her stupid math teacher, the girl who used to be her friend but now isn't, and why she hasn't come to see him lately.

I can picture him so clearly, smiling to himself at this rambling, classic Emily-style conversation. He asks them to come in tomorrow night before choir. Good idea, Dad.

11:30 am

Even in RICU, he has to have his therapies. The miracle is that he feels well enough to do them. His need for extra oxygen is steadily declining, and he hasn't had to be suctioned for twenty-four hours. Cheryl says he's turned a corner. He's sitting up now in a wheelchair, brakes set, in front of a tiny sink, exposed to all passersby as he makes his first attempt to brush his own teeth since the accident. He uses a special toothbrush with a fat, soft handle; I can see that doing it with his left hand is a pain. He can't keep his balance and brush at the same time; the man who is helping him holds his shoulders so he doesn't go face first into the faucets. I stand off to one side, watching, trying to see my athletic, good-looking husband in this thin, needle-armed, hospital-gowned, slumping bald creature who can't quite manage to spit out toothpaste without dribbling all over his own chin.

His physical therapist here is named Jill. She's demonstrating how Bruce can use stretchy rubber exercise bands to work his arms and shoulders, even while lying in bed. She looks like a kindergarten teacher—smooth, straight hair, wide eyes, pretty smile, strong young body. The idea with the bands is for me to hold one end and keep up the tension; I'm shocked at how little tension is too much for him, and I see her notice this. Jill smiles her orthodontist-perfect smile and says that it will only get better if he does this every day. Some of the weakness is from the weeks of illness, and that can be restored. Anybody would be limp as a noodle after enduring what he has. What's difficult to bear is the possibility that most of his lack of strength could be from the injury, and permanent.

He's already lost about twenty-five pounds. He's depleted in every way except in the one that counts the most—his spirit. He motions for me to keep going, and this time we both pull just a little harder.

4 pm

Eileen has good news. While I was at the hospital, Karen called from church. She told Eileen she's figured out the Harborview parking problem, and I now have instructions for how to get myself a space.

"But it makes no sense," she says. "It's the craziest system I've ever heard of."

"Is the space in the parking garage?"

"No, it's a lot, like, across the street from the hospital and down about a half a block. It has nine spaces, and you'll get a tag that guarantees you one of them. It costs $30.00 a month, which your church is going to pay for. The good thing is you get in-and-out privileges. So, you can just come and go whenever you want, no day passes."

"Am I already signed up for it?"

"No, that's the weird part. They give these nine spaces to whoever happens to show up at their office on a day when one of them becomes open. Which happens, like, once in a blue moon, right? I mean, this is a huge hospital, with lots of people staying in it for long periods?"

"And they only have nine long-term spaces? That can't be right."

"Karen swears it is. And, someone is using up their pass today. So, you have to be there, on the first floor at a room marked "Parking Enforcement," at nine o'clock sharp. They'll give you a thirty-day pass."

"What happens after thirty days?"

"You tell them on the twenty-ninth day that you want to renew it, and they give you another one."

I'm glad I'm going to get one, but I don't like the arbitrariness of it. "So I just get this because Karen knew who to ask and how to work the system?"

"Just a privileged white girl."

I think of the people camping up in the NICU lounge because they can't afford to rent a room to live in while they wait out intensive care. I think of the people I've seen all over the hospital, stricken and broke and barely coping. I imagine trying to deal with something as simple as finding a place to put my car without the wall of people who have my back. I couldn't do it.

That night we watch The Gilmore Girls with Eileen. In the old days the girls and I would do this every week, just the three of us, because Bruce had choir practice. I find myself automatically relaxing into the familiar rhythm. I give them bowls of ice cream. I brush their hair: Heather's is fine, straight, and thick, just like mine. She likes getting her hair brushed. She likes me to lift her hair and put the brush to her scalp. Once, she reaches up and moves the brush to the hairline near her ear. I linger there, loving her, grateful to be touching her. Emily is in the middle of a perm, so I have to work gently and slowly through every strand, her blond curls winding sweetly around the bristles.

I get the scissors and trim their fingernails, then their toenails. I get rose-scented lotion and rub it into their feet. In the meantime, the television entertains us all. It's fun to see Eileen watching this show for the first time; it's full of silliness and wit, but underneath is a serious attempt to underline the goodness at the center of this fictional mother/daughter pair. Plus, we are all rooting for Lorelei to open her eyes and see that Luke is really the right man for her. She never does, which is why we have to keep coming back every week: so we can be there to see it when this one thing turns out the way it should.

Day 21: 6:15 pm

The girls, Eileen, and I are driving as fast as we dare into Seattle. They have choir at seven o'clock, and there is just time for a speedy visit to RICU beforehand. Eileen is filling us in about Cheryl's life. Eileen is famous for artlessly getting every single person she encounters to tell her everything. Yesterday I learned from her, for example, that one of the aides in rehab, a dark-skinned, gold-toothed guy named Tsegaw, is from Eritrea—where, of course, Eileen has been, and the politics of which she knows well.

Cheryl, she says, is the daughter of two physicians who practiced medicine in Central America while she was growing up. This explains a lot: why she seems so laid back, how she came to possess such a great, gentle soul, why she seems unhappy to find herself in the middle of an institutional monster like Harborview Medical Center. Eileen has also learned that Cheryl is planning a new career as a massage therapist, and that she only intends to be working as a nurse for a few more months.

"Lucky we got her before she left," I say. Emily wants to know why. I try to explain. "She's just special. She, like, loves Daddy—not because she knows him, but just because that's what she does. She loves people. I bet her patients get better a lot faster than other nurses' patients do."

"That's cool."

Yes, it is.

Fifteen minutes later, we're walking into the disturbing, wide open space of RICU. Eileen and Heather were here for a little while yesterday afternoon, but this is Emily's first time, and in spite of my attempt to prepare her, she is freaking. I'm hustling them quickly into his little curtained area, only to stop cold once inside.

Bruce is having a de-SAT episode, and from the looks of it, a serious one. There's a doctor in here, along with a nurse—not Cheryl—

and an RT, and all three of them have their hands on him in some way. He's gasping, but he looks at the four of us and somehow manages to say, "Sorry, having a little trouble" before the RT orders us right back out again. I'm so pissed at the station nurse for letting me walk my kids into that scene that I can't say anything until we get back outside.

When my breathing is close to normal, I tell them we'll stop back after choir, no big deal. Eileen and I are glancing at each other—what the hell? He's been so much better since Friday, but this looked exactly like what kept happening to him in rehab. The girls are disappointed, but not frightened. They go to choir practice while we sit in the sanctuary. I have adrenaline poisoning again.

8:10 pm

Because the normal entrance to the hospital is locked at eight o'clock, we have to go in through the security set-up outside the ER. I don't think the kids have seen this hallway since the night of the accident, and I didn't want to make them come here. We stand in line with everyone else, waiting while armed, uniformed guards take each past-hours visitor one at a time. You have to give your name, the name of the person you're visiting, and your relationship to them. You have to wait while they call the floor to get the okay from the nurses. You have to turn over your bags and keys and walk through a metal detector, just like at the airport. This is a high-crime neighborhood, and this hospital is where victims (and perpetrators) of gang violence often land.

This time, I make sure the desk nurse who answers the phone knows that I don't want the girls to come in unless Bruce says it's a good time. She checks, then comes back and tells me to bring them on in. Thanks. Emily hasn't seen him in almost a week; she's so happy that his nose tube is gone, she barely notices anything else. It does make a huge difference. We're talking quietly, making plans for the next time, wondering if he'll get moved back to rehab as soon as tomorrow. That's the current agenda.

In a reversal of what used to be a family custom, we decide before we go that the girls should sing him a goodnight song. The kids' choir was working on "Ubi Caritas" tonight, so we do that, just Emily, Heather, and I, without the harmony he would have supplied. Three times through, quietly.

Ubi caritas, et amor.
Ubi caritas, Deus ibi est.

(Where there is charity and love, there also is God.)

He listens with his eyes closed at first, then opens them to watch the girls' faces. *Deus ibi est.*

Day 22: 8 pm

I'm hanging around in RICU, laughing at the way Cheryl and our second-favorite RT are teasing one another. Our second-favorite RT is Chris, a bear of a man with semi-wild hair and a "no-worries" attitude that fits well into the little world Cheryl somehow creates. He's calling her lame—the queen of lameness—because she doesn't get some hip cultural reference he's just made. Neither do I; I didn't even catch what he said. But the word "lameness" rings a bell.

"She's wallowing in lameness," I say.

His head comes up from the chart he was working on. "Wallowing in lameness! Exactly."

Bruce is snickering. "I remember that. Lame, lame, lame, lame!" It sounds so funny when he does it in his pathetic whisper that Chris and I laugh out loud. Cheryl just looks puzzled. I explain. It's a routine from an old local comedy show. In one of the show's more mature moments, there was a circle of guys with very long hair trying to outdo one other in stories of things that suck. After each story, they would all shake their heads sadly and say, "Lame. Boy, that's so lame. That is on the lame list! That's wallowing in lameness." I go on to say that it always ended with a kind of lameness circle jerk, in which they faced the center of their pity circle and shouted "lame, lame, lame, lame!" while shaking their hair vehemently at one another. Chris and I demonstrate..

Then I look around and say, gesturing at where we are, "Guys, we are literally wallowing in lameness here. RICU is lameness land." Bruce laughs at this until he cries, which makes me feel like the queen of everything. Chris then decides it's a good moment for me to learn the quad-cough.

"Me?"

"It's easy. You're going to want to know how so you don't have to wait around for somebody official once he's out of here."

I think of myself begging for an RT. "Teach me."

He shows me where to put my right hand, wrist flexed, just on Bruce's diaphragm, with my left hand pressing on top of it. I get into the lunge position I've seen them use so often. "It's all in the timing," he says. "The idea is that you get a rhythm going by counting to three. He starts by breathing in, and then you push down gently and say 'one' as he breathes out. Do it a second time, and pay attention, so that your push down is right there with his second exhale. On the third time, go for it. When he's breathing out the third time, you shove as hard as you can against that spot."

I'm worried about the stomach tube, but he shows me that it's not in the way. I'm stalling, joking around, scared. What the hell. I crack my knuckles and tell Bruce we ought to be able to do this. I wink at him. "Our timing was always pretty good before."

He smiles a little, and I know he's thinking of those stolen afternoons. "That's true." And then I just do it. Gentle, gentle, hard. He coughs up a nasty wad of snot, sucks it out of his mouth with his trusty wand, and says, "Again."

When we're finished, I turn around, a little shaken but proud of myself. Cheryl is looking at me with so much raw compassion that I almost lose my balance. "What?" I can't make it sound like a joke.

"This should not happen to some people," She says. "Some people, this should not happen to."

"Come on, Cheryl," I say. "This shouldn't happen to anybody."

Day 23: 11 am

Bruce has something to show us. Eileen and I have come to see him together today; it's supposed to be the day he leaves RICU for the medical floor, and we both want to say goodbye to Cheryl. He's up in the wheelchair, slumped and quiet, but ready to roll. Cheryl is giving him a narrow look.

"I'm going to check that blood pressure one more time, Buddy."

He rolls his eyes. "I feel fine."

"Yeah, but you're pale. Wouldn't want you to pass out from the excitement." She straps the cuff on his arm and pumps it up. The three of us wait while she gets the reading. It's okay. "Sorry," she says cheerfully. "I just gotta be sure." She gives me her broad, ready smile. "You look nice today."

Right. The truth is, I'm getting thinner. I keep putting on jeans that used to be snug and watching them slip down to ride stylishly on my hip bones. And I don't bother with makeup, so the circles under my eyes are there for everybody to see. "If I look better," I tell her, "it's because you are making him better."

"He's making himself better," she says. She squats to tighten the laces on his enormous, perfectly white shoes, looking up at him like a proud mom. "You're the man, Bruce. You are."

"All right, all right." Eileen is pretending to be impatient. "Bruce, show us what you got."

He looks up at me, wiggling both eyebrows. "Watch this," he whispers. He plants his palms on his knees and slowly brings his chest all the way forward. And then, under his own power, he rises back up again. He lifts both skinny arms, elbows squared, in the gesture of a weightlifter. "Ta da."

I'm clapping, genuinely impressed. He couldn't do that a week ago, when Josh first showed it to us on his last day in rehab. "Independent in the forward pressure release. Cool. Does this mean I'm off the hook with that tip-back thing?"

"Oh, you'll still have to do that sometimes," he says seriously. "This is hard. Plus I like to look up your shirt when you lean me back."

"Pervert. So, where do you want to go?" I glance at Cheryl. "Is it still okay?"

"Let me walk you to the hall," she says. "Officially, I'm not supposed to let him out of my sight, but he isn't sick. A little tour around the building won't hurt."

"Around the building? I thought we were taking him somewhere interesting."

"The building is interesting, trust me." She pushes him as we go past the other patients. There is a young guy hooked up to a ventilator, strapped to his bed while an armed guard sits, blank-faced, in the visitor's chair. There is the little girl with Down's Syndrome, wearing a medieval-torture-device metal halo. Rich the RT told us she got hurt because she didn't have enough muscles in her body to keep from giving herself whiplash when she tried to sit up. There is another person of indeterminate gender, in two full leg casts, with an oxygen mask like the one Bruce uses. This person has not had a single visitor all week.

Day 24

The room on the medical floor is closet-sized. It has one window with a wonderful view of the sound and the mountains. The visitors enjoy this; Bruce is always prone and never even sees it. There's not room for his wheelchair, so they leave it parked outside his door in the hallway. It's a way-station, a stopping place between RICU and—we hope—a stay in rehab where he can actually take advantage of the therapies. It's Saturday night, and when I walk in, his nurse—a good-looking young guy whose name I don't catch—folds his arms across his chest and gives Bruce a look.

"Another one?"

Bruce is on his side, facing us. "This one is my wife."

"Oh, sure she is."

I laugh. "Has he got something going on the side?"

The nurse gives me a look. "Honey, he's got women coming out his ears. On the side doesn't begin to cover it. Side, front, back, up, down, other side, man! Every time I come in here, there's two or three more of 'em, and never the same ones twice. What is up with you people?"

While he's saying this, he's unwrapping Bruce's legs for the night. Yards and yards of pink/brown ace wraps pile up on the white blanket. The nurse winds it up into neat rolls and sets it on a shelf above the tiny sink. He pulls a little syringe out of his pocket. "Heparin," he says. "Sorry."

"I can't feel it," says Bruce. "It's supposed to burn, right?"

With quick hands, the nurse lifts Bruce's gown and injects the drug into his stomach. "That's what they say, yeah." He disposes of the needle. "You can't feel it at all?"

Bruce says that his middle is the numbest part of him. I don't like hearing this, and I don't like looking at the stomach tube. It's got a flat, clear plastic disc about the size of a quarter that rests like a washer against his skin. Four tiny black sutures hold it in place. The tube itself is three inches long, with a bright red valve at the business end. The other end disappears into his flesh.

After the nurse leaves, I sit on the edge of the bed and take his limp right hand in mine. "It's funny, I was just thinking this afternoon about all these women looking after you."

"Yeah?"

"Yeah, it's like suddenly you have a whole boatload of mothers." I laugh. "That sounds scary, like something Gary Larsen might draw, huh?" I bend his index finger and straighten it out again.

He smiles his loopy oxycodone smile. "It is kind of like that."

"In a good way, I hope." Middle finger. Bend. Straighten.

"Oh, yeah. I liked it when this nurse guy kept thinking everybody was my wife all day."

"Too bad for them, they're not." I still have his wedding ring. I wear mine in the usual place, and I wear his on the middle finger of my right hand. I hold it out to show him. "See? I have proof. You're taken." I match his right hand against my left one, then brace it from behind with my own right hand. His long fingers lie still between mine, and I notice that his palm is soft and smooth, like the skin on the inside of my arms. The calluses are already gone.

10 pm

I slip into Bruce's room. Dark, quiet, and he's snoring. Our friend Jane is sitting in the visitor's chair. She stands up to hug me, then holds a slip of paper under a narrow nightlight. On it, she has scrawled, "He's having periods of up to 30 seconds without breathing."

After she leaves, he sleeps on for a half an hour, definitely snoring, definitely suffering from apnea. I count the seconds of the no-breath periods when they come. There is no particular pattern. He'll breathe restfully for five minutes, then suddenly stop. One thousand one, one thousand two … it could be eight seconds, or eighteen, or, as Jane said, as long as thirty.

I try breathing just as he does, stopping suddenly when he stops, and I can't do it. I can't stop breathing right in the middle of a normal rhythm and hold it for thirty seconds. What fresh hell is this?

Day 25: 11 am

I'm sitting in one of the front rows at church. The sanctuary is full today, which is good because I'm going to get a few minutes to tell them what Bruce has asked me to say. I'm not especially nervous. I've been at the lectern before this group so many times, but never delivering any news so personal or so hard. I'm just hoping I don't cry. When it's time, Tony invites me up, and I climb the steps. Jocelyn and

Sue are in the front row of the choir; I catch their eyes and make a little face.

Then I stand at the microphone. Not everyone knows who I am, of course. It's a big church. I say my name, and that I'm currently on staff as the youth ministry coordinator, and that I'm married to Bruce Hanson. I turn and point to the place in the choir where he usually sits, in the top row with the basses. I tell them he's that really tall guy with the interesting glasses.

I say what happened to him, and when, and where he is now. I say that since the moment he fell, for every hour of every day, our family has been among God, and God has been among us. I say that my old life is gone, that I am grieving for my children's lost innocence, that I have tasted a lot of ashes. I admit that I have been sad beyond description—but that also, often in the very same instant—I have felt blessed, also beyond description. So, how is Bruce? I have a message for them from him.

> ...most of what I find is hope. I don't know how this is going to turn out. I don't know what kind of life I'll have when this is over, but I do know that it will be full and rich. I knew that even lying in the snow. I also deeply know that God is in my life, and the strength I draw from that is tremendous. I don't have to live in regret or in wondering what if. Doing what's placed in front of me, each little step, is what it will take to rebuild my life. I don't know how to do this, except for living a day at a time, or even a minute at a time, which, with God's help, I am able to do. I don't believe in a God who lets things like this happen to people in order to teach them something, and yet I am learning. So, if you're going to pray for me, what I ask for is prayers of determination and hope...

Then I close the notebook. The room is perfectly quiet; the faces looking at me are respectful and sad. Yesterday, I tell them, for the first time in twenty-three days, my husband was able to breathe room air. I lift both hands, palms up. "Room air, people!" I can't help smiling about this; after all those nights of helplessness, he can breathe. The enormous, empty space above the congregation is suddenly not empty, but filled with something ordinary and full of glory. I thank them again, take my notebook, and go back to my seat. The choir members rise, open the red leather binders that hold their music, and wait for Steven to give them their note.

1 pm

We're in his tiny room on the third floor. Heather is nervous and annoying. She plays her flute too loudly, and she won't settle down and try to connect with him. She seems itchy to leave the minute she arrives, marching around the little room, kicking things "accidentally." Watching her, I finally get it. Her strategy is to simply ignore this current version of "Dad" until a more recognizable one appears. She hasn't said so, of course. She may not even know it herself, but this is what her every look and gesture says. It's a measure of how desperately she misses his old self, that she can scarcely tolerate the new one. In the meantime, Bruce is trying, with his tiny store of resources, to somehow be with her. I ache for them both, but I also see that it's all right. Watching them struggle, I think of a favorite line from Gerald May: "In matters of love, there can be no anesthesia."

Emily does better—they actually play three or four games of hangman together. She kind of blows it by misspelling a word in one of her phrases, but she is much more able to hang out and explore this situation. She asks polite visitor questions: How are you feeling, Daddy? Did you sleep last night? Do those poison ivies hurt? When are they going to take them out?

"Poison ivies" is Heather's term for the IV needles still inserted and taped to the backs of his hands. He says, no, they don't bother him, and he thinks they'll be gone tomorrow. Emily says that's great, sounding enthusiastic and phony. She is finding her own way to be his daughter, falling back on her best behavior—on her manners—to see her through. I'm insanely proud of her; isn't this exactly what manners are for? To help us pick our way through delicate, dangerous social territory? Her father—the strength against which she has always tested her own mettle—is helpless. She hasn't really spoken with him in nearly a month. She is going forward blind, willing to believe he's still there for her, wanting him to know she's waiting. She's twelve years old.

4 pm

Now that he can travel without an oxygen tank, it's a lot easier to push him around the hospital. We ride the elevators randomly, trying to get up really high to a place where there are windows. The top of the hospital is a pediatric floor, though, and I won't go up there. Kids sick enough to need a trauma center—no. We're religious about pressure releases. Every fifteen minutes, either I tip him back or he does his seated low bow, once in a while needing a little shove to get vertical again. We don't talk much while we're in motion. I don't like blabbing to the air over the back of his head, and if he speaks I can't hear him. Suddenly I realize he's trying to get my attention, and I stop to lean over and look into his face.

"What?"

"Where are you going?"

"I don't know. Nowhere, just moving."

He makes a face. "Well, let's go somewhere."

This irritates me. "Fine, where do you want to go?"

He's quiet. I wish he could drive the damn thing himself. I wish he could fucking give me directions at least. "I just get so tired of being pushed around," he says. "What time is it?"

I check my watch. Time for a pressure release. I wait while he's tipped forward. Hospital time on the weekends is the way I imagine it would be to live on one of those planets far out in the solar system. Jupiter. Every day lasts four times what it should, and so there is no need to hurry. This time he sits up unassisted, good. We decide to roll up to his old room at rehab, just for someplace to go. He'll be moving back there tomorrow. The floor is quiet, not the way I remember it. I guess only the nurses and aides work weekends.

The door to his room is extra wide and heavy, for soundproofing maybe. It's a long, narrow room, with his bed in the middle, facing a wall lined with whiteboards. A pair of televisions hang from brackets mounted in the ceiling. We drive past the bed toward the windows, which are big enough for me to stand in, one in each corner. They face the street—no view of the Sound from back here. Still, there is the world. Cars. Buses. People walking. He stares out at it for a few minutes, then turns himself around so he can see the clock. He can't turn his head because of the neck brace. Time for a pressure release.

I'm reading him some of the cards we've pasted to the wall, carefully taking them down so the adhesive doesn't tear them. His balance in the chair is so bad that he can't hold a card and read it at the same time. It's a good collection—everything from jokes about doctors (Nine out of ten doctors want you to get well immediately. The tenth one thinks you might have a few bucks left.) to beautiful home-made cards from artist friends, to religious ones. There is a photograph of about a hundred men, apparently at a men's retreat of some kind, with a note attached informing him that they're Methodists, and they're praying for him daily. We have no clue who these people are, or who sent the note.

I find a card from his Aunt Sue and pull it down. "I forgot to tell you, she e-mailed me and asked if I thought you'd like her to come out." She's from the side of his family we know less well—his mom's sister. I've only met her a few times, most recently last fall when I happened to be in Louisville, where she lives. I wanted to get together with her then because it seemed like a chance to learn something about his mom, who died long before we met. Aunt Sue was kind to me, and interesting.

He takes the card and struggles to open it with his left hand, right arm swinging behind him. I wait. Jupiter time. Then suddenly he's got tears in his eyes. He's been sick and paralyzed for almost a month, and this is the very first time I've seen him cry. He says, with difficulty, that he wants her to come, that I should get hold of her and set it up. I get him a Kleenex from the box by his bed.

"You okay?"

He takes a breath. "Yeah. Don't know what that was. Let's go back." I push him through the doorway, wheels soundless on the polished floor.

That night, before I go back to say goodnight to him, Eileen asks me why we all seem so sad. "He's getting better," she says. "I mean, today wasn't a great day, but that's just because he didn't sleep well ..."

"It's not that." We all know he's not as sick. She's told us how upbeat he was all yesterday afternoon, when she was allowed to take him all over the hospital—even, for a few minutes, outside. His first time out of doors in a wheelchair. "I think it's just—it's a new month. Time is going right on. I'm guessing, I didn't talk with them about it. But that's how it feels to me, and I bet to him, too." I pull on my coat and take the keys off their hook in the cupboard. "It's like the whole rest of the world gets to keep going, and we're stalled right here."

Day 26: 1:30 pm

We're in the rehab gym, and David is here with a digital camera to take our picture for today's Great Big List update. I stand behind the wheelchair, one hand on Bruce's shoulder, feeling defiant. He's in his hospital gown and drawstring hospital pants, with ace bandages peeking from beneath the cuffs, and of course, the giant clownish white shoes. His hair is starting to grow back, but I think most people wouldn't recognize him yet. The stiff navy-blue and white neck brace covers him from collar bones to earlobes.

David shows us the image on the camera's little screen. Good God. Worse than I thought. I look like one of those women in the pictures of the Great Depression, haggard and prematurely old. I hardly care. I'm getting anxious about the time. They were going to move Bruce back to his rehab room first thing this morning, but so far, nothing doing. The shift will change at three, and I'm afraid if it isn't done by then, someone will decide to leave him where he is for another day.

It wouldn't matter, except that he wants it to happen. He wants something. He's been so sick and passive, and now he feels well enough to want something. He slept last night. He slept, and his eyes are clear. He slept, and he wants to get going, get back to those therapies, get out of here. He wheels himself toward the nurse's station, but I have to speak for him once he's there. He's too short in the chair to get in their faces, and whispering takes too much breath anyway. We aren't giving up. They have to move him today.

They do, but it takes the intervention of a nurse to make it happen. Her name is Jo, and she's connected to us through Keith's friend, Cate. When Cate was on this floor, Jo was her nurse; Jo is one of the people we were advised to look out for, and here we are, relying again on our special connections. Jo physically chases down the paperwork, gets the orders signed, and delivers them to the appropriate people. It's almost five o'clock in the afternoon, but he's moving. Today.

There is a young cowboy who lives on the range
His horse and his cattle are his only companions.
He works in the saddle and he sleeps in the canyons,
Waiting for summer his pastures to change.

James Taylor

```
Barriers: respiratory
complications.
Decreased right hand
function and grip
strength. Fluctuating
up-times, decreased
strength and
endurance, balance.
```

NINE

Day 26

By nine o'clock, I'm in Bruce's room, watching Tsegaw go through the ritual of putting him to bed. First, the stiff belly binder comes away with a loud Velcro rip, which makes Bruce groan with relief. Then Tsegaw unwinds the endless ace wraps, and finally bends over to execute the delicate maneuver of removing the leg bag attachment and replacing it with a connection to a night bag. The used leg bag, emptied into the toilet, gets tossed into the medical trash bin near the door. Tsegaw smiles at me, showing his gold tooth, and gestures that I should go ahead.

I lift Bruce's left knee all the way to his chest and hold it there for twenty seconds, then straighten it and point his foot at the ceiling. It takes a fair amount of strength to keep that long leg in the air; I have to use my shoulders. I count slowly, trying to do a good job. I lower the leg to the bed and sit down with my back to him, facing his foot. I take hold of the ball of his foot with both hands, pulling hard so that his heel cord gets a stretch through ninety degrees, ignoring the jittering spasm my touch creates. Clonus. Josh has said to just push right through it to make it stop, and so I do. It works. His foot goes from tapping a hard, fast rhythm against my palm to stillness. The room is dreamy and quiet, and I can tell Bruce likes being handled in this way.

After both his legs are stretched, I find some lotion and rub it into his feet, taking my time. Between the toes, bending each one as much as it will go, my fingers working themselves hard into his dry skin. His eyes are closed, his face relaxed. They've already given him the nighttime meds: oxycodone, Benadryl, omeprazole, gabapentin ... it seems to be a winning combination. I am absurdly gratified that he falls asleep before I can say goodnight, as if my hands are the reason. I leave before the night shift even starts, confident that he'll rest.

Day 27

He does. When I arrive at eleven, they're already sitting him up in the wheelchair, and one glance into his eyes tells me that it was another good night. For him, this means four hours of uninterrupted sleep. It means not waking up when the nurse comes in every two hours to shift his position so that his skin stays healthy. It means breathing easily with the boost provided by a couple of liters of extra oxygen delivered through a narrow nose cannula. He says that last night he had his first dream since March 6th.

"It was like—I was a piece of furniture. One of those—like, a footstool, only big and upholstered ..."

"An ottoman?"

"Yeah. I was an ottoman." We're interrupted by a big man with a loud voice who introduces himself as Bob.

Bob is going to be Bruce's occupational therapist, his OT, for the rest of his time at Harborview. He has a strange habit of squinting while blinking his eyes rapidly, as if he were trying to get something out from under contact lenses. After a few minutes, I stop noticing this. I like him. He lays out a plan for the work they're going to do together. Every week, there will be short term goals, and here they are for this week: Bruce will, independently, brush his teeth, put on a pullover shirt, and use a standard telephone. With minimal assistance, he will shower, and he will start learning how to pull a pair of pants onto his numb lower body.

I sit there listening to this surreal agenda, knowing even as I cringe at the idea that Bruce needs special training to do these tasks that he is lucky to be able to do them at all. As I'm thinking this, Bob confirms it.

"You know, I really like working with C6 injuries," he says. "C5, it's hard because there's only so much you can do. C7 and below that, you pretty much know what's possible. But C6—boy. It's different every time. That's a real borderline area."

He's talking about the cervical vertebrae, the neck bones. The numbering starts at the top, at the base of the skull, C1. Christopher Reeve's injury was at C2; the most famous quadriplegic in the world also had just about the worst possible level of damage. A person with a C4 injury or higher is almost guaranteed to need a ventilator to breathe. People with C5s usually can't use their hands at all. My skin prickles at the thought that if Bruce's head had been angled just a little differently when he landed, this man would be saying something else to us now.

Of course, there is also the possibility that we wouldn't even be here, but this does not bear consideration, either.

Bob goes on. "I was reading your chart this morning—and it's not bad. Even if you get no more return, even if all your muscles function from now on just the way they do today, you can get pretty damn near to full independence." Bob has massive arms. He crosses them over his chest, looking like he can't wait for the challenge of helping Bruce find his way to this goal.

Bruce is looking up at him from the wheelchair. He can't lift his chin because of the brace, so he just raises his eyes. "That's what I want," he whispers. "To be independent."

1 pm

We're in the meeting known as "Rounds." They hold it in a conference room down the hall from the gym, every Tuesday afternoon. We sit at a big rectangular table with a dozen or so people; I'm taking notes in my journal. Dr. Smooth Eyes presides, calling on the various therapists in the order they happen to be sitting. After a few people speak, I stop taking notes and just sit there, marveling at what a waste of time and energy this is.

Dr. Shakir, the resident, speaks first, outlining the events that got us all here. Ski injury, airlift, surgery, pulmonary issues, premature attempt at rehab, RICU, a couple of nights on the medical floor, and now back here. He's quiet-spoken and careful with his words, not a native English speaker but very clear—the kind of man whose authority comes from a dogged intelligence. He also has a certain warmth that makes me glad he's here.

A young woman with big, dark hair named Maria then says a sentence or two about how she hasn't yet had time to speak with us much. She's our assigned psychologist. I'm wondering if she's a student; she looks so young. Then a speech therapist who is not Fleur but someone else says that Bruce is strictly forbidden swallowing until he passes an exam, which will not even be scheduled for four to six weeks. I already knew this, but hearing it still makes me sag in my chair.

We stop so Bruce can do a pressure release. He unlocks his brakes, pushes his chair back a couple of feet, and lowers his face to his knees. I doodle in my journal. They wait, shuffling their papers, having private conversations.

Next is Bob, who tells the whole room about the short term goals he and Bruce agreed to work on for the coming week. I suddenly understand why we're all here. This meeting is one of those institutionalized solutions designed to fix a problem that happened sometime in the past. I can almost see them inventing it. (You know, what's wrong is that not everyone is on the same page. Right. We need to make sure everybody on the team has access to all the information. What if we were to get everyone together, including the patient and caregiver, if there is one, and run down the picture. How often? Weekly, I'd say. Good idea.) Now Josh is talking, laying out the short term goals for physical therapy. I start to pay attention again.

He addresses Bruce, ticking them off on his fingers. "Sitting on the edge of the mat without support, balanced, for thirty seconds. Rolling over on the mat with moderate assistance. Going where you want to go in the chair on your own." He pauses, checks his notes. "Oh, yeah, and demonstrating independence with Kate in range of motion."

"I did it last night," I say.

He picks up his pen and checks it off. "Goal met," he says, and people smile.

Next is a woman named Jody whose title is "Recreational Therapist." Her job is to get the patients out into the world— "integrated into the community," is the way she puts it. She'll be talking with Bruce about some places they could go, and later, about outings with me and the girls.

Finally, Dr. Smooth Eyes wants to nail down a discharge date. Eight weeks is what they figure he'll need to be well enough to go home, and eight weeks from now is the fifth of June. A current passes between me and Bruce. June 3rd is Heather's eleventh birthday. He'll want to be at home by then, and I say so to the group. A woman named Norma volunteers that we have some issues with insurance coverage anyway. His rehab benefits will be used up less than three weeks from now. She says there are ways to get around it, and that she'll be in touch to help us negotiate. And then they let us go.

I'm on the phone with Dave and Mim, our regular afternoon call. We sneak it in every day at 2:25, just before Heather gets home from school. I've given them the latest news: Bruce is off the oxygen tank. He can breathe. The pneumonia is over, and he's back in rehab. Eileen will be on her way home at the end of the week; she's seen us through the hardest part, and I can't find any more odd jobs to give her. The week after that, the girls are flying to Minnesota to be with them. Mim wants to know what sorts of things she should plan.

"Well, they'll want to go to the Mall of America."

"We can do that. Do they need anything? Should we shop for anything in particular?"

I consider this. Even after fourteen years, it feels odd to be among people for whom money is never the primary issue. It isn't that they flaunt it, or spend it just to be spending it—quite the opposite. Bruce's folks are sensible, careful, and kind. They just happen to be able to afford things like flying their granddaughters out for a week, and taking them shopping on top of that is not a problem. These are special circumstances, after all. So I say that the girls could use some clothes for Easter, and remind them that Emily is turning thirteen right after she gets back home.

"I thought about that," Mim says. "We were wondering about a party for her here, with her cousins ... do you think that's something she'd enjoy?"

In many ways, Mim is the woman I want to be when I grow up. Thoughtful. Reasonable. "She'd love it," I say. "We'll be trying to figure out something here, but—it's bound to be tough on her."

"Okay, that's set, then." I know she is taking notes. "What else?"

"Um, I don't know. Are all the cousins on spring break next week?"

They don't know for sure, but they will check. They will have the tickets sent to our house, and they will be at the gate to meet the girls when they arrive. They want me to use the time to get some extra rest; they're sure I must need it badly.

"Actually, I'm doing okay," I say. "Having Eileen here has made everything so easy ... okay, maybe not easy, but manageable. I do sleep."

We go over the home front schedule for the next few weeks. Starting right after the girls get back, I will have someone staying with me for all the nights until Bruce gets discharged in June. First is Mim herself, followed by Dave. As soon as Dave leaves, my youngest brother, Bob, will show up to take his turn, then Bruce's aunt Sue, then Dave again, and so on.

It's also time to start gearing up to make our house accessible. I tell them that two of Bruce's therapists will be coming out next week to see how we're set up now and make recommendations. Dave perks up.

"They come out to your house?"

"That's what they said. I gather it's the usual procedure."

"If they give you a written report, can you have them send me a copy?"

"Sure."

"Because that would be really good, to have that right away." His tone is meditative and interested; this is his area. When it's time, he and both of Bruce's brothers will come to do what has to be done to our house.

I find talking about this difficult. I don't want to make our house accessible—actually, to be precise, I don't want to have to. I want Bruce to walk through the front door. I fantasize about standing at the kitchen sink, watching him come down the driveway, where he will disappear from my sight as he goes up the steps and comes through the front door. I will walk out of the kitchen to meet him, and I will say ironically, "Where the hell have you been?" And he will smile.

Day 28: 1:45 pm

Bruce and I are loitering in the wide hallway outside the rehab unit, talking about the girls. Eileen and I are planning to bring them up tonight after choir, their third visit in four days. On Saturday they leave for Minnesota, and this will be his last chance to see them until they get back. He's frustrated.

"It's like there's still, I don't know, a wall between us," he whispers.

He's right. They don't like to touch him, especially Heather. I don't know if they think they'll hurt him, or if it's too gross, or if he just seems unfamiliar, or what. "They don't show it when they're here, but they miss you so bad. Maybe tonight they could, like, lie down next to you and have a real cuddle." I've done this, slipped into his bed once he's all set for the night, and I know how good it feels—not anything close to how it was, but still a lot better than leaning over for a one-armed hug.

"What time are you bringing them?"

"After choir."

"That's right, it's Wednesday. So, 8:15 or somewhere in there?"

"Yeah, by the time we get up here. Can they get you all ready by then?"

"Fuck, I don't know. I can't exactly make them."

7 pm

Eileen and I are in the kitchen, putting away the remains of our donated dinner while the girls get ready to go downtown. Eileen is looking over the lists of dinner-makers Lisa has been sending home with Emily. "Your support system is so amazing," she says. "Who are all these people?"

I glance at the names. "Mostly parents of the girls' school friends. Some are my students."

"And the people at the hospital? Are they all from your church?"

"A lot of them. Some are from where Bruce used to work, some are twelve-step folk he's known for a long time. And some artists. They're mostly from church, though."

"The nurses keep talking about it … I get the feeling they don't see it work this well very often. I've sure never seen anything like it."

"Well—it's not like we just show up on Sunday and listen to the sermon. We're hooked in. I work there, and both of us have volunteered so much time. I co-chaired two pledge drives. He taught in the church school for—I don't know—years. Plus, both of us were on boards, God." I tick them off. "Mission and Community Service, Fellowship and Recreation, Worship, the Music and Arts Committee, the Brother-Sister Church Committee … we go to all the camps and retreats. We chair the retreats. Plus choir. He sings in the choir, and both the girls are in the children's choir. People know us. They know our kids."

Suddenly I remember that she's used to working with medical issues, like, on a grand scale. Eileen has been doing AIDS work for ten years; she went to Africa for an international conference. She's been to the White House. "Eileen, how many people do you know who've died of AIDS?"

"How many do I know, personally?" She puffs her cheeks, blows out air. "A lot, God, how many … maybe a couple hundred?"

"Personally? Really?"

She looks at me, then away. "For years I refused to get a new address book. Then it got to where I would go to look for someone's number, and there would be whole pages of names crossed off. Pages and pages." Her fine-boned hands are open in front of her, empty. I am silent.

"Have you ever been there when it happened?"

"Sure."

"More than once?"

She says, "Oh, yeah, probably more than—I don't know, a dozen times."

I didn't know that. How could I not know that about her life? "That's a lot of funerals."

She runs her fingers through her spiky hair. "I've been to so many goddamn funerals. I've spoken at so many funerals."

We're quiet, knowing how easily it could have been a funeral she came here for. And then she moves right on; she needs my help to fill out a twelve-page form for social security disability insurance. Her face, bent over the papers, is beautiful.

8:30 pm

In fact, Bruce is ready when we get there. He's unwrapped and changed into fresh night clothes, lying in his bed, propped on his right side facing the windows, with enough space left next to him for one of the girls. Emily goes first. Heather stays out in the "living room" with Eileen, looking as if she's about to go to the dentist. I close the door behind us and tell Emily the plan: just slip your shoes off and climb in, and then you guys can have some time alone together. She looks dubious, but she's willing.

She lies on her back, tucked snugly against him, and I know she's thinking about the stomach tube and the catheter. I do, when I'm there. He puts his arm around her and closes his eyes, inhaling. "Emily," he whispers. "Oh, my God." She relaxes a little, but it's awkward. They're not quite comfortable, either of them, but of course he can't wiggle himself into a better position, and she's afraid of jostling him. She's looking straight up at the ceiling. I can hear the gurgling in his lungs from six feet away. Oh, please let him get through this visit without needing to be coughed.

"Daddy, you have butterflies."

He makes a noise. "Aren't they ugly?" There are garish, enormous butterflies painted on the ceiling tiles just above his bed. He hates them. This is going to work, apparently. I tell them I'll be back in a few minutes and leave them alone.

It's almost the end of Heather's turn. Emily, Eileen and I have run out of things to talk about, and it's past time to leave. I open the door and walk over to Bruce's bed. He's whispering the Cowboy Song to her, and she's lying there in the circle of his arm, crying with her mouth open in a square, not making a sound.

He stops, his good hand gentle on her face. "Honey, is this too hard?" I can see the effort he's making to keep his breathing steady and shallow. The gurgle is louder.

"No," she says. "It's okay. Keep going." She's nearly choking, and she seems to be trying not to let him know it.

The song is really called "Sweet Baby James." It's a waltz, and the lyrics are about a lonely young cowboy, singing to himself by a campfire under a starry sky. Heather has been in Bruce's arms thousands of times listening to this song; I stand there crying as he goes into the second verse. His whispered voice is a thin line of yellow light, visible beneath the closed door of her childhood, now officially ended.

Day 29

Eileen, Bruce and I are looking around for a place with a table where we can be private. She needs him to help her finish the Social Security paperwork. She's leaving soon; this is her last official job as my personal slave / maid / childcare person / secretary / gofer. There's a conference room down the hall from where the computers are; the sign on the wall next to the door says it has to be reserved with the nursing staff.

"Fuck that," she says cheerfully, and walks in. I follow her, pushing Bruce's wheelchair carefully through the doorjamb so I don't smash his feet into anything. She closes the door behind me and hangs a little sign in the window: Room In Use. "There we go."

She's all efficiency. She has folders labeled in her careful, distinctive script. She has a couple of big manila envelopes, already set to go with their destinations printed. She has stacks of official forms, which she now sets in four neat piles. I'm across from her, and he's in between us, trying to keep his balance.

I've noticed that his secret to not tipping over is to let his bad hand swing free, straight toward the floor and behind the chair; this maneuver gives him a bit of a drunken look. It also makes his stomach tube, currently plugged while not in use, poke out the front of his shirt where nothing should be poking.

Eileen is running him quickly through a list of past employment questions that I've already answered. He stops her, careening forward a little as he reaches for the page. "This isn't right," he whispers. Eileen gives me a look.

"Sorry," I say. "I tried." Eileen rolls her eyes.

He's still looking at the page. "Most of this is wrong." Eileen is unfazed. She has a bottle of White-Out already on the table, and together they start correcting my guesses. When did he work for US West, then? What was his title at WatchMark in 2000? "Geez, Kate," he whispers. "Don't you know anything I've been doing?"

"Apparently not. Maybe I'll just go get a latte. Eileen, do you want anything?"

He makes a face. It's an ongoing misery to be barred from the simple pleasure of swallowing so much as a sip of water. I don't bring food into his room, and I don't eat in front of him anywhere if I can help it. But lattes are another whole thing. They're expensive, bad for me, and completely necessary. The baristas at the Bistro on the second floor know my name, what I'm going to order (a double-tall, nonfat latte), and how I like it (hot and extra foamy). I made a decision at some point not to feel guilty about drinking so many of these things, no matter who doesn't like it, or what kind of faces he makes.

Day 30: 2:00 pm

I'm at home, alone, Eileenless for the first time since March 21st. I left her at the United gate a couple of hours ago, and the house is quiet. Quiet and orderly, thanks to her. All around me is the evidence of her touch. The countertops are clean. She sorted all that paper, threw away what she could, paid what had to be paid, filed what had to be filed, filled out, dear God, all those reams of forms. Thanks to her, my wash is done, my girls have gone to sleep for weeks with the same person in the house, and the cars have both been in for oil changes. She even arranged to get the crack on the van's windshield repaired. All this, plus taking double shifts at the hospital during the worst nights. She'd make a hell of a wife, I told her as we said goodbye. She laughed at that. "Gawd, don't even think such a thing."

The phone rings. Jocelyn. She wanted to tell me, she says quietly, that Bob Burkhart died in his sleep last night. I'm in the hallway when she says this, and I sink down onto the steps that lead upstairs.

"He couldn't have. Tell me that's not true."

She sounds so broken. "It is, Kate. He had a heart attack, and Carol apparently got up in the morning not even knowing it had happened. She found him later."

"He was just up at the hospital … he spent the night with Bruce in RICU."

"I know."

Of course she knows; she's the one who put his name in the schedule. But I can't stop talking. "He wrote this beautiful entry in the journal, did you see it?" I know I'm hurting her by saying this. I'm hurting myself. I seem to have to say these things to make myself believe her. "He wrote that Bruce asked to be rocked, and that he tried, but it didn't work." This does it. Now I have this news in my cells, absorbed. I get it.

"I'm just so tired of things being sad," she says. "I just want all this sadness to stop."

"Yeah, well—"

"I shouldn't say that to you," she says. "But I can't help it. I just need it to stop. I need it to be over."

"I'm glad it was you who called me," I say. "You were brave to do that. I wouldn't have wanted to hear it from anybody else."

7 pm

Bruce is sitting in his wheelchair, patiently allowing a young researcher from the University of Washington to attach dozens of electrodes to his scalp. Luckily, he still has hardly any hair, so it's a fairly simple procedure. He's being a guinea pig, a participant in a study to test some new gizmo for sleep apnea. Tonight he has to sleep with these wires attached to his head so they'll have a baseline record of his breathing patterns without the gizmo. Next week they want to have him test their new equipment, first here in his room and then in a more controlled environment.

Right now, this means two things to me. First, that I'll be asked to leave soon because they'll be taking him somewhere else for the night to hook him up, and second, that I need to tell him about Bob's death right now, for the same reason Jocelyn told it to me earlier. So that he doesn't have to hear it from somebody else.

The researcher is working swiftly, making conversation as he goes. A friend is with us, Margaret, and it's obvious that she hasn't heard. I listen to the researcher smoothly move from one subject to another,

144

wishing he would be quiet. Finally, he turns away to find something in his briefcase, and I get my chance.

"Something bad happened last night." They look up. "Bob Burkhart died in his sleep." I just say it, and they both react as if I've punched them. The researcher pauses in mid-motion, his graceful hands suspended above Bruce's wired head. I tell them the rest of what I know. It's bizarre, this conversation, in this situation, the way the researcher goes back to plugging away, almost done, a few more ... hands flying while the three of us weep and try to get our bearings. Finally he asks if we want a few minutes.

Bruce, wiping tears off his nose, waves a hand. "Just get it done."

I sit next to Margaret on the bed. She's rocking herself back and forth, trying to get her head around it. Bob was a force in our church. Not a follow-me-I-know-the-way kind of man, but still a man you'd want at your side. We say the useless things that must nevertheless be said, and then it's time for me to go.

I leave with a bad feeling. Bruce shouldn't be letting them do this study. He 's finally getting some rest after all these weeks; now is the wrong time to be volunteering for a nighttime experiment. I wanted him to say no, you can do it to me later, when I'm stronger. It's too late. I kiss him goodnight, avoiding the tangle of plugs. I'll be up later than usual tomorrow, after I put the kids on their plane.

Day 31

I'm at the airport again, waving cheerfully to the girls as they march off down the jet way, beginning their big adventure. They are flying alone for the first time. The moment they're out of sight, I head for the restroom. I lock myself in a stall and sob for five minutes, too bereft and raw to care who hears me. I'm sending my kids away because I can't take care of them properly. I know it's temporary. I know they'll enjoy themselves, that they'll be with family. Still, it makes me ashamed. Bad mother. I also understand, walking alone back to my car, that their very presence has been an imperative to keep going. A portion of my strength is on its way to Minnesota.

Tell me about despair, yours, and I will tell you mine.

Mary Oliver

```
Wife of patient
appears tearful
today, making
comments suggestive
of depression and
attempts to cope with
husband's injury.
Psych contacted to
intervene.
```

TEN

Day 31: 1 pm

"UE Group" is what Bruce's whiteboard says for this hour. "UE," it turns out, stands for "upper extremities," which is the Harborview word for arms. The word, "group," refers to the fact that for the first time, he is not doing therapy all by himself. He's one of three people, in fact, parked in their wheelchairs before the Monark machines. These are small, table-mounted appliances with a pair of handles sticking out on either side and a switch for adjusting the resistance. They're like stationary bicycles built for arms, made to build endurance and strengthen the upper body.

To Bruce's left is an Hispanic guy named Jose whose face has the slightly confused, dreamy look I've come to associate with head injury patients; he also has what appear to be multiple physical disabilities. Jose used to be a carpenter. He's been here in rehab for two months already, and before that he spent a whole season in a nursing home, and before that he was in a coma in intensive care for more than two months. I learn all this from his older brother, whom I have been saying hello to around the unit all week. He tells me now that Jose should not be alive. The brother is very proud; Jose is a miracle.

On the other side of Bruce is a young woman who wears a brace on one hand, a bicycle helmet in case she falls, and another brace around one of her knees. She is Wendy. She is attended by her husband; I watch them often, and see between them a bond so strong it is nearly visible. They're quiet people. Like Jose, she is doggedly turning the cranks of her machine. Behind us all is an OT named Pauline whose perky comments make me long for a roll of duct tape, or at least an errand to send her off with.

Bruce is struggling. His right hand is ace-wrapped to its handle. He turns the wheel for two minutes, then takes a one-minute break, then does it again. Twenty minutes nonstop is the goal. At every break, he closes his eyes and slumps forward, breathing hard, right arm dangling from where it's fastened to the machine. He's tired today; apparently it was hard to rest with all the electrodes fastened to his head. He needs a nap. I sit beside him, waiting to take him back to his room. Before us Puget Sound sparkles, and the Bainbridge Island ferry glides serenely into its mooring. Today he is one month post-injury.

3 pm

It's the change of shift, so we have two nurses in the room. Ann has been with him for the day; she is one of those interesting, clear-eyed, physically strong women who seem to hit their stride in their fifties. She wears her hair in a salt-and-pepper crew cut—the exact same hair style my brothers all had when we were kids. The other nurse is Diva, a tiny Philippina woman we are just getting to know. She's going to be taking care of Bruce most nights from now on. Ann is usually the "charge nurse," the one in charge of staffing. She doesn't spend much time with the patients, and this is the first time I've seen her in Bruce's room.

She's messing with the end of his bed, tidying up the sheets and looking over his nighttime boots. There are two of these: one is knee-length, black, and sturdy. Made of tough plastic, it's lined all over the inside with sheepskin, even on the adjustable straps, in the places where they press against his skin. The other one is white and much smaller, only ankle-high. Its inside is padded with thick foam, and it looks to me like a white boxing glove.

Ann tells Diva to be sure he wears both of these at night.

"I thought we could leave this foot free," Diva says, taking his left toes casually in her hand. "This one is moving a lot now." Bruce wiggles his toes, then slowly, slowly lifts his left knee an inch off the bed, something he's been practicing with me at night.

Ann shakes her head. "It's more important to protect his skin and make sure he doesn't get foot-drop. He's going to be a walker, so we can't let anything happen to his feet."

"What did you say?"

She gives me a direct look, not sure what I want.

"About him being a walker."

Her face softens. She says that she's been doing this for a long time, and she's read his charts, and anyway, you can tell. You can just tell that some people are going to walk.

"No one in this hospital has said that to us." I want to nail her to the floor and have her say it again and again.

She shrugs, disgusted but resigned. "Oh, well—they can't really say anything they aren't absolutely sure of, you know." She looks at him again, gives his knee a little shake. "But, yeah. You're going to be back up on these legs."

"If it's possible, I'll do it," he whispers.

After they leave us alone, we stare at each other.

"Did you hear that?"

"Yes. Did you?"

6 pm

Tidying up the cluttered top of his little bedside table, I hand him his C-harp, just because I don't have a good place to put it away. He lifts it to his mouth and blows a couple of quick riffs, plaintive but strong. His nurse, Chris, has been talking to one of the respiratory therapists while she hustles around the room. She stops in her tracks. Chris has "adopted" Bruce, which means that whenever she's on the floor, she wants to be assigned to take care of him. She's a mom—a tall, loosely built woman with unruly dark hair who is quickly becoming one of my favorite people.

She stares at him. "Bruce! Did you just do that?"

He wipes his mouth, takes a breath, and tries again, this time with them watching. The notes coast, climb, howl sweetly, and fade. He makes his delicate, old-man cough.

"Shit, man, you should be doing that every day," the RT tells him. "That's great therapy for your lungs, better than this dumb thing." He flips his thumb at the bong.

"Wow." Chris is beaming. "I just had no idea."

I'm really happy because it is so good to hear even this tiny bit of his music in this room, but there's more. It's wonderful to see these people finally start to understand who he is.

Day 33: 10 am

I don't go to the hospital on the morning of the home accessibility evaluation. It's the first time in weeks that I've been alone in our house at this time of day, and it feels both familiar and unsettling. I look around the kitchen, wondering stupidly if our house will make a good impression on Bruce's therapists. If it does, they don't show it; they're here to work. I show them the way to our bedroom. Bob has a clipboard; he's taking rapid notes while Josh dictates.

"Open design, front to back split, four levels. Seven steps between the entry level and the master bedroom. Door to master bedroom opens in with a turn-style knob"—he drops to one knee and slides out his carpenter's tape—"width, twenty-seven inches."

Bob is looking around our bedroom. "This is wide open. This space will work fine. Platform bed, plenty of room. This his side?" I nod. "Doesn't matter—it is now if it wasn't before." He pokes his head into our bathroom, leans against the doorjamb and writes again, telling me that the bathroom will need heavy modifications. The door isn't wide enough for a chair, Bruce will need a shower that he can wheel into, and the toilet is right in the way. He points. The wheelchair can't get in the room with the toilet here. It will have to go there, probably, in that corner. The tub is history. I'll have to gut the room and start over.

Josh leads the way out into the living room, kneels and puts his hand into the carpet. "You'll have to take this up—this, and what's in the bedroom, and what's downstairs—wherever he'll be. With his arm and shoulder strength the way it is now, he couldn't push himself across it." I just sigh. "He's going to get a lot stronger, but it'll take awhile." They glance up the second set of stairs.

"What's up there?"

"The girls' rooms."

"Okay. He won't have to go up there for now." They head back down toward the entryway, leaving me on the landing. They're so straightforward. To them, it's just an interesting construction problem. It's purely a matter of thinking through how to make a particular house accessible to a guy whose disabilities they both know intimately. I'm glad they're on it, too—but it's our home they're discussing with such detached enjoyment.

We have a tiny porch with two concrete steps. No good. We could put a ramp here, but Bruce would be exposed to the weather coming in and out. They open the door to the garage and look around. "Plenty of space for a ramp in here," Bob says. He smiles, knowing what I'm thinking. "You'll have to move all this stuff, of course." He takes the measurements, nods again. "Plenty of room. Nice house."

In the kitchen, he quizzes me about what Bruce likes to do in here. "Does he cook?"

"Sometimes, yeah."

"Do the dishes?"

"Nah. Hardly ever."

Bob goes through a pantomime of Bruce trying to get to the phone, trying to use the microwave, trying to open the sliding door to the deck. They measure the height of the stove, the distance between the refrigerator and the sink. They have answers for everything. This microwave won't work, it's too high. He'll need his own, just a small one. It could fit right here, maybe. Bob is pointing at a corner in the kitchen where a row of my cookbooks now stands. Our table is measured and pronounced too low for the height of the wheelchair. It will need to be raised up, somehow. Not hard, just get somebody to make something stable for the legs to sit on.

The faucets are the push kind; that's good. We might want to think about switching the refrigerator door to open the other way. We might want to think about the smoke alarms. We might want to think about installing a burglar alarm system. They measure the opening to the half-bathroom next to the front door. Way too small. He won't be going in there anymore.

These are all small, fixable issues, according to them. The only big question remaining is how he will get from the entry level to the next one, where our bedroom is. We talk through some options. A long ramp from the kitchen to the backyard and up to the little deck that hangs off our room? There is a pause when I suggest this.

"Kate, he'd have to go outside every time he wanted to go upstairs." Josh looks at me as if I haven't comprehended how much trouble Bruce is going to have, just being out in the world. He's right. I haven't comprehended it.

How about making his living space be on the entry level? Could the garage be adapted to turn into some kind of bedroom/bathroom area for him? Possible, but a lot of work. Bob is standing in the dining room with arms folded, looking at Rocky's giant kennel.

"What do you use this room for?"

"Passing through, mostly, and using the computer. It's supposed to be a dining room, but we've never needed one. Sometimes we've kept a couch in here … it's a cozy place to hang out and read."

"Does the dog kennel have to be there?"

"No. We used it to crate-train him when he was a puppy."

They shove it out of the way, measure the space, and exchange a satisfied look. Problem solved. There is enough room right here for a platform lift, an open electric elevator. It will be easy. Bob will give me a list of local suppliers for this kind of lift; he says I should call them today and place an order.

"Bruce's dad is coming here next week to help with the house. Are you going to make a written report?"

Bob hesitates. He is, but there's no time to lose now. The house needs a lot of work, and I need to be looking now, today, for a contractor. I tell him that Bruce's family will help me. He studies me, eyes blinking rapidly, then shrugs. "You really don't have much time." I turn on the computer, copy out Dave's email address, and tell him to make sure Dave gets a copy of the report. They drive away, and I take off my shoes and walk barefoot on our carpeting, wondering what kind of floor is underneath.

Day 34: 6 pm

With the girls gone, I'm spending a lot more time at Harborview, and often there seems to be nothing to say. Right now we're sitting silently together in the "living room," waiting for the baseball game to start at seven. There is a patient a few doors down from Bruce named Brett, who has been walking slowly around and around the unit, using a four-legged walker for support. His walker has a thick gray pad attached to the place where he rests his arms, and this time when he comes around the corner, he stops to visit, leaning on the padding as if it were the edge of a counter in the neighborhood bar.

He talks for thirty straight minutes. Whenever he pauses for breath, Bruce tries to reply, but his whisper isn't strong tonight, and anyway it's clear Brett requires no response. He tells his whole story. He was with this crazy woman, see, and they were both fucked up on cocaine and pretty drunk to boot. She was driving, and he was in the passenger seat, laying out some more lines. She ran a red light and then drove straight into something, and he slammed into the windshield, head first.

He ended up in her lap, and he couldn't move. He was hollering that he was paralyzed, goddammit, paralyzed. The bitch didn't believe him! She just kept telling him to get the hell off her lap. Bruce and I listen to this story, smiling inwardly. This guy is colorful, a welcome change from the dull routines. What I want to know is, where is his injury?

"C6," he says proudly. He's wearing a navy blue and white neck brace just like Bruce's, a Miami J, except he wears his loose, like an old necktie. "God damn, those first few days, when I couldn't move anything, I was one scared motherfucker."

"Did you have to have surgery?" I'm guessing that he didn't.

"Sure did, two weeks ago. Cut me right here." He points to the same place on his neck where a scar has now formed on Bruce.

He starts off on a new monologue, but I'm hardly listening. Two weeks ago? Brett can walk, and talk, and eat, and he's probably going to be discharged soon, without a wheelchair. I think of all those people telling me that it would take six weeks for the swelling to go down, and that things might look a whole lot different by then. Six weeks is now just eight days away. I want to un-know this. Brett is what they were talking about. Brett is the most positive scenario, the rosy picture they couldn't promise. This crazy guy with the drug problem, with the rotting teeth, with the same injury as my husband's, drew the lucky card. I want not to know this.

Day 35: 10 am

We're downstairs with Fleur, where a doctor who looks like a Keystone Cop is about to have a look at Bruce's vocal cords. The doctor has straight red hair, parted on the side, and a thick mustache clipped to a bristle over thin lips. He's spraying some Afrin into Bruce's throat, humming to himself. He takes up a metallic tube and slides it into Bruce's mouth, impossibly far. Bruce lifts his left hand and waggles it; the doctor slides the device out. Time for a cough.

He bends forward with the effort, producing a thick wad of slime, which I catch in a paper towel and dispose of. By the time I'm back in my seat, the metallic thing is once again inside. On a pair of colored television monitors appears a double image of Bruce's vocal cords. They look vaguely like genitalia, strands of wobbling pinkness. Fleur says she sees some movement, a little improvement over last time. The doctor withdraws the tube and slides a flexible instrument into Bruce's nose, down and down, and there again are the vocal cords.

Even I can see that it's not good. They ask him to make an ahhhh sound, and he tries, but one of the cords is still, and the other barely wiggles. No dice. They tell him he'll have to wait another couple of weeks to try again, and we are dismissed. Waiting for the elevator to take us back to the fourth floor, he tugs on my sleeve. I bend over to hear him whisper, "I didn't want to drink a radioactive milkshake anyway, you know."

Dealing with email has become much easier since our friend David set up a giant list. He produces daily updates about what's happening, and directs people toward Jocelyn if they want to get plugged into the vigilante roster. He's got Lisa's email on there, in case anyone wants to join the dinner-delivery efforts, and he reminds everyone that Bruce's sense of humor is intact. I hardly ever read his version of "what's happening," though, without wincing. I know he's trying to be upbeat, but I'm afraid he's giving people a false impression of what is still a relentlessly grim scene. I'm sitting at my desk, reading his latest "news:" Bruce's voice is getting stronger all the time, and his right hand seems to be coming back, too.

Bruce still has no voice at all, and his right hand is completely limp. I tap out a message to David, asking him to be careful. I know that everyone wants this to turn out well; every single day we get five more beautiful cards in the mail, each one assuring us that prayers and thoughts are pounding away at God's ears to that end. These cards now fill most of the available wall space in his room, and are starting to spill into the hall. What I don't like is the combination of these cheery emails and the knowledge of all those people, reading them and praying away.

I don't believe in that kind of prayer.

I can't imagine a God inclined to give this one guy a break, but only on the condition that enough people beg very hard. My own intercessory prayer is much simpler, and always follows the same pattern. I think of God, then I think of Bruce, then I think of God, and so on, until the process gets the two of them together in my head. It's very calming, which is the point of prayer, as far as I can tell. It's beneficial to the person who is praying.

Day 36: 7 am

I wake up alone in the house, alone in our bed. I've just dreamed that I was outside the doors leading into the rehab unit, looking at Bruce coming toward me in his wheelchair from all the way down at the end of the hall. It's a very long, wide hallway, probably fifty yards from end to end. In the dream, he's sitting up straight, smiling at me. In his old voice, shy and dear, he says Hi, Kate. I smile to myself, stretching in bed and remembering the sound of his voice, and then all at once I get the dream-pun: he's at the end of a long hall. A long haul. This is what we face.

11 am

I happen to be present the first time he gets to shower. If the idea of finally getting completely bathed excites him, he is doing a fine job of not letting anybody know it. Bob helps him get ready, removing the belly binder but leaving the ace bandages on. It would be dangerous, Bob says, if he had a low blood pressure event in the shower chair. I picture Bruce all slippery and soapy, keeling over while Bob tries to hold on to him long enough to get him in the bed ... no, leave the wraps on.

The shower chair is a monster, bigger than the regular wheelchair, with a special air-bubbled cushion fastened to its seat. The seat itself looks like a toilet lid; he'll also use this chair to position himself over the top of a regular toilet. There is a pair of little black footrests, and wide gray armrests. Bob does the pivot-transfer to swing Bruce into the shower chair, then fastens a wide adjustable belt around his sunken chest. The collar stays on, of course, but except for that and the ace wraps, he's naked. The catheter snakes away from him to a bag hooked over a rail underneath the chair. Blood pressure check. It's good. Okay, ready.

Bob wheels him into the tiled bathroom he has never used. I hear the water running, and then Bob's voice calling out comments and instructions. "Feels pretty good, huh? That's it, use the armrest to hold yourself up. You want to be sure to use a lot of soap there ... watch out you don't slip sideways, there you go. You're smiling! Everybody likes this first shower. Okay, now use the washcloth on your feet if you can ... good job."

A few minutes later, the two of them come out in a cloud of steamy air. Bob's shirt and pants are splash-marked. He's focusing on getting Bruce safely through the door. Bruce has damp white towels all over him. Across his lap, around his shoulders, draped down over his legs, and, most endearing of all, on top of his head, framing his pink, scrubbed face. He looks so happy, just like a little boy coming out of his bath.

Noon

As always, we spend the lunch hour in his room, with the door closed so the sight of the laden food cart will not remind us what he can't have. He has wheeled himself over to the supply rack that stands against the wall, and he's trying to get the lid off a little pot of lip balm. It's a screw-on, and it doesn't look like he's going to be able to do it; the thing is the wrong shape to be managed with one hand. Finally he succeeds in grabbing it with his teeth.

I'm thinking that I'm glad I didn't offer to help. Independence. "Sorry," I say. "Did I screw it on too tight?"

He's smearing it over his lips. "Of course," he whispers, bitter.

"Of course?" I'm surprised how much this hurts me. "Of course?" As if I'm constantly screwing things up for him? As if these thousands of small acts on his behalf are poorly done? As if I'm a thoughtless, inconsiderate ... "of course?"

He finishes coating his lips, carefully puts the lid back on, loosely, and wheels around to face me, looking contrite. "No, not of course. Sorry. I just get tired of not being able to do anything." He can see that I'm still stung. He shrugs, which hurts me even more. I feel like he's just given me notice that he isn't going to use up any of his energy looking after me. Knowing that it has to be like this—that he can't take care of me, that it still takes everything he's got just to keep afloat—is no consolation.

9:55 pm

The fast-talking researcher is back. This time, having learned from the night of the electrode experience that Bruce does indeed have moderate sleep apnea, he has convinced him to go ahead with Step Two. On the bed is a black suitcase, out of which he is taking one thing after another, smoothly describing the function of each as he attaches it to Bruce. First are two blue straps Velcroed firmly around his head, one across his cheekbones and the other around his forehead; these will hold the blower in place. He demonstrates. The blower is part of the machine he wants to test, called a C-PAP. It will cover Bruce's nose tightly, and it has a very accurate sensor that will know when he isn't inhaling.

I'm watching, thinking to myself that besides being completely insane, this won't work. Bruce always breathes through his mouth when he sleeps; I want to stand up and insist that the researcher pack up and get out right now. This is when he produces a truly heavy-duty-looking white Velcro strap, which, he says, not giving us any time to protest, will go around Bruce's head, just so, to keep his mouth firmly closed so he can't cheat. He attaches it tightly, lengthwise, from under Bruce's chin to the top of the head.

Now, my paralyzed husband is fitted with a little conical mask that completely covers his nose. A hose leads away from it to a machine set up at the side of his bed; this contains the computer that will know when he hasn't taken a breath in awhile. It will activate the equipment to send a blast of air up his nostrils. I can't even look at him. He's strapped up like a pig, and this researcher is describing how well this will all work, how much some people love it, how rested they feel after giving it a try. I want to slap him. I already know what's going to happen.

Bruce is going to force himself to give it his best shot. He's going to lie there making a superhuman effort to stay calm, fall asleep, and let the machine do its job. It won't work. This thing is going to drive him absolutely crazy, and I'm astonished that he doesn't seem to know it. If his lungs start gurgling in the middle of this madness, what then? I won't be here to help him cough; they've said I have to leave for the night. They want him to be completely undisturbed, to give it a chance to work. Diva is scurrying around, finishing her nighttime tasks with a frown on her small face. I hope to God the night nurse isn't the Nurse-Who-Is-In-The-Wrong-Line-Of-Work.

Day 37: 10 am

So now he's exhausted again. He managed to last with the C-PAP for two hours, says it was complete hell. Says he felt sealed into a pressure chamber, unable to speak or even open his jaws. Every so often the sensor would kick in and blast him with cold air, shooting hard up his nostrils. Very restful! And then the night nurse—not the one who is in the wrong line of work—took her sweet time to come and get him out of the cage. Six times pressing the call button. All therapies are cancelled for today; he stayed up all night and can't deal.

Chris hangs a DO NOT DISTURB sign on his door and closes it behind her. All of us—me, Josh, Bob, Chris, Diva, even the aide, Tsegaw—are feeling mad at ourselves for letting this oh-so-persuasive sleep study guy get within a block of Bruce. I step out of my shoes and my jeans, then slide into the space next to him.

It's heaven. His long bare legs are against mine for the first time since March 6th. He's sleeping already, exactly like he used to, when we got off to ourselves during the afternoon. I lie there for two hours, happily listening while he breathes evenly, on and on.

3 pm

It's time for Chris to leave, but she's sticking around for a few extra minutes because she wants to advocate for Bruce. The sleep study guy has checked in, heard what happened last night, and scheduled a meeting. A meeting! I'm out of line, I know, but I speak up.

"He's taken enough of your time," I say. "Let me tell him to buzz off."

I'm not remembering that Bruce is a scientist in a large part of his soul. He believes in science. He understands the method, the necessity of designing careful experiments and completing them according to plan. He was looking forward to doing his part. He ignores me.

"Really, you don't have to talk with these people."

He's lying on his other side, facing away from me. One wobbly hand rises from the bed and swats in my direction. Shut up. It's not your call.

It's enough to take me down, this simple, casual dismissal, this wave of a shaky hand. I leave the hospital as quickly as I can, trying to get out before I go completely to pieces. It's the second time in two days he's hurt my feelings, and I feel like lying down and not getting back up. This is the risk of feeling so close to him. I have no defenses.

Day 38: 10 am

We're going to buy Emily a present. Harborview has a gift shop; it's down on the first floor, and Bruce wants to go in there himself and find something to give her. She'll be thirteen tomorrow. The first obstacle is the door to the shop. It's just barely wide enough for the chair; I have to make a couple of runs to get him aimed straight at it. Then there is carpeting inside—not thick, but still adding to the difficulty of maneuvering. He wanted to do this himself. I walk away, looking over racks of useless, expensive gifts.

The narrow aisles are lined with glass shelves holding breakable objects, and the store is crowded. Apparently this is a popular gift-buying time. Bruce can barely push himself along, and when someone is in his way, he can't make himself heard over the Muzak. He finally has to tug on a fat woman's dress to get her attention. She looks down at him, apologizes, and hurries around a corner as if what he has might be catching.

You think he's scary now, I say silently to her broad, retreating buttocks, you should've seen him a couple of weeks ago.

At the counter, he tries to get his credit card out of his wallet, but needs my help. The clerk can't hear him when he asks her to gift wrap the present, a pair of stars-and-moon silver earrings. He's whispering as loud as he can, but there is too much noise. The clerk is impatient; she asks me what it is he wants, dismissing him. Finally he has the present, wrapped and paid for, in his lap. He lets me push him out of the store and back to the elevator. Then he takes the wheels into his hands again, positions himself, and reaches for the button, struggling to keep his balance. We wait in silence, and when the doors finally open, there is no room. The elevator is full of able-bodied people, who stand looking blankly at us until the door slides closed in our faces.

Day 39: 8 am

It's Emily's birthday, and Easter Sunday. The girls are still on Minnesota time, so they're wide awake hours before we need to leave for church. We decide to take Rocky on his favorite walk through the woods that run behind our house, and once we're out there, we're all glad. It's a beautiful spring day, fresh and peaceful. I tell them I did this with him every day they were gone, even when it rained. Rocky's been gaining weight. Bruce used to take him for five-mile runs two or three times a week, but now for more than a month he's been kind of a slug. Today, he's joyful to be out early, galloping out of sight, then appearing at the top of the trail with his tail wagging. I'm back to being a mom, thank God. When they aren't looking, I examine them for signs. Is Emily ever going to sleep well again? Her eyes are dark. Is Heather ever going to talk with me? She takes off after the dog every time the conversation turns serious.

The church is crammed, front to back, with extra chairs set up along the side aisles and everywhere else they will fit. There is a full orchestra; trumpets are necessary for Easter music. In front of the choir, in the center of the space between the first row of seats and the steps to the chancel, there is a bare wooden cross, seven feet tall. As people come into the church, they're invited to take a single flower from the overflowing baskets of lilacs, lilies, tulips, daffodils, roses, and candytuft that stand near the doors. When the time comes, the whole congregation will walk in slow procession to fit each flower into the chicken-wire that is wrapped tightly around the cross.

Slowly, the cross will be transformed from a stark grey symbol into a cross-shaped fountain of color and scent. Easter. The girls and I are sitting on the far right side of the sanctuary, holding our daffodils and waiting our turn. When I get to the cross, I decide to find a spot way up near the top. It's corny, but I'm going to put my flower in a place Bruce would have been able to reach. It will be for him. What I don't anticipate is how it will feel to raise my arms … the familiar posture of giving myself to his embrace. This is how high I had to reach to get my arms around his neck. Shaking, I work the stem beneath the wire and step away.

We're in the hospital cafeteria, the place where Heather drew us a picture of the accident almost six weeks ago. Two dozen people have come here to help us celebrate Emily's birthday. She sits at the center of a long table, looking beautiful with her blond curls and round, smooth cheeks. People have brought balloons, and there is a cheery tablecloth, a huge cake, and a pile of presents and cards. I'm with Bruce at one end of the table. He's having a hard time. People are eating grilled cheeseburgers and fries from the hospital deli. We've all just been to church together; the music was stunning, the sermon provoking. Bruce has been here in the hospital.

He's a little dizzy, and he's having trouble keeping his balance. He tries for awhile to stay in the conversation, but no one can hear him. Now people are eating cake, licking the frosting off their forks, and it's too much. He needs to get out of here, he says; can I take him out of here for a few minutes? I tell Emily we'll be right back, ask a friend to keep things rolling, then push him out into the hall.

"Do you need to go back upstairs?"

"I don't know. I don't want to sit there watching people eat."

"We could go outside ... there's that little patio off NICU."

"Whatever. Is it cold out?"

I can't get used to him worrying about being cold. Shivering while other people are perfectly comfortable is my job. Our family joke is that whenever someone asks him if he's cold, he answers, "No, I'm Norwegian." Now he can't be outdoors without two blankets when it's seventy degrees. His body can't regulate its own temperature. So we go first to his room for wraps, then back down to the second floor.

It's not fair, but I'm irritated. Couldn't he fake it for one hour, so that Emily can have him at her damn birthday party? Isn't it enough that she has to turn thirteen with her dad in a trauma center? He stops to do a pressure release. My anger vanishes. It's not like all this is fun for him. The distance between what we want and need from him and what he's got to offer stretches out in front of me, wide as Lake Washington. There's no one to be mad at. It just is.

We roll toward the paved patio outside the NICU lounge. I scan the room as we go slowly by. Most of the people who were camping out here in March are gone, replaced by a new set of desperate, sad faces.

Day 40: 9 am

I'm standing in front of my first period class, not the same person I was when they last had to listen to me talk about conic sections and the rules for solving third degree polynomials. The kids are subdued and respectful. They've missed me, I know. A few of them have taken their turn on the dinner list. Someone asks quietly, "Is it hard?"

"Harder than pre-calculus," I say. I have them show me where they are now in the text, pick up my chalk, and start talking. It feels good to be with them, to be making sketches on the board, to be immersing myself in the simple job of teaching. The material itself is a comfort: predictable, orderly, useful, and above all, familiar. I'm surprised at how glad I am to explain it all again.

Day 41: 11 am

Today for OT, both of us have to pass a test. We have to go into the little computer room, watch a video about skin breakdown, and then take a test. Because we've both read the chapter in Yes, You Can!

about pressure sores, this feels insulting. Do they think he's been so careful for all these weeks about pressure releases just for the fun of it?

After I see the video, I know why they're being so anal. The color images are revolting and scary. These things are ridiculously easy to get; as little as twenty minutes of sitting or lying with bone pressed into skin will start one. And they're a bitch to get rid of. If he gets one and doesn't notice it, chances are high that it will spread deep into his flesh, all the way to the bone. Then, think surgery, permanent scarring, high likelihood of a repeat performance on the same spot in years to come.

As long as he's in the hospital, his nurses, doctors, and therapists will check his skin every day, but at home it will be our job. My job. We both pay attention, and we both get a hundred percent on the test.

Hope, faith, love, humor, and a strong will to live offer
no promise of immortality, only proof of our
uniqueness as human beings ... even under the
grimmest circumstances. Far more real than the ticking
of time is the way we open up the minutes and invest
them with meaning.

Dr. Norman Cousins

Skin Problem #1
(Pressure Area):
Sacral/coccyx
pressure sore.
Interventions/Actions
: Site appears less
red than yesterday's
observation. Tagaderm
remains intact to
prevent worsening of
sacral split. Patient
up in wheelchair for
therapies. Pressure
releases every 15
minutes. Continue to
monitor and evaluate
after being out of
bed.

ELEVEN

Day 42: 11:30 am

I can't believe it. He's got a pressure sore, right on his tailbone, which appeared sometime between yesterday afternoon and this morning. He's lying on his side when I arrive, just as the video said he would have to. Chris is trying to use this as a teaching moment for me, carefully lifting his gown and showing me a red spot the size of a quarter. She touches it gently with her index finger, but it doesn't blanch. That's how she knows it's a pressure sore. All day, this little patch of red skin is the main topic of conversation.

How did he get it? Isn't it wonderful that he knew something was wrong? That's a really good sign, that he could feel it, even there, in the numbest part of his body. But how did he get it? It's not in an area that gets pressure while he's in the wheelchair, and anyway he's always doing those releases. But isn't it lucky he's got enough sensation to feel it?

I shudder at that last question, thinking how scary it would be to know that his flesh could literally decompose without him feeling a thing. His own theory is that he got it earlier this morning, when they had him propped up in the shower chair for a long time, trying to see if he could go to the bathroom sitting up for a change. Oh, God. I suppose that's next. Sooner or later, I'm going to have to be trained to help him deal with the bathroom issues. I close my mind to that, resolutely refusing to think of it until the moment I have to.

The girls picked up a new game from their cousins in Minnesota. It involves being the first to spot any one of long list of cars, shouting out the name of the find (Slug Bug!! PT Cruiser Bruiser!!), and then hitting whoever is in the car with you. For the first few days, I put up with this, glad they're acting like kids again. They're especially fond of making up new categories, something their Uncle Paul seems to have a gift for. (Car-with-a-green-and-purple-paint-job-and-tape-over-the-back-windows!! Orange pickup-truck-hauling-a-beat-up-lawnmower!!)

After a few days, though, the out-of-nowhere shouts and punches start to wear on my nerves. I promise them that when their Uncle Paul shows up in a few weeks to help us fix the house, I'm going to kill him for teaching them this game. I make them laugh by screaming like a banshee in labor every time they spot one of the cars. This works too well. They do it more and more, and depending on what's going on at the hospital, it gets to a point where I really can't stand it. I'm taking them to Seattle one night when the solution occurs to me.

"Maybe you guys could just say it really softly, and kind of stroke me … that would be soothing."

"Sssllllluuuug buuuuug!" Heather says in a silken, slow-motion voice. Her hand touches the side of my head in a tender gesture.

"Oh, that was so nice. I hope you find another one."

Day 43

The gym is empty, except for us. Josh has asked me to stay later than usual; he needs to start training me to do "assists." The chair must be staged properly at the edge of the mat, angled about twenty degrees away, with one of the front corners just touching. It's easiest to do when the mat is level with the chair, so he has adjusted it accordingly. Later I can learn how to deal with uneven transfers.

He has a "sliding board" ready. This is a smoothly polished piece of blond wood, roughly the shape of a flattened skateboard. Steadying Bruce with his left arm, Josh shows me how to lean him over, slip one end of the board all the way under his butt, and set the other end firmly on the mat. He takes Bruce's feet off the footrests and sets them on the floor. He has me stand square in front of the chair, slip both hands under Bruce's bottom, and bend my knees.

"Keep your back straight," he says. "That's the most important thing. Let your legs do the work."

It's awkward because the footrests are sticking out where my feet want to be. Bruce leans over my left shoulder. I count to three, rocking him the way I've watched them do it, then lift and swing him two inches to the right, halfway onto the board. I'm scared. Josh is encouraging me to keep going, same thing again. Okay, squat, straight back, count, lift, move. This time he lands almost at the edge of the board.

"That's good. Be careful you lift him all the way up; you don't want to drag his bottom against that wood."

"Oh, hell no," I mutter into Bruce's ear. "Wouldn't want to do that." I lift him again, feeling it in my hamstrings, and this time he lands all the way on the blue mat. Josh climbs behind him to help him balance, and I straighten up, stretching my shoulders.

"How's your back?"

I twist, feeling for a twinge. Nothing. "Seems fine."

"Good. Why don't you move him back."

We do it a couple of times, each one a little easier. Josh goes off to answer a page, leaving us alone. Bruce can't lie on his back because of the pressure sore, so I get behind him to give him something to lean on. Another therapist and patient have come in; they're right across from us, working on a mat just like ours. She's not cooperating, though. She's got a lot more to work with than Bruce, but she's moaning that she doesn't want to, it hurts, she's too tired. The therapist, a tall, dark-haired guy who could pose for GQ, is trying to convince her to give it some effort.

"This is for you, you know. You won't get well if you don't try."

"It's not for me," she whines. "It's all for you. I'm tired." She lowers herself to the mat, one hand over her brow. "I need to take a nap. I want to go back to my room, now."

Bruce shifts his shoulder to let me know he wants to say something. I lean over close to catch his whisper. "If I ever act like that," he says meaningfully, "give me a dope slap."

Even with Mim in the house to help me, there is too much to do now. In the mornings I get the lunches made, drive the carpool, and teach my classes. I stop at the espresso stand strategically located just before the on-ramp to I-90 for a latte, which I drink on the way to Harborview. I walk quickly from my parking lot to the Emergency Room entrance and take the stairs to the fourth floor. No more elevators for me. Upstairs, his room is no longer the deadly quiet place it was a month ago.

Fleur might be there, pushing him to learn something called "stacked breathing." Bob might be making him try to use the wretched tenodesis splint, a clumsy metal-and-plastic contraption that seems not worth the painful effort of wrestling it onto his stiff right hand. Jody might be in the room, making a date for an outing. Does he want to go to an art museum? A pool? And, there is still the possibility of finding one of the RTs in there, doing the quad-cough to clear the lung secretions that still sometimes plague him. I stay every day through the lunch hour and on into the afternoon.

I have to learn, quickly, everything the nurses know. I have to learn everything the whole collection of therapists knows. I have to know what his medications are, how to recognize a dangerous headache when he gets one, how to trim his toenails so they don't get ingrown and infect him. I have to be able to help him do every single thing he can't do for himself yet, and the list is long.

When I leave the hospital, I'm always in a hurry to get somewhere else. Emily needs a ride home from art club, or Heather's' flute needs to be brought to the music store for some repair, or there's a soccer game. There is a band concert, a teacher conference, a dentist appointment. There is a dance, or a play audition, or any of the dozen things I want the girls to keep doing. It's time to sign them up for summer activities, or all the spaces will be filled. I don't know where the forms are; I worry about the paperwork that is starting to pile up again, but I can't ever seem to get to it. We're still getting dinners delivered every couple of days, but the house cannot run itself. I show Mim as much as I can, hoping she doesn't feel put upon; I am not able to take the time to sit down with her and find out. I try to use the time driving the girls around to hook up with them. Sometimes it works, but often I'm too distracted, thinking hours or days ahead, trying not to blow it.

This afternoon, I have to take Heather's flute down to the music store in Bellevue Square; something is wrong with one of the pads. I'm sitting in the car on Bellevue Way, across the street from the Art Museum. The museum has an unusual entryway; a two-story-high cube is cut out of one corner of the building, forming a kind of open portico.

The ceiling of this space is a white square with twenty-five foot sides, and on this surface is a continuously repeating video clip Bruce made last winter. He was so excited to get this commission—his first as a working artist. One of the things on the clip is an image of Bruce himself, striding toward the camera ... I'm sitting in traffic, the museum visible in my peripheral vision, waiting for the endless light to change. And then, sudden as thunder, I break down and howl. The pain is physical and huge. I ought to pull over until this passes, but I don't. I hold onto the wheel and drive through the intersection, screaming and screaming.

In the evening, when everyone is home, fed, and settled for the night, I go back to the hospital. Jocelyn is still scheduling visitors to be with him every day from four to eight, but it makes sense for me to be there after that, when his nurses get him into bed. I need to know how, for one thing, and sometimes Diva is too busy, for another. Tonight, for example, I walk in to find him slumped, exhausted and alone, in the chair, in the dark. He is staged next to his bed, just waiting for someone to come and put him in it. He's already called them, but they just keep saying they'll be right here. I'm not actually checked out to do it, but I know I can, so I do.

I set up the sliding board, make sure the brakes are locked, and move him over. I lift his feet and lay his upper body down, careful to support his head. He groans with relief. I unlock the brakes and push the chair out of the way. I help him get his shirt off, then the binder. I untie his shoes, pull off his socks, remove his pull-on pants. I shove him halfway onto his side and stuff pillows behind his back to hold him up; he can't lie flat because of the pressure sore. I cover him with the quilt to stop his shivering.

Diva hustles in, giving me her broad smile. "Oh, ho, ho," she says cheerfully. "So, you can do this all by yourself, now, good. Hello, Bruce!" She's about five feet tall, a slender, dark-eyed woman with a charming, musical accent. Her words come out soft, crisp and light, like pastry. She wears clean white running shoes with her dusty blue uniform, and, usually, a red fleece vest just like mine. She's one of the people I absolutely trust, along with his day nurse, Chris, and the therapists, Josh and Bob. Bruce has told me that Diva has a magical way of knowing just how to arrange his limbs and pillows so he can sleep.

Because I've just done some of the work she came in here to do, she has a few extra minutes to spend with us. She takes Bruce's limp right hand in hers and makes his index finger touch the tip of his thumb, then straightens it, then repeats the procedure with the other three fingers. She says it's important to do this. We want to keep his fingers moving.

"Every night, see?" She starts over again at the first finger, then puts his hand in mine. "Now you."

"Diva, where did you learn to be a nurse? Did you go to school here in the U.S.?"

"I did," she says, bent over to work the fastenings on the catheter. "But I was already a nurse when I got here."

"From the Philippines, right?"

"That's right. I was working on spinal cord patients there, oh, for years, a few years, before I got the chance to come to New York."

"What was that like? Is it the same here as there?"

She rolls her expressive eyes. "No way! We don't have all this OT, PT, respiratory, psych—we are that! We are everything, all at once. And this"—she holds up the leg bag she's just replaced—" this, we washed, yes, us, the nurses." She tosses it into the trash. "We re-used them, see? Here, we just throw them away. There's more, always more! The storage room is full of them. But you know, you pay for that." She's got the ace wraps off his legs. She starts to wind them into rolls, then stops herself and drops the pile on Bruce's chest. "Here, Bruce, you do this," she says. "Is that okay, huh?"

He's not as zoned as usual because she's just now dropping the meds into his feedbag. "Sure," he says, "I'll try." With his left hand, he feels around for an end, finds it, and starts rolling.

She watches for a minute, then says, "Bruce, this is why we all like you so much. Always the same from you: I'll try, I'll try. That's good. That's what's gonna make you get better." She drops a washcloth into the white canvas bag and says, "We did the laundry too, in Manila. And for all our patients." She shakes her head. "It was nothing like this. They were all together, in one big room." She gestures, her right hand indicating a long row of beds. "And the nurses, we did everything. Here—this is easy!"

She's watching me rub lotion between his toes. I ask her how many patients she had to take care of there.

"A lot! Here, people complain if they got, I don't know, five. Five! And there's not that much to do." She turns the lights up. "Okay there, Mr. Bruce, I'm gonna have a look at your sore. Kate, you come over here. You gotta know what these things look like."

I don't want to. "I saw it this morning," I say. "And yesterday."

"Well, good. Then you can tell me if it looks any different tonight." She's staring at the spot and frowning in a way I don't like. Shit. I walk around the bed and there it is—a dark red coin at the base of his spine. Diva touches it a couple of times with the tip of her little finger.

"How does it look?" Bruce whispers.

Diva is silent, then says she doesn't believe in giving people false hope. "It's a little darker, Bruce. And I think there's a tiny split starting."

I can't really tell. I tell him that to me it looks just like this morning. "Maybe a little more—concentrated. Smaller, but darker."

Diva just frowns and goes off to get his meds.

I walk back around to see Bruce's face. "It really doesn't look bad. Compared to the pictures in that video, I mean."

"Did I tell you about the butt conference today?"

"Excuse me?"

"Oh, it was quite the show. After you left this afternoon, Josh and I were finishing up, and he decided he was going to take a Polaroid of the sore."

"Gakk!"

"So, he pulls the curtain around the mat, right there in the gym, lays me down, and drops my drawers."

"Oh, for Christ's sake."

"But when he comes back, he's got, like half the hospital with him … that other PT guy, a couple of doctors, a nurse or two."

I'm laughing now. "What, no one from CNN?"

"Right, you get the picture."

"A butt conference. Well, that's a first. So, did Josh get it on film?"

Bruce yawns hugely, his chin flattening against the Miami J. "Camera didn't work."

Diva has come in and finished her chores. She's smiling at the two of us from across the room. "I shouldn't say this, maybe. When I first got here, I couldn't tell the white people apart. They all looked so alike to me!"

Bruce and I crack up, and I ask if it's still a problem.

"Well," she admits, "Sometimes it is." We laugh again, and now she's embarrassed. She waves her tiny hands. "Not as bad, not as bad! Especially when I get to know them a little. Like you guys." She pauses for one beat, and in that space I understand that, like Chris the day nurse, Diva is claiming us. Then she goes on. "But in the beginning, forget it! Everybody looks exactly the same." She is standing at the door, her small, sturdy shape silhouetted in the light from the hallway. Bruce is arranged on his side, facing the window, space enough for me left next to him. "Good night to you both," she sings out, and closes the door.

In the dark, I take off all my clothes. I lie down next to him, facing him, loving the feel of his long thighs. His hand lingers over the shapes of my face, fingertips tracing my cheekbones, my jaw line. He touches my hair, pushes a strand behind my ear. I wait, breath held, for him to find the rest of me, but he isn't interested in that tonight. Slowly, I let him teach me this unfamiliar story. The minutes pass, unbelievably tender, and whatever space has ever been between us is, at least for this moment, filled.

Day 45

The girls' favorite person at the hospital is Nurse Bob. Nurse Bob is built like a barrel, with a squat, round torso and beefy arms and hands. He looks deliciously deranged in his dusty blue nurse's uniform—like a hell's angel dressed up for Halloween. When Diva isn't working, he's often assigned to take care of Bruce. He has a long, skinny ponytail, he's partially bald, and he knows how to make kids laugh. As soon as Emily and Heather catch sight of him, they start to laugh.

He puts his meaty hands on his hips. "You're back again? Don't you have homework to do?"

They assure him, thrilled, that they already did it.

"Well, they must not give you enough." He shakes his balding head at the incomprehensible incompetence of teachers. "I'll have to assign you some extra work. I want a typed essay, next time I see you."

"An essay! What's an essay?"

"See, you don't even know what an essay is. Okay, a story. Write me a story. I expect double-spaced, with no spelling mistakes." He pulls his round, stubbled face into a stern frown. "Are you good spellers?"

Emily insists that she is; Heather informs him that she sucks at spelling.

He says, disgusted, "Suck? You suck at spelling? What kind of talk is that? My mother would wash my mouth with soap for saying that. You probably just use spell-check, anyway."

"Well, duh. That's what it's there for."

He turns away as if Heather is beyond help. "Spell gorgeous," he says to Emily. She does, impressing him in spite of himself, but he recovers quickly. "I can't even spell that word," he tells her. "So I don't know if you're right!"

"I am." Emily is making the face she makes when she's trying to stop herself from laughing so hard she cries—her lips stretched out over her top and bottom teeth. I see Nurse Bob's lips twitch, but he controls himself.

"Okay, then, you don't have to type your essay." He frowns at Heather again. "You do." And he lumbers off happily. Protesting, they chase him down the hall, leaving me and Bruce to trail along behind.

Day 46: 9 pm

I've been at the hospital all day, and I'm waiting for the girls to be delivered by the friends who've had them for the weekend. They're an hour late, which is about fifty minutes more than my raw nerves can bear. I roam around the room looking for things to put right. Rearrange the CD collection. Blues, Santana, gospel, rock, more Santana. Go through his closet, looking for things that need washing. Stand in the doorway, looking down the hall. Not yet. My skin is starting to crawl; I have a surge of resentment for this new anxious-mother routine. I am not like this. Except that now, I am.

It vanishes the moment they appear, flushed and happy from a day spent outdoors. I drink up the sight of their faces for a few minutes and then start making noises about needing a latte. This is a cover, a way to leave them alone with him for a little while. We've learned that as long as I'm in the room, the girls speak to him mostly through me, and he lets them. Not okay, not necessary anymore.

Ten minutes later, I'm sitting on the sofa in the Bistro, listening to the jazz this barista favors with my legs curled underneath me. Emily is suddenly there, pulling me to my feet.

"Mama! Daddy has a voice!"

We race back to his room, where I approach the bed. He's lying there with his left hand on the front of the Miami J, fingers spread over the place where his vocal cords lie, as if he could feel them vibrate through the hard white plastic. He looks at me, tears standing in his eyes. "I have a little voice," he says.

10 pm

In the car, I ask them the question I've been asking every few weeks. "So, how much of Daddy is there now?" The first time I asked this, Emily said, loyally, ninety percent. This was while he was still in RICU. Heather just snorted.

"Ninety percent! What's ninety percent about him? He can't eat, or talk, or walk, or ..."

He can barely breathe, I thought.

"Okay." Emily's voice was quiet. "Fifty percent?"

"Ten," said Heather bitterly. "No, five."

"That would be practically dead!"

"Duh!"

Now I pose the question again, and this time they agree: twenty percent. He's a fifth of the person he was before.

Day 47: 11:15 am

Bruce and I are posing for another picture. This time we're in his room, both sitting, he in his wheelchair and me in a chair next to him. We're holding hands. He's wearing his street clothes, and his hair has grown a half an inch since the last photo. I'm relaxed and smiling, legs crossed. Not shown in the picture is the reason I look so confident—Dave. He's standing right across from us when this picture is taken, having just flown in this morning. Something in me expands, loosens at the very sight of Dave. He's the real grown-up; with him around I can stop faking it.

He's in town to help us make plans for fixing the house. The hospital people all call this work "home modifications," which makes it sound to me as if our home is about to become part of the hospital, or at least, a sort of extension of the hospital. Our friends from church and most of our family call it "remodeling," as if we've simply decided to re-do our kitchen, or add a deck. In my mind, what we are doing is "fixing the house." It's as if I'm pretending that the house is what is broken. Maybe if we can just "fix it" properly, our family can live there together again.

Do people seem silly and frivolous to you now?
Because everybody I know, we spend most of our
time just whining about everything. Now you know
something that we don't know, don't you?

David Letterman, to Christopher Reeve

```
To help us establish
a plan of care, we
outlined what we
believed would be a
"typical day" at
home. It is probable
that the patient's
morning care would
take approximately 3
to 4 hours.
```

TWELVE

Day 48

The negotiations with Premera Blue Cross are complete. Our policy has coverage for sixty days of residency at a "Skilled Nursing Facility"—a nursing home—which Bruce, thank God, does not need. They have proposed that we exchange these sixty "SNF" days for half as many at Harborview Inpatient Rehab, thus giving him thirty extra days here. Since he's only got two days left of regular rehab coverage, he'll be going home thirty-two days from now—on May 21st. Discharge is less than five weeks away.

When I get home and tell Dave that they've moved the discharge date from June 5th to May 21st, he gives me one sharp look, then studies the lists spread out in front of him with even more narrow focus than usual. His voice, though, stays casual. "That's going to be interesting," he says slowly. "There's going to be quite a lot to do around here." I've made him a snack from leftovers and given it to him. Waiting on Dave is automatic, almost reflexive. He's just that sort of man. He says that these renovations are going to make a huge mess. He says our house will be full of dust, especially once they start tearing all the doorframes apart. He says I'll need to call my crew of helpers and get them organized, then sees my face and stops.

"Maybe you ought to find somebody to put in charge of running this project."

Good idea. I'm going to have enough to do getting trained to be a personal care attendant. I haven't said much about this, and I don't want to. I'm still in a kind of fierce, private not-until-I-absolutely-have-to mode on this subject. "I can probably come up with somebody for it," I tell him. "We know a few retired guys at church who might be able to help."

"That would be perfect," he says, making himself a note. He's already in the process of turning this into an engineering exercise, a complex set of overlapping mechanical problems that must be solved simultaneously. I can see that in spite of everything, he's going to relish the challenge of getting it done.

Day 49

This is what Bruce can and can't do: he can push himself in the wheelchair all the way from his room to the gym. He can maneuver the wheelchair into position, angled correctly toward the mat, left front corner of the seat just touching. He can set his own brakes. Then someone else has to lift his feet off the footrests, slide the board under his butt, move him over to the mat, lift his up his knees, swing his feet up on to the mat, and pull his heels forward into the position that is called "long-sitting." He can then balance by leaning back and bracing himself with his arms out straight.

Once in that position, he can get himself lying flat on his back by going down first to his elbows, then slowly inching them forward, careful to keep his head steady as his upper body goes down. It has taken Josh three days to teach him how to lie down safely. When I try it myself to see what's involved, I realize how tough everything becomes without abdominal muscles. From lying on his back, Bruce can roll himself to either side, then all the way onto his stomach, then back again. This move is hard for me to watch. He reaches both arms high over his head and grabs his right hand in his left, then uses his shoulders to rock himself a few times, slowly building momentum. It reminds me of the way you rock a stuck car to push it out of deep snow.

On about the fifth rock, over he goes, hips leading, long legs tangling. Getting back is less awkward because he can push off with one arm. The thing he can't do is get from lying down to sitting up. Josh is all over him, certain that if they just get his limbs properly arranged, he'll be able to do it. Bruce's eyes are squeezed shut. He's growling through gritted teeth, pushing with all he's got, and still it doesn't work. Weeping with frustration, he asks for a second to get his breath before trying again. Josh is running one hand through his hair, clearly frustrated. "This should be doable," he keeps saying. "You're going to get there. You're so close. Okay, let's see." After a few minutes, he comes up with a new plan, and they start over.

Day 51: 9 am

We're having a super-special, extra-heavy-duty Rounds meeting today. Except for us, every single person in the room is wearing a narrow, sober expression. The social worker named Susan is about to show us why.

She stands at a large whiteboard, marker in hand, and lays out the events that will constitute a typical day for Bruce at home. Just for the sake of this exercise, she begins his day at seven am. His very first job is to give himself the suppository that will make it possible to move his bowels. He'll have to catheterize himself. He'll be sat up, get transferred to his wheelchair, use the bathroom, and be helped to take a shower using either a shower chair or the commode chair.

After his shower, he'll be transferred back into the wheelchair, then be transferred back to bed, where his skin will have to be carefully checked for pressure sores. In bed, he'll be helped to do his range of motion and strength exercises, and dress his lower body. He'll then be moved back into the wheelchair to put on his shirt and brush his teeth. He'll take his morning medications, and it will be time for another catheterization.

As Susan describes each of these activities, she's writing them down in a brisk column at the far left of the whiteboard. Now she makes a second column, marked "time intensity," where she fills in the probable duration of each task. At the end, she does a quick tally. So far, he's four hours into his typical day, and he hasn't been downstairs yet. Almost every single thing on the list is something he can't do without help. I sit there looking at it, not particularly upset, because it is much too surreal to take seriously. I know that I will when the time comes, but for now I just watch it unfolding, like a slow-motion pie smashing into my face.

Susan fills in the hours between eleven am and six pm with his afternoon activities. Three times a week, he'll be coming back here for outpatient physical therapy. The PT itself will only last for two hours, but the process of getting to the hospital and home again will use up a large chunk of the rest of that time. On other days, he can work on art or whatever personal projects appeal to him. It is hardly worth noting that he won't be going back to work anytime soon. He will have to be vigilant about doing a catheterization every few hours, and he will have to remember his pressure releases.

He'll find that he needs to sleep a lot more than he used to; she thinks that he'll want to be in bed again by nine pm. This will mean going upstairs about seven, since the nighttime routine of medications, undressing, skin checks, in-bed-exercise, catheterization, and range of motion will probably take about two hours. During the night, she reminds us, he'll need to be turned over frequently, and probably catheterized at least once. Gosh Bruce, what a high-maintenance guy you've turned out to be.

Now she draws a third column: "Equipment Needs at Discharge." Moving across from the list of activities, she names the items we will have to buy or borrow to make the schedule she's outlined possible. One by one, she writes them down: the wheelchair, a shower/commode chair, a transfer board, an adaptive communication device, a blood pressure cuff, a bag for use in carrying what he needs while in the wheelchair, and urinary supplies. Then, just in case he still needs them, she adds tube-feeding supplies and an oxygen delivery system.

I picture the aluminum pole that stands next to his hospital bed, with the feedbag full of cream-colored liquid food. I imagine it standing in our bedroom at home, next to his side of the bed. I imagine myself, every night attaching the line to the plug that sticks out of his stomach, the whirr of the machine delivering nutrition—and once again I simply refuse to confront that scenario until I have no other choice. His voice has started to come back; it's possible—not likely, but possible—that he'll be able to eat by May 21st. Looking at the list, I tell myself firmly that these things will either become routine, or they will go away.

Now we have to discuss what issues need to be addressed in the next twenty-five days. The list makes it painfully obvious that taking care of him at home will be more than a one-person job. We'll have to hire a personal care attendant. We'll need to conduct interviews. Susan is in the middle of telling us how one goes about checking references when Bruce interrupts her with his tiny new voice.

"I've hired lots of people in my job," he says. "It's not a problem."

I wonder if they can hear, as I can, how tiresome he finds it to be treated as if he's just sprung into the world, a silent, badly disabled guy with no history, no resources, no life experience to get him through what's ahead. Susan, for example, is clearly not convinced that he's aware of how important it is to properly check references. She's explaining why this matters when he shifts in his chair. I think of the stacks of resumes he used to wade through in search of a qualified candidate for some position at his office.

"He's hired people before," I say. "So have I. We've fired people before. It's not an issue."

She moves on. What about transportation? Jody volunteers that she's in the process of getting Bruce signed up to use public access transportation. She will see that he gets a chance to practice on the metro bus. What about an emergency communications system, in case his voice is still weak? Fleur reaches across the wide table and hands him a big silver whistle. I have to bite my lip so I won't laugh. It's so innocent, so sweetly low tech. It's a playground toy, a thing the soccer coach uses to make the kids listen up. This is his emergency communications system.

It's time to go around the room. They discuss the pressure sore, which has, amazingly, healed almost completely in only a week. Josh reports that Bruce is making progress in PT. He can now roll over on the mat. He's close to being able to get from lying to sitting independently, but he isn't there yet. He still requires a lot of help to transfer in and out of the chair.

The nutritionist named Vickery tells us it's time to start paying close attention to his weight. Bruce's ribs show, not just from the front, but from the back, too. His hipbones are suddenly sharp blades; all these weeks of tube feeding have kept him alive, but they aren't enough. If he keeps losing weight, what will they do? I don't think I want to know.

"The safe range for weight loss is from ten to eighteen percent," Vickery says. "Bruce, you've lost thirty pounds as of yesterday, which puts you right at eighteen percent." She says that he'll have to be weighed every few days from now on, and I see Dr. Smooth Eyes making a note.

Bob says proudly that Bruce is a star at mastering personal self-care. He could do about half of lower body dressing on the very first try! I was in the room when this happened. Bob was slouching against the sink with his arms folded. Bruce was in his bed, leaning back on his stiff right arm, struggling to hold himself up while shoving his mostly dead legs, one painful inch at a time, into a pair of pull-on pants. It took him half an hour, and a bit of assistance. When he was finished, Bob whistled in approval. "You did that without a single reminder." He turned to me and said that the process has, like, forty separate steps, and that they have to be done in a very particular order. "I only showed it to him once," he said. "That was truly amazing." I wanted to tell him that Bruce can still recite lines of computer code he wrote ten years ago, but I didn't. My husband remembered a sequence of forty consecutive steps? Gee.

They ask if we have any questions. We do, actually. Bruce would like to get to church. It's eight blocks away, down a treacherous hill and across a freeway overpass, so probably too far and too hard to attempt by chair. He would need a ride in Jody's van. Can this happen? No, Jody doesn't work on Sunday mornings. Okay. Can we bring our dog in for a visit? They'll have to check. Maybe. Where is the custom splint? He needs the custom-made tenodesis splint in order to use his right hand; it's been promised for weeks. They don't know, they'll have to check. Speaking of his right hand, does anyone have a theory about why it worked for a couple of weeks after the injury and then became paralyzed? No, but they're trying to schedule a test that will show whether any signal is getting to it from the cord. When is the test? They don't know. They'll check.

Anything else?

Alone together in Bruce's room, we are both quiet. I'm thinking about Susan's whiteboard list, and I know that he is, too. "What are you afraid of?" I ask.

"About going home?"

"Yeah."

He sighs. "I'm afraid I'll get there and it will be just another place."

I take his right hand and begin bending the fingers in the way Diva taught me. "It won't," I tell him. Here it is—the enormity of what he confronts, all the time, all by himself. I'm afraid I'll get home and it will be just another place where I am like this.

Day 52

We're at the hospital, trying to get ready to go on Bruce's first outing. Jody and one of the OTs are taking Bruce, Dave, me and the girls to see a Cirque de Soleil film at the Seattle Center IMAX Theatre. It's freezing outside, and Bruce is anxious about being cold. I'm crouched in front of him, trying to get his blue windbreaker zipped, conscious of the girls watching. Daddy can't zip his own jacket. Finally I get it, and we go out to load into the accessible van.

I hate the ride to IMAX. Dave and the girls and I are sitting on bench seats along the wall, facing inward to that we can't escape looking at Bruce, who is in his chair. Heavy gray straps bolted to the floor of the van secure him dead center. He's too tall to see out the windows, so for most of the trip he just rides along, blank-faced. Heather and Emily are doing a half-hearted version of the slug-bug game, which Jody joins a little too enthusiastically.

The show itself is a miracle. We're wearing 3-D glasses to create the illusion that the gymnast/dancers are right in front of our faces, and they work almost too well. Once, when a juggler tosses a ball, it flies directly at me, then hovers just within reach. In spite of myself, I put out my hand to grab it. All of us do. Some of the scenes are set in the desert of southern Utah, in places Bruce has camped. Some are in a forest just like the one behind our house, so vivid I can nearly smell the sycamores. At one point, a pair of dancers does an intricate, erotic dance. Their bodies are an astonishment of strength and grace; they move gently, powerfully around one another, sometimes locking their limbs together in feats of breathtaking balance. They're so intimate, so intensely involved with each other, that watching them feels voyeuristic. During this part of the movie, Bruce surprises me by reaching across the space between us to take my hand.

Day 53: 6 am

I wake on the family room futon, too early. I've been dreaming something that left me with a sense of needing to hide. I lie still until the dream takes shape again in my head. I'm making the girls drive cars by themselves. Heather is parked in hers a little way up the street with the engine running; I am putting Emily behind the wheel of another one when a policeman drives up and tells me I can't do this. I'm trying to pretend I wasn't really going to, trying to avoid looking at Heather in her car so he won't discover that I already have.

10 am

I'm driving Dave and the girls in to church. He's been working his lists all week, and now he gets out a pen and makes a couple of notes. He and Jocelyn have decided to manage the house-fixing themselves. The guys I had in mind to be designated as potential onsite project managers are both unavailable, so Jocelyn is going to recruit worker bees and pass along specific marching orders from Dave. He'll be going back to Minneapolis in the morning, and my youngest brother, Bob, will be flying in on Tuesday.

Dave wants Jocelyn to be absolutely clear about what needs to be done, in what order.

I am thinking about a conversation I had with Heather yesterday. She's been sad and quiet at home, especially when her Grandpa starts discussing the plans for the house.

"No more changes," she said, looking wretched. "I like our house. I like our carpet. We have enough changes."

Dave went into a rational explanation about how her dad couldn't come home unless—but I could see that she already knew all this. She was simply trying to say how much she hated it, and wanted to see the end. Me too, kid. I followed her to her room.

"Heather, I think we have to hold on to good thoughts now."

"I try."

"Doesn't it help at all?" She looked so hopeless, sitting on her rumpled bed in her messy room.

"I don't know. I keep expecting good things to happen, and they keep not happening."

"Some people go around expecting bad things to happen, and then they say 'of course' when they do happen."

She just sighed.

"I think your way is better. Listen, I read something good the other day. I read that always, in every single moment of your life, you always have whatever you need to get through that moment. It made me think of you and Daddy on the mountain."

She turned her face away.

"No, listen. You had your courage, and your good sense, and you had Jill, and you had Dr. Huseby, and you still had Daddy, conscious and telling you what to do." I cocked my head at her. "You had everything you needed in that moment ..."

She didn't even look up. "Yeah, well, I had a lot of stuff I didn't need, too."

Right.

When we get to church, I keep my head down and try not to meet anyone's eyes. Church is exquisitely painful now. The language of our

185

faith grabs hard and won't let go; I've had to stop singing the hymns. Today a soloist sings about the balm in Gilead (to make the wounded whole). Today the text is the story of a few disciples walking, heartbroken and grieving the loss of Jesus, unable to recognize him when he suddenly comes to walk along with them. Today, three different times, old friends burst into tears at the sight of my face. I understand that I've come to represent something here, that some people look at me and see only the reflection of whatever terrifies them. I am not myself; I am the image of the unthinkable. In a strange way, this grotesque, spectacular tragedy has erased me.

Now a woman—the second one today—is telling me tearfully that she can't imagine what I must be going through. I say brightly. "Oh, sure you can. It's easy! Just think of the person you love best in the world, and say out loud, '_____is a quadriplegic.' Then see how you feel." There is a silence. She steps back, shocked, and I am ashamed. She is trying to be kind. "Sorry. It's just that it's taken me until last night to say that sentence myself." This is true. I wrote the words into my journal, twice over, like a schoolgirl being made to learn a new language through repetition.

Day 54

Dave has gone home again. He has things to take care of in Minnesota before coming back here in ten days to oversee what I'm beginning to understand will be a frenzy of activity in our house. The girls and I are on our way home from Harborview.

"Tonight Daddy said 'I love you, my dear' in the exact same way he always said it," Heather tells us from the back seat. She sounds thoughtful, not sad. "He's the only one who can say it that exact way."

"Remember when he used to say, 'bonehead driver'?" This is Emily. "I wish I could hear him say 'bonehead driver' again."

"The other day," I tell them, "I got to hear him say 'dope slap'."

"Dope slap! I love 'dope slap'!"

"I want to hear him make that little noise he makes when he's annoyed." They both start doing it, aiming for just the right intonation of disgust. "Pteh. Pteh. Pteh."

"He does that a lot these days, actually," I say, swinging the car off the freeway.

"I miss him." We are all silent. Yes.

"When is he going to be able to eat? I wish he could eat."

"They're giving him another test tomorrow morning, to see if he can swallow without having it go into his lungs instead of his stomach. If he can, they'll start letting him eat."

"If he can eat, let's make him a banana cream pie! Tomorrow after school!"

"Oh, totally! He would love that …"

Banana cream pie is what I always make for Bruce on his birthday; he likes it better than cake. While I drive slowly through the neighborhood, they go into a long list of all his favorite foods, every one of which they are going to make and bring to him in the hospital.

Day 55: 11:30 am

He's already failed the swallow test by the time I arrive. He's not nearly as disappointed as the girls will be because he was pretty sure something wasn't working quite right.

"I aspirated some water and didn't even feel it," he says.

"Shit."

"It's okay. They'll do it again in a couple of weeks."

We both know that he has to pass that test or be on tube feeding at home. Please, God. Please. We're sitting in front of some windows in the long, wide hall just outside the rehab unit. I want to change the subject, so I show him the latest broadcast from Jocelyn to the Great Big List. Working from Dave's instructions, she's made an itemized summation of ten things we need done at our house by the time "the Hanson Men" show up to finish the job. He reads it in silence.

"Ambitious."

"Yeah, that's what I thought. Did you see this? Your dad said they're going to put a bathtub in the laundry room for me."

He gives me a look that is part kindness and part seriousness. "You couldn't survive without a bathtub."

I've been thinking this same thing, but I never would have asked them to add yet another job to the list—especially not one with the sole purpose of accommodating my favorite self-indulgence. "This was your idea?"

"I know you," he says.

2 pm

Rounds. We come into the conference room and take our places at the head of the big table. Dr. Smooth Eyes invites Bruce to help himself from a dish of chocolates.

Jesus. "He can't eat," I say crisply. Would it really be so hard for her to track the fact that this patient hasn't been able to swallow in almost two months? She apologizes all over the place and tells us how just the other day she did something equally dumb—which does not reassure me. Then she helps herself to another chocolate. This meeting, in fact, is all about eating. Each person around the table expresses regrets that Bruce failed his swallow eval as if he hadn't made it into his first choice grad school.

"There's still a good chance you can pass before your discharge," Dr. Smooth Eyes tells him. "Of course, you'll have a long way to go after that before you'll be able to get all your nutrition from your meals."

I shift in my chair. Stupid. She's just said that Bruce will definitely need tube feeding at home, and I know there's no way she could be sure of this. Would it kill her to offer a little window of hope, just to break up the monotony? I think of the day, now weeks ago, that she caught me as I was leaving the hospital after an encouraging PT session. It was the day after his left quadriceps muscle woke up.

She asked me how I thought it was going.

I was upbeat. "Really well. He's planning to walk out of here, you know. He's planning to be kicking the soccer ball in the front yard again."

She frowned. "He may walk again, that's impossible to tell … but I don't know how coordinated he'll ever be. I just think he's going to have a lot of spasticity." She shook her dark curls, an oh well gesture. Then she saw my expression. "Of course, I'd never say that to him."

Then why say it to me? That was the day I stopped wanting to hear her opinions.

A picture showing specks of black paint scattered against a white background—this was the image that set in motion the current era of spinal cord regeneration ... It was these specks that in the early 1980s allowed scientists to demonstrate definitively that cut spinal fibers were capable of regrowing.

Luba Vikhanski

```
Patient statement:
Discouraged at lack
of strength for
functional mat
mobility and poor
results of swallow
evaluation. "I can't
push this wheelchair
around. I can't turn
or get my feet on and
off the footrests."
```

THIRTEEN

Day 55

It's my day to learn the car-transfer. I've got the Prius parked behind the hospital, in a turn-around area that is, I've just discovered, supposed to be the main entrance. To my left is a huge new parking garage, straight ahead is a new helicopter landing pad, and beyond all of is the city, Puget Sound, and the Olympics. Far away to the south, the giant white cone of Mount Rainier shimmers. The day is postcard perfect: sunny, clear, and warm. I've been here for twenty minutes, waiting for Josh and Bob to show up with Bruce in his wheelchair, and the little worry-rats are just beginning to gnaw at my insides when they appear.

They get him staged next to the passenger seat. Brakes locked, wheelchair angled in as close as possible, feet off the rests and on the pavement. The problem is that the car door is in the place where the person who moves him has to stand. They puzzle over this for awhile, running over possible arrangements. Could he be lifted from behind? Maybe, but not all the way into the car, unless the assistant has a back that's twice as strong and twice as long as a normal one. Is the back seat any better?

Bob climbs in to check. Nah. Same door problem, less leg room once inside. What if the assistant lifts him from behind to get him onto the sliding board, then climbs over and just guides him into the car, no lifting required? While they have this conversation, I watch carefully so I'll be able to do it when it's my turn. Bruce sits, squinting in the sun at the helicopter pad and the view behind it. He's wearing his blue baseball cap that says "Atomic Skis" and a white tee shirt with a black and white sketch of a heron playing a harmonica on the back.

Finally they agree to try the two-stage approach: major lifting done from behind the chair, actual insertion into the passenger seat done while squeezed into the space in front of the chair. Josh does it, and it works. He picks up Bruce's feet, one at a time, and sets them on the floor under the glove box. He's in the car! No time to waste, they go right to work figuring out how to get him back out. Bruce is touching the dash of our car; I want them to shut up and let him just sit there for a minute, but they don't. Josh has moved the chair away from the door. He takes Bruce's two feet and sets them back on the pavement, then helps him get his body angled properly. Bob moves the chair back into place, and they set the transfer board firmly beneath Bruce's butt. Josh has almost no room to maneuver.

Part of the problem is that the seat of the car is a couple of inches lower than the seat of the chair, which means that this isn't a level transfer. Bruce will have to be lifted uphill. Josh keeps making little adjustments to his own posture, until at last he figures out that if he starts out with his knees wider apart than usual, there will be room for his feet on either side of the corner of the chair. He sticks his head into the car, takes hold Bruce's bottom, reminds him to lean way over so his head clears, and lifts him halfway up the board.

Now Bruce has to steady himself and wait while Josh climbs awkwardly out from the space in front of the chair and dashes around to stage himself behind it. Once there, he easily moves Bruce the rest of the way up the board and into the chair again. "Whew."

Bob offers a few pointers about minor changes to the procedure. Bruce has a giant coughing fit, which ends with him trying to spit a wad of nastiness on the ground. He doesn't have enough wind to spit, and some of it lands on his shirt.

"Pteh." It is his trademark expression of mild disgust.

Bob and Josh are snickering like third-graders. Suddenly it's funny—just another guy thing, gross and stupidly wonderful. "That's great," Bob says to Bruce, who is laughing. "If you couldn't laugh at a little snot on your shirt, now that would be pathetic."

I'm going to put him in the car. I do everything Josh did, which isn't too hard since we are just about exactly the same size, and he is dictating instructions rapidly. Leaning over to take hold of Bruce's butt, I say softly into his ear, "Let's nail this so we can get the hell out of here."

"Good plan."

He is in. I put his left foot in, then his right, and close the door behind him. Josh looks at me for a couple of beats. "Go ahead and take him for a ride," he says.

Yeah! This is clearly against all the rules. We don't have anybody's permission, no doctor has said he's ready, but we're going. I hop behind the wheel, turn the key, and together we drive past the ER entrance, past the parking lot where this car usually is, past the light at James street, and down into the city. We're out!

On the floor that night, we're messing around in the hall with nothing much to do. The Mariners have won again. They've been playing for a month now, and they haven't lost a single series—a few games, but not a single series. I'm wishing their games were all home games, all starting at seven pm local. This afternoon they beat the Yankees in New York, and so there's nothing to entertain us. Bruce is in the wheelchair, and I'm sitting on the floor. I do this a lot because I like to mess with his feet, and even more because I need to look up at him. I ache to stand before him, looking up, and this is the next best thing. I have his shoes off, and I'm rubbing his toes.

"Does this feel good?"

"I wouldn't say exactly good. It feels interesting."

How many times have I done this, rubbed his feet and assumed that he was feeling what I would be feeling if he rubbed mine? What a dope I am. "Interesting how?"

"It's hard to describe."

I wait.

"Kind of ... crackly."

"Really." That is interesting.

"Yeah, almost like, electric. It's not unpleasant."

After awhile I put his socks and shoes back on, but leave his feet on the floor. This chair has individual foot rests, the kind that can be flipped up. He moves his left foot idly, then reaches to unlock his brakes and does it again. The chair glides backwards. I sit there on the floor, watching him. He's moving himself around with his left leg.

"Can you make it come back?"

He tries. "It's a lot harder."

"Must be different muscles."

When we show Diva this, she claps her hands. She says she's going to chart this, and that now he has a new exercise which he must do, every day. "Little bit, and little bit more, and little bit more after that," she says. "That's how you're gonna get better."

Day 56: 2:30 pm

I'm standing in our living room with Bob. My youngest brother arrived last night in a cab, having just flown in from Sarasota. He's got his hands in the front pockets of his work jeans, and he's pleased with his first morning's efforts.

I am stunned. The living room carpet is all gone. The floor underneath turns out to be beautiful—perfectly finished dark-stained hardwood floor, expensive and lovely. Why did they cover this up? Bob takes me to the garage where he has stacked the carpet in fat, neat eight-foot rolls for hauling to the transfer station. We walk back upstairs, where we both kneel to put our hands on the incredible floor. Our voices ring and echo as we talk. I think of Heather, who begged me not to let them take away our carpet. She'll be unhappy today.

Bob shows me where he's lifted a corner to check the floor in our bedroom—it's the same dark wood. This afternoon, he says, this part will be done. Tomorrow, the little area downstairs, and then he can start painting.

"It's so much work ..." I can't get over him coming all the way out here prepared to spend his vacation days doing all this work. I left home when Bob was nine years old; we haven't shared a house in thirty years. He's the youngest of my five brothers.

"You don't know me now," he says.

He's right. The Bob I used to know is a party-animal, a ladies man, and always a lot of fun, but he was not a worker. "The jail thing changed you." Two years ago, he got busted for drug use.

"Yeah, it'll do that. And, I'm just too old."

I snort at this, but it's just for form's sake. He's nearly forty; it's long past time to put a life together. He tells me he got himself a work ethic, and describes his business in Florida. He has employees. He deals all the time with super-rich people, every one of whom goes away a happy customer. Nobody, nobody can get a job done as well or as quickly as he can. He likes working.

"Did you lose the tongue stud?"

He shows me. Nope.

"Let me see your tattoos." He bends his shaved head and there they are: a three-inch high devil just behind one ear, and a matching angel just behind the other. "You're still you," I tell him. "Just smarter."

He shrugs. "Pretty hard to be much dumber."

That afternoon I get a phone call from a man who identifies himself as the Washington State Elevator Inspector. He says he's been advised that I'm having a lift installed in my house and wants to verify the information.

"My father-in-law ordered one last week," I say.

"Do you happen to know the make?"

"No. Wait, he might have left the brochure here." I rummage around and find it. When I read the product description to him, he stops me.

"You can't have that lift in your house. It's not legal in Washington."

I don't know what he's talking about. I tell him that my husband broke his neck, and we have to have a lift because our house has stairs, and that my father-in-law ordered it from a list of suppliers that he got from the occupational therapists at Harborview Medical Center. To me, this settles it. Surely Josh and Bob wouldn't have recommended equipment that isn't legal.

"I'm sorry," he says. "The lift your father-in-law ordered isn't up to code. It won't pass the inspection, and you will have to have it inspected."

I'm done. I get out my phone book and give him Dave's number in Minneapolis.

Two hours later, Dave calls, as angry as I have ever heard him. He says that of the four suppliers whose names he got from Harborview, two were out of business, one was the supplier he ordered the lift from, and the last one was some character named Kevin. Dave, scrambling to make the arrangements for the lift last week, had asked Kevin to come out to our house and see if he had any equipment that would work for us.

"When this guy came to the door," he says, "I'd already found the lift I ended up ordering. I told him thanks for his time, but I'd solved the problem." Dave pauses, remembering. "And then he asked what I'd bought. I did something stupid and told him. He said that I couldn't buy that one because it wasn't approved for use in Washington, and I told him I already had."

"What does he care?" I ask.

"I think he was just mad that he missed out on the business. Kate, he turned you in. This Kevin. He called the inspector's office in Olympia and gave them your name, and that's how this inspector got wind of it. It's the only way he could have."

"You'd think people would have better things to do than make this harder," I say.

"Apparently not. I think the inspector would just as soon have never heard of you, but once he'd been given your name, he had to follow up. Damn bureaucrats." He says that it's all solved, but he's pissed. He's already cancelled the first order, found a supplier who checks out with the state of Washington, and ordered a lift from him. It's not ideal. The first one was ideal. The first one was also $2,000 cheaper than the one we're going to get. "Damn bureaucrats."

7 pm

Bob is painting the ceiling over our dining room. He works fast and clean; his hands are so steady that he doesn't even bother with tape. He doesn't look tired, in spite of having been in motion since the moment he arrived. Twenty feet up on his ladder, he can look down on Emily, who is practicing her cello in the living room. She plays the same page over and over again, for half an hour. It's one of those little tunes that burrow into your brain cells and won't come out. While she's loosening her bowstrings, his voice suddenly floats down, putting words to the melody.

"I am wa-ay up here, wa-a-a-ay up here, I-I-I hope I do-on't fa-a-a-a-a-all down!"

There is nothing he won't do. He convinces Heather to give up her "Get Out of Broccoli Free" card for one night, then makes a dish of broccoli covered with home-made cheese sauce that she actually likes. He teases them, takes them to their soccer games, and paints like a fiend. In between runs to Home Depot for supplies, he takes phone calls from his crew in Sarasota. His presence is a gift.

Day 57: 9 pm

The range of motion ritual for Bruce's legs is to have him move whatever he can. Lying flat on his back, he does tiny little knee lifts with his left leg, pulling his heel a couple of inches toward him, then letting his foot slide forward again. He wiggles all the toes on that foot. He turns his ankle side to side and points and flexes the foot itself. All these movements are weak and small, but this leg is clearly not paralyzed. On the right side, nothing ever happens. We know only that if the right leg is fully extended and I pick it up and pull it out a foot or so away from his body, he can make it come back toward him. Nothing else.

I'm at the end of the bed, facing away from him, getting ready to do my thing with the lotion. His right foot moves just before I touch it.

"Did my foot just move?"

"Yes." He does it again. His foot goes from pointing straight at the ceiling to aiming at the top of the wall. Again, and again. I move up to kiss him. "Another exercise, huh?"

"I guess. Thank God." We're quiet, in the excited way. "How many days has it been?"

I count in my head. Twenty-four days in March, thirty in April, three in May. "Fifty-seven. So much for the six-week thing."

"It was always just an estimate."

"I know. I still think they shouldn't say it." I stressed for a long time over that deadline. I knew the exact day that would mark six weeks, now long past. That was the day by which he was supposedly going to have most of the return he would ever get. This is what they told us. The muscles that were firing after six weeks could maybe get stronger, but if they weren't firing by then, they probably never would.

Day 59: 8 am

The doorbell is already ringing. Today is the day of the first work party. I don't know what to expect, who will show up, or even what they'll be doing. The man at the door is our friend, Jim, whom I normally see at church, dressed in business clothes. He's a lawyer, I think—right now a lawyer wearing the most hopelessly ripped up, paint-splattered tee shirt I've ever seen. He's looking down at me with a kind, almost apologetic expression, saying that Jocelyn said today was the day.

It's one of those crashing moments. His arrival marks a whole new phase, in which our lives will be even more open to public inspection. I make the appropriate welcoming, grateful noises, but inside I am getting shivery. I go to look for my brother, who is, naturally, already working. I find him in the garage, pouring paint from an enormous bucket into a smaller one.

"The worker bees?" he says.

"Well, one of them, at least. Can you give him something to do?"

Bob walks past me with the rolling, straight-shouldered gait my whole family shares. He shakes Jim's hand, at ease and in charge, and I relax. At least I won't have to direct the dismantling. Within an hour, the house is full of people. They are removing screws from the doors leading to the kitchen and the garage, then hauling the doors themselves out to be disposed of. They are using screwdrivers to pry the doorframes loose, piece by piece. They are clearing the clothes out of my closet and carrying them up to hang in Heather's room. They are trying to sort out what is obviously junk in the garage, and then making run after run in pickup trucks to the dump. I walk into our bathroom at about ten o'clock, and there is Jim, kneeling in front of the now-empty cupboard under our sink. Before him is a cardboard box full of whatever used to be loose in this room: Comet, Windex, stiff old sponges, soap, a set of electric curlers, toilet paper, makeup, Bruce's shaving lotion collection.

"I'm not sure where you'll want to put this," he says.

Neither am I. I take it from him and walk off, feeling confused and fragile. The girls are in the kitchen with both doors closed, watching cartoons. I carry the box upstairs to their bathroom, but there isn't anyplace in there to put it, and finally I just set it down in their hallway. These people are from church, from Bruce's old office, from my school. Some are from his twelfth step group. One is from the Men's Group, and there is even a woman and her husband from the Vermont College class he graduated with last February. At one point a neighbor we've barely met wanders over to see what's going on, and ends up staying to help.

Bob decides that there is enough manpower to get the bathroom cleared. Just before I leave for the hospital, I see a few guys hauling my old bathtub out the front door.

That night I have another bad moment in Bruce's room. I'm struggling to get his foot organized in the giant black boot he has to wear every night to prevent foot drop. I'm tired, and I'm tired of doing this. The straps aren't cooperating; there are three fussy little metal clasps that always give me trouble. I'm tightening the last one when he mentions, casually, that his foot feels like it isn't in there quite right. Okay. I start over, undoing the straps, lifting his foot out, then setting it back in.

"Is that better?"

Silence.

"Bruce?"

"Yeah, I think that's okay."

How nice. My fingers seem to be twice as thick as usual. Finally I get all three straps snugly fastened. Fucking thing.

"My right leg needs to be straightened just a bit more."

This request, delivered in a languid, distant tone, sends me into a white rage. I look at him, lying on his blue egg crate, his hospital pajama top crumpled where it touches the stiff neck-brace, his face restful from the drugs they give him every night, and the sight fails to soften me. The strain of the last two months is right up against the knowledge that I'm in for an untold future time doing this, and I don't want to move.

Day 61

Another dream wakes me up. Bruce and I are standing together in front of the nurse's desk. He's on his feet, I keep saying, but they aren't interested. He's on his feet, but he's exactly the same height as me, a full foot shorter than his real height. He sways and wobbles. They ignore us both.

An hour later, I'm struggling to write a note to tell my brother thanks. He's leaving this morning, and he stayed up most of the night laying tile in the part of our bathroom where the sink used to be, leaving a space in one corner for the toilet. Yesterday he figured out what wood we'd need to rebuild our torn-up deck, ordered it from Home Depot, had it delivered, and made a detailed sketch showing whoever will finish the job how to do it. He's finished painting all the rooms, including two accent walls and both of the tricky textured ceilings. The house is lighter than it's been in years.

I take up my pen and tell him about the time that I was at a church meeting. People were discussing the reasons to bring small kids to church. (They need to hear the stories. They need to form the habits and practices of faith. They need to see their parents at worship.) I write to my brother that I stood up at that meeting and said that I bring my kids to church because I want them to know they're not alone in this world—that they can count on the people here. I said that everybody gets their turn in the fire, and when it comes around for my kids, I want them to know they're not alone. I write that as long as Bruce or me or Emily or Heather is alive, he's not alone, either.

11 pm

I've just blown a couple of hours watching Jocelyn's tape of the last two "West Wing" episodes. In the second one, there is a scene in which the political aide, Josh, is talking with a pollster, played by the deaf actress, Marlee Matlin. The aide is asking the pollster to do something which I gather from both of their behavior will be very difficult. He's asking her to do it in secret and in extreme haste. Even more difficult, maybe impossible. The deaf pollster questions him closely, her understanding of the gravity of his problem dawning visibly on her beautiful, angular face. There is a quiet between the two of them, pregnant with the implications of trouble. Then she nods and says firmly in her thick, impaired speech, "No problem."

I've reversed the tape and watched this little moment three or four times, and each time it makes me weep. Such a simple scene: in the face of catastrophe, one friend saying to another, No problem. Oh, Jocelyn, Sue, David, Bob—all of you.

Day 64: 8 pm

Now Heather wants to come with me to the hospital, just to get away from the chaos in our house. Her grandpa Dave is back, along with her Uncle Keith and her two Salt Lake City cousins, Josh and Christian. Bruce's Aunt Sue is also with us. Until this week the girls had never met her. Now this stranger is sleeping in her parents' bed. The rest of them are staying at my friend Judy's house—a circumstance that makes the whole circus just bearable—for them, I suspect, as well as for us. Tomorrow Bruce's brother Paul will fly in, and next week Keith's wife Tracy will join the party, on the same day that Aunt Sue leaves.

We're in Bruce's room, and he and Heather are trying to create a complete map of the United States from memory. She's sketching on the corner whiteboard as he dictates, trying to fit in the names of all those tiny eastern seaboard states. They get confused in the south. "Wait, isn't that where Mississippi is?"

"I thought Mississippi was over here."

"No, that's Missouri ... I think. And what about Alabama?"

In the end she fills in the gaps with jagged script that reads "all those states where nobody I know lives." Then she starts a new map, which she labels "Hansonetteland," a name that comes from combining their last name and mine. She gives each of us our own section: here is the state of Bruce, and this is the state of Kate, and this is ... I'm taken by the poetry of it. The state of Bruce. What sort of a territory is that? What is its capital? What are its exports?

We talk together whimsically, the three of us relaxed and ordinary. She finishes her drawing by surrounding our country with the Sea of Sophie, and then it's time to go. I pull on my coat, turning in time to see them exchanging a hug. He always closes his eyes at her touch, as if he is trying to memorize the feel of her.

"I love you, my dear."

"Goodnight, Daddy."

Day 65: Noon

Tomorrow is the next work party. I'm in our garage, sorting through boxes of things that belong to Bruce, trying to be philosophical. Over the years of our marriage, we've tried a variety of approaches to our two different ways of dealing with clutter. He doesn't like to sort things. No, he really, really doesn't like to sort things. I really, really don't like to be surrounded with things I know should be thrown away. He doesn't trust me to sort his things. Many foolish dollars have been spent on fruitless efforts to get one therapist or another to help us develop a mutually satisfying solution.

About a year ago, we agreed that he could simply "have" the garage. If I found myself stressing too heavily about this or that pile of his unsorted belongings, I could simply gather them up, drop them in a box, label it with the date, and set it in the garage. Andy Warhol used this method; his boxes of old junk mail are archived in the basement of some museum. If it worked for him, it could work for us. We'd park our cars in the driveway, where, we rationalized, there was plenty of room. Tomorrow, though, the people are going to finish clearing the garage. We need all this space back again.

In the parking space that's by the door leading into the house, there is going to be a wide, railed ramp with a switchback. The other parking space will be where the Prius has to go. In bad weather, we won't want to be doing the difficult choreography of getting him in and out of the car in the driveway. This means that these boxes and bags of things belonging to Bruce must be sorted out at last—and I'm elected to do the job, after all. Oh, well.

I sit in the sun on an upturned paint bucket, slowly making piles. Ten-year-old Mountaineer magazines. Inserts to the church bulletin from when the girls were toddlers. Old photographs, homemade Father's Day cards, dull-tipped pencils with no erasers, dried up markers, bank statements, minutes from a church board meeting he chaired years ago ... and art supplies I can hardly bear to look at. Boxes of water-color markers, expensive brushes, calls for entries to juried shows.

I'm flipping sadly through a sketchbook filled with careful, beautiful pencil drawings he made in Paris at the Louvre in the mid-nineties. Toward the back of this book are a series of drawings of women's naked torsos that are not from the Louvre. Their bodies are carefully—lovingly—detailed. The women are posed in the thrusting, come-and-get-me language of porn. In the sketches, none have faces, or hands, or feet.

I'm moving through odd, intense layers of emotion, studying these images. Deep sadness that the hand that made these drawings can't hold a pencil. Resentment that he made them at all. Curiosity about the particular kinds of bodies he chose to focus on. Exhaustion at the idea of confronting all my insecurities and jealousies and confusion again. Irony. I close the sketchbook and find a sturdy, medium-sized box. I label it: Bruce's Art Things, and set the book inside.

One day the hero sits down,
afraid to take another step,
and the old interior angel
limps slowly in
with her no-nonsense
compassion
and her old secret
and goes ahead.

David Whyte

Patient continues to
make significant
daily and weekly
progress, with noted
improvements in
mobility skills and
lower body dressing.

FOURTEEN

Day 66: 3 pm

The work party is in full, roaring swing. My whole youth group is here, doing the yard work I've neglected; they've pruned the rhododendrons, laid down new bark, raked and mowed the front yard, and are now at work turning over the garden so I can plant. Inside is bedlam. Inside is Bruce, home on a day pass. I can see that he's wishing for a little peace, but there is not a room in the house where that is possible.

Dozens of friends keep stopping their work to squat at the side of his wheelchair and say hello. I put my head close to his. "You doing okay?"

"I'm getting tired."

"It's pretty hellish."

"I'm, like, trapped. Everyone keeps touching me ..."

I know how much he hates being handled. The gentle touch most people think is appropriate can trigger a wave of neuropathic pain. He's described this to me as being kind of like the pins-and-needles feeling you get when your foot goes to sleep, only more intense, and hot. "They mean well," I say. "We'll leave soon."

"I know. Could you get me some water?"

I fill a fat plastic syringe with water from the tap and unscrew the fastener on his stomach tube, then slowly squirt it into him. I lift his pant leg to check the bag. Full. I get a plastic bottle and drain the contents into it, then flush them. The phone rings; it's for me.

My sister Sue is saying that she just talked to our oldest brother, Mike. Our dad has had a stomach aneurysm. He's at the hospital. She's crying so hard I can hardly understand her, especially with all the background noise. I keep having to make her repeat herself, which makes her cry harder. Finally, I get what she's saying. Our dad is dying, right now, at a hospital far away in upper Michigan. Our dad is dying.

Day 67: 8 am

I'm alone on our front steps, hugging the phone to my ear and listening to my mom. She's saying that it was over last night, that he didn't survive the surgery. She sounds broken.

"I can come," I say. "Of course I can come."

"Katie, you need to stay there. I'll understand."

"Mom, just tell me when it is." She says Thursday, Thursday at eleven am will be the mass. Wednesday night a viewing at the funeral home.

"Okay, I'll make the reservations. I'll see you in a few days, okay? I'm really sorry, Mom."

When I take the girls downstairs to my futon to tell them the news, they panic.

"What? What, Mama, what's wrong?"

"It's not Daddy, okay? Nothing's changed with him. My father died last night, guys." I'm weeping, and so are they. "I'm going to have to go to Michigan next week, just for overnight. I'd bring you with me, but I think it's better if you stay here and go to school."

They're trying to comfort me. Heather says she thinks our family is going to be having so much good luck from now on ... both of them say they're willing to stay at our house with all these relatives, without me. They've only met my dad a few times, so this isn't much of a personal loss for them. Okay, wipe your eyes. Thanks, Honey, I'm okay. Yeah, it's rotten this happened on Mother's Day. Next year will be a lot better.

4 pm

Bruce, his Aunt Sue and I are going to the Bellevue Art Museum. She's been so lovely to have in the weirdness of these past few days—a near stranger to me and the girls who managed nevertheless to fit right in and find unique ways to make herself useful. In addition to spending many hours with Bruce at the hospital, looking after Keith's two kids and mine, and keeping order in my kitchen, she took on the job of nurturing our poor, neglected pets.

Our cat, Sophie, who hates everybody except us, has been spending a lot of happy time in Aunt Sue's lap, and our dog is crazy about her.

She's been walking Rocky all over the neighborhood. She's also been feeding him, brushing him, and training him to heel. She even took him to the vet when he got a hot spot. This afternoon's outing is the only relief she's had from the necessary mania Dave, Keith, and Paul have created in our house.

We all love being at the museum, which turns out to be a perfect place to take Bruce in his current state of health. The spaciousness and quiet are a balm, and the exhibits are cool. The three of us linger for a long time in front of a Bill Viola piece. He's set up a video camera to capture in extreme close-up the image of a single drop of water hovering at the tip of a copper pipe. The drop trembles and elongates on the screen in a process that is both poignant and oddly erotic. Gravity gathers it in at last, and it falls to a flat drum fitted with a microphone, so that the impact fills the darkened room with a deep, resonant boom. We watch this mesmerizing process five times through before moving on.

I notice that both of them are acting as if I haven't suddenly just lost a parent. So am I. It's impossible to comprehend. Today is Sunday. I'm going to Michigan on Wednesday morning; my plan is to start believing my father is dead when the airplane takes off eastward.

Day 68: 8:45 am

Bruce is coming home a week from today, and it can't be delayed any longer; Chris the nurse is giving me the morning care instructions. I've skipped school today so I can be here for this training, and I have my journal out so I can take notes. She's heard that my father died, but Chris is a perceptive woman. One look at my face tells her to leave that subject alone. Instead, she gets right down to business.

The story with his bowels is this. They can be trained to behave themselves, but it takes awhile to find the right combination of tactics. Right now he's been having good "results" from daily use of a certain kind of suppository, combined with "digital stimulation." "Results" is the hospital word for shit. "Digital stimulation" is how they refer to someone sliding a glove-covered finger up there to circle around looking for poop stragglers.

The good news is that he's able to do both the suppository and the finger thing himself, something he just mastered last Friday. What this means is that my part of the process is to: (a) hand him a little foil-wrapped suppository, opened and ready to insert, (b) put a glove on him so he can push it in without infecting himself, (c) hold him on his side so he can reach behind and get the job done. At that point, I'll have an hour to catch up on other tasks while the suppository does its work.

I'll be giving him his morning meds, which consist of something to keep him from getting dizzy when he sits up (ephedrine), something to help keep the pins-and-needles neuropathic pain bearable (gabapentin), and something to make his "results" come out soft (docusate). If he needs help to clear his lungs, we can do a few rounds of the bong and a little quad-coughing, followed by an injection of blood-thinner into his numb stomach.

I should put on his belly binder next, followed by his support hose and his big, white shoes. By that time, the suppository should have done its job, and he'll be needing to sit up and be moved onto the ugly commode chair. He'll ride that into position over the toilet, at which point I'll put another glove on him, coat the index finger with xylocaine gel, and wait for him to be done producing his "results" for the day.

As Chris has been explaining all this in her straightforward, matter-of-fact way, I've been watching her do each thing she describes. There is my husband, naked except for his neck-brace, his belly binder, his white support hose, and his shoes, riding off on the commode chair with catheter hose dangling and stomach tube protruding. He's giving me a look that says, you ain't seen nothin'.

When Chris walks away to get something, I ask furtively, "Have they been doing this to you every day?" It's the first time I've heard about the bowel program.

"Oh, yeah."

"Wow. Thanks for not telling me sooner."

"No problem."

After the "results" appear, I'll peel the glove off his hand and throw it in the trash. Now it's time for a shower, but since he's not actually having one today, she just gives me the quick description. I should take off his shoes and socks, make sure his feet are up on the footrests, shove the monster-chair under the faucet. I should set his brakes, and make sure his soap and washcloth are where he can reach them. I should wash his back, make sure he's rinsed well, and then help him get dry. By that time, he'll need to go back to bed for some more sleep. She doesn't say what I'll need, but I'm thinking some good drugs of my own might be in order.

5 pm

By the time I get home, the ramp in the garage is almost finished. It's been raining all day, the kind of cold rain that makes your body ache. Here is our friend Bill, whistling and pounding nails into the rails that line this beautiful, complicated piece of carpentry. Keith is standing in the doorway to the house, looking like he's just spent the day wrestling dust-covered crocodiles—which is to say, tired and filthy.

His expression is happy, though. "Bill, you are my fuckin' hero."

Bill smiles wearily. "It's comin' along pretty good."

"My absolute fuckin' hero." Keith and Bill hadn't met before this morning, but they're definitely two of a kind.

The house project is moving at breakneck speed; Keith has the task of installing all our new plumbing, and it's been one headache after another, involving many extra trips to Home Depot. If Bill hadn't showed up, competent and content to take on the layout and construction of this ramp, Keith would have had to worry about supervising it, on top of everything else he's worried about. And he clearly is worried.

Seeing me notice this, he tells me these things are always a bitch, but that it'll go together in the end. I say I never doubted it, which is true.

Day 69: 11 am

I didn't sleep again last night. I went downstairs when everyone had left and lay there with the purring cats, wishing for oblivion that wouldn't come. As a result, I'm fragile and weepy. I have to leave for Michigan tomorrow on a six-thirty am flight; the reality that I'm going to be traveling alone to bury my father is out there, waiting to get me. I want Bruce to notice that I'm starting to be in trouble. I kneel at his feet and set my head awkwardly in his lap, but he doesn't seem to know what's going on. He doesn't speak. He doesn't lift his hand to touch my hair. It's as if I'm not here. It isn't fair.

2 pm

Rounds again, our last one. I'm holding on to myself, feeling more wounded by the second. I shouldn't be here, trying to deal with this today, but I didn't know that until I got here. The Barbie-doll psychotherapist who has been so useless is taking her turn, saying, "You guys have been so amazing! I've hardly been needed at all." Big Miss America smile. Shut up, Barbie.

When it's time for Johanna the speech therapist to talk, she starts to tell the group that Bruce's voice is very much improved. He interrupts her in a normal voice, then shouts, "And I can yell, too!" She congratulates him on having voice and volume. Just in time, he's finally met his goal. I want to tell the group that Johanna has met her goal, too, by being ten percent less patronizing than she was last week.

I imagine going around the room myself, doing a mawkish, patronizing imitation of their mawkish, patronizing behavior. Josh, you've met your goal of spending eighty-two percent of your time with Bruce in an effort to fit him in the perfect wheelchair, thereby successfully avoiding forever the possibility that he might have spent his $1,500 per day here in rehab working his leg muscles so that he doesn't need that wheelchair. We're so proud. That could not have been easy. Congratulations.

Dr. Smooth Eyes, your one hundred percent effort to be both negative and clueless has certainly paid off over the past week. You haven't had a single episode of either clarity or hope. Way to go. But my insane, bitter ranting is keeping me from tracking what Dr. Smooth Eyes is actually saying. She wants Bruce to think long and hard about setting up an oxygen tank for nighttime use at home. Does he fully understand the implications of sleep apnea? Let her explain. His heart has to work harder whenever his brain sends the message that it isn't getting oxygen because the only way his heart knows to help that situation is to send more blood into his system. Does he understand? And in the long run this could mean wearing his heart out long before it would normally happen. At these words, I'm off again.

Dr. Smooth Eyes, he hasn't been using oxygen in his room for weeks, did you know that? This is your patient, right? Your job is to keep him healthy while he's in the hospital, and if apnea is such a concern, why haven't you written orders to make him do it here, where you have control? My brain is full of acid, furiously producing whole paragraphs of venom. I'll tell you why. Because you're not really concerned about this at all. You just want to sound knowledgeable and in charge. Shut up, now.

Finally it's time to talk about the home visit. He has to have a one-night stay at our house before discharge, so that we'll have a chance to figure out what problems we might run into before he's let loose for good. They're looking at their calendars. Dr. Smooth Eyes wants to have it this weekend, either Friday or Saturday.

"Friday," Bruce says. It's a knife in my stomach. He's forgotten what's about to happen to me. Too hurt to speak, I put one finger on his arm and shake my head. He glances at me. "Oh, yeah." He looks at the team. "Kate … has to go out of town. We'll do it Saturday night." Gosh, thanks, Honey. Sorry to mess up your schedule with my problems. I have to get out of this hospital before any of this starts spilling out of my mouth. I know very well I'm being insane; from the moment I started telling myself it isn't fair, I was lost.

3:30 pm

He's just finished a spin at the Monark machine, which he can now handle for the full twenty minutes, at least on a good day. I'm saying goodbye. I'm telling him that I can't come back tonight, and that I'll be in on Friday at the regular time. Again, it's as if I don't exist, as if my situation is not worth mentioning. He replies, vaguely, that he hopes he passes the goddamn swallow test later today. Empty, I am so empty. I kiss him on the cheek and walk out.

4:30 pm

I'm at my own doctor's office, sitting on the exam table. When he comes in, I'm going to tell him that I need something to help me go to sleep. I can't afford to be this fragile, and I know a lot of it is from lying awake so much in the last few days. It's the only way I can think of to take care of myself. I'm breathing slowly, practicing how to describe what's happened to me in the last couple of months. If I sound too crazy, he might get suspicious that I'm going to try to commit suicide, and then he won't give me the pills. I'm not suicidal, though. I just have to be able to sleep.

5:30 pm

Keith is looking up at me from where he's just finishing installing the drive-under sink that's been such a colossal pain in the ass. He's pleased that he got it working, and he says that Bruce could do his home stay tomorrow, if he wanted to. Enough stuff will be ready. I say that I'll still be in Michigan, and he puts his head in one dirty hand.

"Christ. I'm sorry, I forgot all about that. God."

Day 70: 5:25 am

The pills to help me sleep worked too well. Last night, I set two alarms, and I just slept through them both. I drag myself upstairs; I'm supposed to be at the airport in thirty-five minutes, and it's a twenty minute drive. I stand in the shower in the girls' bathroom, get out, get dressed, and drive myself to SeaTac. I park the car, make a note of the stall number, and walk calmly into the terminal. I'm acting as if I'm not late at all. I stop in a store near the gate to buy some deodorant, which I just realized that I forgot to pack. I linger over the selections.

6:15 am

At the gate, the last flight attendant is in the process of giving away my seat to a stand-by customer. I hand over my ticket; the attendant gives me a look and says, "Thirty seconds later and you'd have missed it." The standby customer sags, and I walk through the jet way door with the attendant locking it up right behind me. Okay, I almost missed my flight. Whatever.

Family relationships strongly influence life satisfaction of people with spinal cord injury ... closeness to family, the level of family activities, and blaming oneself for the injury were the three most important variables ...

Dr. Wise Young

> Patient judged
> appropriate to begin
> trial modified diet
> given improvement in
> swallow function
> demonstrated during
> barium pharyngogram
> today.

FIFTEEN

Day 70: 4 pm Central Daylight Time

They've just announced that my flight out of O'Hare is delayed for one more hour. I'm sitting on the floor in the terminal with my back against the wall, arms wrapped around my knees. I'm thinking that it's stupid to expect Bruce to be able to take care of me now. I'm telling myself that what feels like indifference is preoccupation, and who can blame him for being preoccupied? I'm watching the crowds flow past, suddenly hyper-aware of wheelchairs.

Most of them hold elderly people clutching their carry-on bags in their laps while maroon-vested skycaps shove them through the terminal. One is a guy about my age, flying past in what I now recognize as an Ultra light. A spinal-cord guy, long past his injury trauma, by the look of him. I watch him with equal parts hope and despair as he vanishes smoothly into the crowd. A man who looks like Bruce lopes across the space in front of me and takes his place in line at Starbuck's. I watch him hungrily, eyes narrowed. Look at the casual way he stands, six and a half feet tall, as if it weren't a miracle of muscles and balance. Look at the big, easy health of him, his shoulders so effortlessly square. Look at his dark hair, curling around his collar. After awhile, I have to cover my face with both hands.

4:30 pm

I'm back in the air at last, flying north over Lake Michigan toward Iron Mountain, where a rental car will be waiting for me. On the ground, I'll have a two-hour drive to Escanaba, where my father was born, where I was born. If all goes well, I'll still be in time for the viewing. I get out my journal. I've agreed to deliver the pastoral prayers at the service tomorrow morning. I sit in my narrow seat, watching the silver water far below and searching inside myself for a voice in which to address God at the funeral.

6 pm

Almost there. I stop at what looks like a strip mall an hour away from my mom's house to buy something black to wear tomorrow. I have a dress, but it was in Heather's closet and I didn't want to wake her up this morning. The store doesn't have any dresses. It's a strange store, somewhere in the middle of Michigan's upper peninsula, with racks of clothes that all look alike in a dull, tasteless way. I have to try on the pants because I don't know what size I am now. It turns out the eights are too big, but I buy them anyway; I won't be this scrawny forever.

7:10 pm

It's him. It's my father in the casket. Oh, Daddy. I kneel down on the little bench in front of it and hold onto the polished rail they've thoughtfully placed here for people like me, people who might fall on their faces when this time comes, if there weren't something to hold on to. It's a good, sturdy rail..

Also, it's not him. He looks plumped up, at least the top half of him does. The bottom half of him is oddly flat beneath the covering they've arranged to his rib cage, as if his belly and legs and feet aren't even under there. His hands look just as they always have, with broad, short fingers and a certain thickness through his palms. Someone has artfully arranged a black rosary in his hands. My brothers, Mike and Charlie, are on either side of me, my sister Bette hovering just behind us. All of them are crying. They've been here all afternoon. I ask where Mom is; they say she just went home with Pat and Dan. Okay. Then that's where I have to go now, too. This place is closing in ten minutes anyway.

8 pm

My brothers and sisters, I'm very happy to see, are still the absurd, beloved characters I left behind thirty years ago. There are eight of us, and we're not much in the habit of staying in touch. We don't gather for reunions, don't remember one another's birthdays, don't exchange Christmas gifts. We are still us, though. We are still the people who endured those frozen winters with Monopoly marathons, who fought over whose turn it was to do the dishes, who looked after one another in ways our parents didn't, or couldn't. We were children together, and we know the deal.

Surrounded by my siblings, I settle immediately, like a dog circling its bed and sinking down into it. I know who to be here. I am Kate, eldest sister, smartest mouth, the one who took care of the house and babysat the littler kids—the one who got clean away. Someone is telling me there is pineapple upside-down cake in the kitchen, which causes a swell of laughter. It seems I am still famous for eating an entire cake, long ago ... they don't believe me when I claim not to remember this event, but I'm not lying. I don't remember it.

The queer thing about this gathering is that it doesn't feel queer at all. It feels familiar, and comforting. My mother sits in a corner of the couch, exhausted and wan. By turns, like all of us, she laughs and then cries and then laughs again. At one point, I make a call to Seattle. Bruce passed the swallow test this afternoon, while I was in the air over Illinois. He's ordered his dinner—all mushy foods, but food. He finally gets to taste food, and I won't even be there to see it. When I hang up, everyone is looking at me.

I tell them the news, but regret it immediately. It isn't that they don't care what's going on; they just can't understand it. They don't even know why eating is such good news. Most of them have only met Bruce one time in the fourteen years we've been married, and they probably wouldn't recognize him if he walked into the room right now. Only Mike, Charlie, and Bette have email, and they've been getting their news from David's Great Big List updates, which means their version of the story is relentlessly optimistic and very general. At this moment my brother Bob arrives, giving me a chance to change the subject. We exchange a hug and a rueful look. "Didn't expect to see you again so soon." And then he moves smoothly into his own familiar spot in our line-up: youngest brother, best-looking, the one no girl can get to settle down.

Day 71: 11 am

The distance from the funeral home to the church is one block. The boys have set the coffin into a white hearse. My sister Sue and I are on either side of my mom, holding her hands as we all follow the hearse to the front steps of the church. The boys lift it again and carry it up the stairs and into the vestibule, where they set it gently on a wheeled cart.

My mom is shaking; a breeze has come up, and it's cold. I get the Jesus-feeling briefly, the warm sense of a nearby presence that makes me pay attention.

The coffin is taupe-colored metal with raised-relief images of the Last Supper over each of the six brass handles. We're standing just outside the sanctuary, where three priests in white robes wait to meet us. My cousin Lynn's clear soprano voice floats down from the balcony above, singing a sad pop song I almost recognize. Good old Lynn. She's the daughter I wasn't, the girl my father wanted me to be. The priests shake vials of holy water over the casket, and then it is wheeled up the center aisle to stand at the foot of the altar. We follow and take our places in the front row, inhaling incense.

It's the worship service of my growing-up years, deeply rhythmic and soothing. When the time comes, I take my prayer and walk, straight-backed, to the lectern.

The next hours go by in a rush. We all file downstairs, where a post-funeral brunch is underway in the church basement. My mom points out a man she knows who has stigmata, wounds in his hands like those of Christ. She wants me to meet him so he can lay his hands on me and say a prayer for Bruce. Okay. He does have marks in his palms, and I try to be still and open to any possibility while he touches me and murmurs. Around us, people are dishing up orange Jell-O and potato salad and sliced ham.

We still have to take my father's body in its coffin out to the mausoleum. That will be the last thing. My flight home leaves around dinner time, so I can stay for this, though I don't want to. I'm restless, feeling in-between, knowing the mountain of tasks waiting for me in Seattle, which I'll get one day to finish before the home visit. I also don't want to see the little door close forever on my dad.

Because he was a veteran, there is an honor guard of old men in uniform standing by to pay their respects. Crying, my mom leans over and puts her lips to the top of the closed coffin, and there is an endless moment of stillness. Then the man with the keys to the crypt slides the coffin smoothly into its custom-fit darkness and closes the door behind it. My dad's little slot is one of dozens forming a giant array in this gleaming brass and marble place.

Back at my mom's house, I'm suddenly in no hurry. I take a long walk down to the lake with my sister, then take my time saying goodbye to my mother. One of my brothers' wives has been talking about what she thinks my mom should do now. If she sells this house, she could move in with us next winter, and then ...

My mom is saying that she's been praying for me and Bruce. She apologizes for not coming out to help us. I tell her I knew she couldn't, which is true. My dad was doing rehab himself last winter; she could no more have left him alone than I will be able to leave Bruce. Around us, the others are still discussing her future. I lean over and say, "Do what you want, Mom. Don't listen to them."

She surprises me by whispering back, firmly, "Oh, I do. I let them talk, and then I do exactly what I want."

This makes me laugh softly, and so I am able to leave her.

Driving twenty miles an hour over the speed limit the whole way, I make it to the tiny Iron Mountain airport exactly three minutes before my plane is scheduled to take off. My suitcase is not closed, I'm not sure where my ticket is, and I haven't refilled the car's gas tank. I walk up the moveable staircase at the very last second, still rummaging in my purse ... do I have my cell phone? Sitting on the plane, I close my eyes and acknowledge the truth: I don't want to go home. I came within inches of missing my flight yesterday because I didn't want to bury my dad, and now I've come equally close to missing this one because I know that the "home" I'm headed for is going to feel like foreign ground for a long, long time.

Day 72: 5 pm

In Bruce's family, Paul is the one whose job it usually is to keep people laughing. All this week, he's been filling this role with admirable consistency, even while working fourteen-hour days in a frantic race to be done with the house by tomorrow night. He is unfazed by Keith's frustration with the knotty plumbing problems, by Dave's impatience, or even by the occasional whining of Keith's kids, who are a little unhappy at being made to spend their spring break in this madhouse.

He is not bothered when Emily plays her groaning cello pieces, when Heather steals his stash of Girl Scout cookies, or when his projects keep getting interrupted for emergency planning sessions.

Keith calls him "Sparky" because his task is to re-wire our bedroom. They've decided that we need a ceiling-mounted fan—a lucky notion, as it's turned out—because when Sparky went up to breathe hot dust in our attic for a few hours so he could install it, he discovered that there were live, open wires up there. This led him to decide, cheerfully, to go over our whole electrical system. The possibility of a fire in our house, with Bruce trapped inside, does not bear consideration. Paul also takes it upon himself to make sure we have a functional fire-alarm system, and to add its installation to his long list of jobs.

Paul's favorite joke is Keith himself. Keith wants to get this done and get his family the hell out of here, and I don't blame him. The rest of us steer clear of Keith when he's storming around with a visible cloud over his head, but Paul behaves as if nothing could be more great than watching things go bad for the one-man plumbing crew. A few days ago, Keith went to the trouble of taping a sign on the girls' toilet: DO NOT FLUSH!! Not wise to the ways of boy cousins, Emily allowed herself to be talked into flushing … within minutes a soggy Keith came raging up the stairs into her bathroom, ready to haul the culprit out to the front yard and tie him to a tree.

When he discovered a bewildered Emily and his two triumphant sons instead, he didn't have a lot of disciplinary options. Paul has been laughing about that one ever since. His other favorite joke is the way he can piss Keith off by shutting off the juice to whatever part of the house Keith is currently attacking, so that, for example, his drill goes dead in his hands and he's forced to wait until Paul turns the power back on. "I just follow him around and see what he's got planned next," says Paul happily. "Then when he's just getting going … I go down and shut off that switch."

Right now Paul is in my laundry room/office, building a plywood enclosure for my new bathtub to sit in. The bathtub is in its final position, tucked in a corner behind the washer and dryer. It's deep, and I know it will save my sanity to have this goofy little refuge. Paul takes a marker from his pocket and writes a note in his blocky print on the inside surface of the board he is about to nail into place: "Hey, Bruiser! If you're reading this, it probably means your willie is working again. Way to go! Love, Sparky"

Day 74: 3 am

It is the eleventh hour of our home visit, and our alarm is going off. I've set it to wake me up gently to a Neville Brothers tune called "Yellow Moon," but I needn't have bothered. We've been awake off and on for hours, trying to find the magical arrangement of Bruce's limbs that will make him comfortable. I'm kneeling beside him, tucking a pillow between his bony thighs. He's on his left side, facing away from me. His right arm is in the "resting splint" that makes it seem like he's wielding a white club. He's breathing pretty well, and everything seems to be okay, except that his right leg keeps having spasms. It's as if he's getting a giant charley-horse from his hip to his ankle. Every muscle in the leg contracts so tightly and suddenly that I can feel the bed jerk from two feet away, and then, after about ten seconds, the leg relaxes. One minute, or two minutes, or five minutes later, it starts over.

He can't sleep while this is going on, and neither can I. The tantalizing possibility of finding a position that will make his leg stay relaxed has a death grip on my brain. I'm going to make him comfortable if it takes me all night. I try bending his knee a bit further and propping a pillow under his foot. We wait. One minute. Two. Maybe this is it. Clench. Damn thing. Okay, how about if I straighten it out a little more, and move the pillow to here. More waiting. Another spasm. On and on, all night long.

"Did this ever happen at the hospital?"

"No, not like this."

"No fucking fair." This is a mistake. Don't go there. Okay, try again. "Do you have any ideas?" I ask.

He lays the white club across his eyes. "I wish I did."

It's hell. The home visit night is purely hell. After all the anticipation, all the heroic efforts of so many people to make our house ready to receive him, all the long weeks of feeling sure that home would be so much better than the hospital, this first long night is more than a disappointment. It's a horror show.

Day 75: 4 pm

Dave and I are hauling everything out to the cars. He has the van, and I have the Prius. We need both—the Prius to carry Bruce, and the van to carry all the gear. It's hot outside, and we're sweating, making trip after trip. There is a lot of stuff. In spite of our demoralizing night on Saturday, Bruce and I are upbeat. Today was weird from the get-go, but we don't care. The first thing was, Chris noticed that his right ankle was swollen. She's too good a nurse to let a patient be discharged with even the remote possibility of a blood clot, so she called the doctor, who ordered an ultrasound.

Getting transport to and from the ultrasound clinic, having the test done, and waiting for the results turned out to be how he spent most of his final inpatient day at Harborview. By early afternoon, all was cleared. No blood clot, no nothing, but the discharge paperwork was slowed to a near halt while he waited for the diagnosis. Now we're hanging around while they get the last signature.

Bruce has decided to do one final workout in the gym. On Friday, he and Josh had their last PT session here, and Bruce finally got to stand up in the standing frame. He drove into position in front of it, and Josh set his feet in the footrests. Josh slid the harness under his butt, then attached its canvas straps to arms on the frame. When Josh turned on the hydraulic jack, the machine lifted Bruce in his sling to his feet. He was vertical for the first time since he fell. Josh went to get his Polaroid, and I snapped a picture of the two of them, standing side by side. Josh's head was level with Bruce's ribs. There. He stood up for all of ten minutes before he got out of here, but it still counts, and we have proof.

Now he's in his wheelchair in front of one of the weight machines, slowly and painfully working his triceps with a set of five-pound weights. I wander back to Room 464 to make sure one more time that we haven't left anything. It's odd to see it so bare. It looks just like everybody else's room. Hundreds of cards, long chains of bright paper cranes, books, magazines, dozens of family photographs, CD collection, potted plants, posters, balloons, and his special Mexican quilt are all gone. We have taken the ugly commode chair and its special inflatable cushion. We have taken both his night-time leg splints, and his monster collection of pills. We have taken dozens of bottles of liquid Tylenol, and a case of thickened apple juice.

He's leaving with clearance to get all his nutrition from eating, but he isn't supposed to drink clear liquids. The thickened apple juice is the consistency of honey; it comes in little juice boxes just like the ones I buy for the girls' lunches. I check the closet and his night table one last time, then sit on the bed to wait. Finally he arrives with a couple of nurses.

"Is it time?" I'm on my feet.

"Wellllll," says the red-haired nurse named Jean. "We need to get him into a different pair of pants. No big deal."

I make a face at him. Say it's not true!

He makes one back at me. It figures. Goddammit.

Jean and the other nurse already have him back on his bed. They're pulling the privacy curtain closed around him, efficient and calm. I know all about this drill. I've been told over and over how common it is for people with injuries above a certain level to have "accidents." He hasn't been much troubled by this, at least not yet.

"Hey Bruce," I call past the closed curtain.

"Yeah."

"I was just trying to decide how to think of this. It could be an omen of bad things to come, or it could be that your bowels needed to make a final statement to this place in the only language they know." Laughter from behind the curtain. "What do you think?"

Jean swings the drapes back. He's dressed again, this time in a pair of hospital pajama bottoms they're prepared to let us keep, which clash horribly with his shirt. She's finding a plastic bag for the soiled pants she just took off him. "I think," she says to me, "that you guys are going to do just fine." I take the bag. Easy for her to say.

He leaves Harborview Medical Center in the late afternoon, the same time of day he arrived here eleven weeks ago. On March 7th at 4 pm, he was in critical condition. His body was numb and still from his nipple line down, and there were four or five ways he could have died in the first twenty-four hours alone. He's leaving in a wheelchair, without much use of his right hand and without control of his bodily functions—but he is leaving. We'll take it. Dave pushes the chair to the waiting Prius, and I start the process of getting Bruce safely into it. Let's go home.

Spinal cord injury disconnects the brain from the
spinal cord below the injury site. If they have not been
damaged, spinal cord circuits below the injury site
become hyperexcitable and this manifests in spasticity
(increased reflexes) and spasms (spontaneous
organized movements).

Dr. Wise Young

SIXTEEN

Day 82: 11 am

Her name is Sarah; she's a big-boned thirty-something with long red hair, a tranquil, patient person who is easy to have in the house. When I leave in the morning for school, she's in our room with Bruce, and when I get back three hours later, she's usually still there. She's employed by a special division of the same temporary agency for which I once did secretarial work—Kelly. Her presence costs us $21.75 per hour, and even though he is barely awake for most of the time she's here, it's worth the money. Without Sarah, I wouldn't be able to leave the house. We're living the daily regimen we saw laid out on the whiteboard in Rounds about a month ago, only we've found out in the last eight days that there were some crucial points omitted.

Night spasms, for example, weren't even mentioned but they are without question the biggest of our burdens. Every night so far has been a repeat of the home visit debacle. The only difference is that now both his legs get spasms all night long. We haven't been able to sleep. So far, no life is possible—not even the limited, slow-motion one we had tried to prepare ourselves for.

Then there is the struggle with the bowel "program." His morning routine doesn't reliably produce "results." Instead his bowels move themselves in a more or less random fashion, often early in the evening, just when it might be possible to share dinner with the girls. Into the category of "better than expected" goes food. Bruce, it turns out, has scaled this hurdle without incident. He eats. He even drinks plain water, right from the tap, in open defiance of Fleur's strict orders to confine himself to thickened liquids.

I am in the kitchen with him now, watching wearily as his left knee bounces meaninglessly in the rapid-fire rhythm of clonus. I wait for him to press down on his thigh to make it stop, but he's staring out at the backyard as if nothing's happening. I walk over and take his left foot off its little shelf.

"You want to move?" I say to his leg. "Move."

Bruce sighs and starts working himself down the length of the kitchen. He can just barely do this, by using both hands to lift his leg and set his foot a few inches in front of himself, then pressing his foot into the floor so that the chair glides forward, then lifting it up and setting it down again, over and over. From the table to the refrigerator and then, since he can't turn around with this maneuver, backwards in the same way. I take my coffee and go out to sit on our front steps. It's a perfectly glorious day, fresh and breezy.

"Hey, Kate!"

What. Back in the kitchen, he's sitting up closer to the edge of his chair.

"Look at this." He lifts his right thigh with both hands and then his foot kicks forward and plops on the floor. He can kick his lower leg. His right quad is working. Both his quads are working.

"Hasn't anybody told you that you aren't going to get anything back after six weeks?" I make a show of taking down the calendar. "That date has passed, Buddy. See? April 18th, that was it. Six weeks."

He kicks his right leg again. "What was happening to me then?"

I have to think about it. "Uh, that was about the time you got your little pressure sore."

"Oh, that." Still kicking, now trying to move himself along using alternate feet. "Did I ever tell you about the butt conference?"

"Remind me."

He gives me a smile that will keep me going for days, a flash of his old self. He tells the story, even though he knows I remember, and finishes with another smile. Wow. A week's supply.

An hour later he's sitting in his wheelchair at the kitchen table, leaning over the newspaper, sound asleep and swaying. A long thread of drool goes from his lower lip to the sports section. The Mariners are still winning, but even that good news doesn't keep him awake. He can't get enough rest. I pull the chair away from the table and drive it through the widened kitchen door into the dining room. I jimmy it around until it's aimed straight at the lift, then shove hard to get him up the little ramp.

I climb in with him and hit the arrow that points up. The noise reminds me of the sound a garbage truck makes when its big claw is hauling something up to be dropped into its belly. We stop with a clunk, and I move the chair into the bedroom and arrange it next to the bed. My meticulous father-in-law has made sure that our bed is exactly the same height as the wheelchair, so I only have to move him across a level space. I set up the sliding board and get him over.

"Sorry," he says, and then he's snoring. I check the leg bag. Not full, okay. He can nap for an hour.

"Is Daddy asleep again?" Emily looks anxious, her blue eyes examining me closely.

"He's just napping. It's hard for him to sleep at night." She'd be more anxious if she knew he only lasted two hours up today.

"Spasms suck."

Tell me about it. "Emily, is that girl still bothering you?" Lately every time she gets a chance, Emily has been talking about a girl in her class who seems to have it in for her. Just what she needs.

She makes a face. "Patsy? She like, hates me. Oh, my God. On Friday, we had bowling, we went to that bowling alley by the Safeway? And—okay, she is a really good bowler. Which, I am not."

I pick up her backpack and set it where it won't be in the way of the wheelchair. "You have other talents."

"No, I don't care, but—they have this thing with, like these red pins, and if you knock one down, you get a free liter of Pepsi. And she got three of them!"

"That's a lot of Pepsi."

She nods. "Three liters. It's a lot of Pepsi. So she's, like, sharing it with everybody? Except me."

"You're kidding."

"No, she was! She hates me. Oh, and—she's the best bowler, right, so when we're there she's just, like, the boss of everything. She makes the lists, and she decides who goes when, and of course I'm always last. She'd make me go to another lane if she could. She'd make me go home."

I'm getting pissed off. "Isn't there a teacher there?"

"He always sits up by the tables, working on his papers. He doesn't even know what's going on."

"You shouldn't have to put up with that." Emily doesn't know how much this troubles me. She doesn't know how worried I am about her and Heather, how afraid I am that I'm failing them. She doesn't know that I'm just itching for a problem I can actually solve, and she sure doesn't know how ready I am to attach my monster rage to someone besides Bruce. I encourage her to keep talking, and she does. There is a lot more.

Patsy, it turns out, has been routinely mistreating my daughter in the openly cruel way of certain thirteen-year-old girls. Emily is an easy target, ironically, because of me. The other teachers can't favor her; she can't get special treatment just because her mother works for the school. Instead, I become convinced, the opposite is happening. She's being left to fend for herself because she's my daughter. It's not fair. Death words.

5 pm

This time when I check, Bruce's eyes are open. "You're awake."

He clears his throat. Gag. Why does he still produce all that thick crud? He isn't sick. He doesn't have a cold, but his lungs are a phlegm factory. "What time is it?" Still in the neck-brace, he can't turn his head to see the alarm clock on his night table.

"Time to get up." I unlock the chair's brakes, shove it out of the way, and stand next to him. "Bruce, I need you to do something." I slide one arm behind him. "Ready?" He nods, face serious, and we slowly get him upright. He still can't do this alone, but he's closer. My job is to give him only what help is necessary until the day comes when that is no help at all. I don't do anything for him that he can do, no matter how long his efforts take or how awkward they are—which is why I stand still now and watch him pick up his legs and heave them, one at a time, over the edge of the bed. He sways but doesn't lose his balance. Good.

He sits for a minute, arms at his sides, making sure he isn't dizzy. His back is curved into a shallow "C," his head thrust forward. His left knee rattles away until he sets a hand on his thigh, and then it is still. "Okay. Think it's okay." I get a plastic jug from the bathroom and undo the fastener on the leg bag, kneeling at his feet. While it empties, I ask if he can make the phone calls about Heather's birthday party.

"Guess we gotta do that."

"Well, if it's going to be Saturday ... we should've sent invitations two weeks ago." Two weeks ago I was on my way to Michigan, and he was hoping to pass a swallow test.

"Right." He clears his throat again, then gestures at the chair. "Think I'm ready."

I roll the chair into position and hand him the board, which he's just beginning to manage. He can lean over a little, and set one end under his bottom, and lay it across the gap to his chair. He can lock his elbows, plant his hands, and help lift as I guide him over.

"Good job." It was good. My legs know exactly how much effort I supply; this time, it wasn't much.

"Slowly getting better," he sighs. "Does she have a list?"

"Oh, yeah." This is Heather we're talking about. She's known who she wanted to invite for months. "With, like, twenty names on it." Calling all these parents is something I could have done myself. I didn't because it's also one of the very few things he can actually do—and therefore he has to. The less I do for him, the more likely it is we'll get through this part without hating each other.

"Okay. I'll do it after dinner."

And he does. He sits at the phone for an hour and a half, painfully keeping himself upright, looking up every number. He works from her list, crossing off the names one by one, making illegible notes in his awkward left-hand scrawl. He describes the plans for the party over and over. They're going to see Shrek, and from there down to the Old Country Buffet in the mall for dinner and ice cream. Where to drop them off, when to pick them up, thanks so much, and yes, I'm glad to be home. He keeps an eye on the clock, does his pressure releases every fifteen minutes, and tracks the baseball game playing silently on the television in front of him. The 2001 Mariners are still winning.

Heather is a constant worry. She goes quietly about her business: soccer practice, school, Girl Scouts, homework, children's choir. When she's in the same room with her dad, which is rare, she tends to look anywhere but at him. Their old life together was all about doing. They were the ones who wanted to run the dog, who wanted to kick the soccer ball, who liked to challenge each other. It's all gone. He can't even come up to her room to kiss her goodnight. He can't read her a story, or play his guitar, or tickle her. When she leans over his chair to give him what passes for a hug, his good hand pats her back awkwardly, and her face says she hates it.

There is more. She knows that I worry about her, and so she tries to help me by pretending to be content. If she needs me, she isn't saying so; maybe she thinks I have nothing left for her, and she can't risk finding out. Maybe she's right. She doesn't see that for him to sit here and make all these phone calls is evidence that he's not going to let her down. She can't even be sure which part of this horror is temporary—none of us can. She looks at me bitterly after he's finished the phone calls. I've put him into our bed, and I'm down in the kitchen, cleaning up and sweeping in the way I always have. I'm feeling glad about the party. Every single kid said yes.

This is when she says, voice cold: "You got used to this pretty fast."

I'm not too exhausted to be stung. "I'll never get used to it," I tell her, furious. "Never. What do you want me to do? Ignore him, like you always do?"

Now she's hurt. "I don't know what to do." She kicks at the black risers that make our table too tall for us but the right height for his wheelchair. "He's so different."

I don't know what to say to her. The truth is that she's desperate to be convinced her dad is on his way back. What she can't know is that part of what's going to bring him back is her. He desperately wants to get back for her. All she needs to do is find ways to let him know she's waiting. I'm thinking through this while we stand the way she likes to, with her back snug against my chest and my arms wrapped tight around her. I want to tell her that he needs her, but I'm afraid of saying something that will make her feel more burdened.

"I just keep telling myself that he's still in there," I say. "And that if I act as if that's true, eventually it will be true."

"Eventually."

"Yeah." I'm so not up to this. She's so withdrawn, and I'm suddenly not even sure I'm guessing right about what's in her head. "Heather, you know, there might come a time when you want to talk to somebody besides me about this."

"Like who?"

"Like—somebody whose job it is to help kids figure out stuff this hard. A therapist." She's quiet, but I can tell she's interested. "It could help." We talk about this quietly for a few minutes, still standing so that we can't see one another's faces, and then I send her to bed. Alone in the kitchen, I finish sweeping the floor, absorbing the news that my buoyant, confident daughter is in trouble, and I don't know how to help her.

Day 83: 11:40 am

Bruce is still in bed. It's Tuesday, and he's been saying all week that he wants to try to get to his lunch meeting today if he can. The meeting starts in twenty minutes, and he hasn't been up yet. Thanks to Sarah, he is dressed.

"Do you still want to try to make it to your meeting?"

"What time is it?"

"You have twenty minutes."

"Better get up, then."

The Tuesday lunch meeting has been part of his routine for seventeen years. It's at a Mexican restaurant in downtown Bellevue, about a ten-minute drive from our house. I help Bruce get into the chair, then wait while he rides the lift down. Because he isn't strong enough yet to control the chair on any kind of a slope, I have to stand in front of him and grab the handles while he rolls off. If I weren't here, the chair would slam right into the dining room wall. I push him into the garage, where I again act as brakes against the gravity of the ramp, this time from behind the chair. I wheel him to the car, go through the business of getting him in, and then take the wheelchair apart. First, remove the special gel-cushion seat. Next, fold the back down flat where the seat was. Next, unlock the brakes and remove both the wheels. Next, put all the pieces into the back seat.

We drive to Azteca. Do I know the best way? Probably not. He gives me directions, blinking and pale in the bright daylight. Once there, I pull into a turn-around area right in front of the doors and get out to put the chair back together. I stage it and help him out, then push him up to the wide wooden doors of the restaurant. I pull on the door, and a maitre d' comes to hold it open for us. Inside, there is red carpeting—bad, I think, hard for him to roll himself over. Bruce is telling the maitre d' that he's with the group, and he knows the way to their meeting room. I start to push him forward.

"I got it," he says.

I stand there while he rolls himself off without so much as a see you later, thanks for the ride. He's late and anxious to get in. He's determined not to look helpless. He's out of bed and out of the house. All these things are good, but I'm still standing here, dismissed without a backward glance.

I go to the car and drive it to a parking place at the very back of the lot. Crying, I'm sick of crying, but it's all I seem to be able to do. I'm thinking about last night. For the hours between 2:30 and 4 am, I was down on leg duty with the feather bed. He kept dozing off while I tried to get him to help me figure out what to do. Whenever I'd realize he was asleep, I'd start to crawl back to my pillow, and then he'd wake up again and ask me to just move his leg a bit more over there. I'd move it, then wait ... then realize he was out. Again and again. At 4 o'clock, I gave up and left the room in a white-hot rage, done resting for the night. He was asleep, and still asleep when Sarah came at 8:30. Not fair. The death words, again.

When it's time for the meeting to end, I drive back to the turn-around and help him into the car. People are standing around watching and telling him how glad they are to see him out. They say cheerily that they'll see him next week, and then walk off into the sunshine. I put him into the Prius, take the chair apart, pack it into the back seat, and drive us home. I don't speak to him at all, not on the ride home, not that afternoon, not that evening.

I do all the night time things in silence. I help him get his clothes off, clean the skin around the stomach tube, and move his legs through their range of motion exercises. I unhook the leg bag, empty it, and replace it with a night bag. I give him the heparin shot. I measure the doses for the 3 am medications and set them up on his night table, so I'll be able to find them easily when the alarm goes off. I set the alarm, raise my eyebrows to signal that now is his chance to say so if he needs anything else. He doesn't. I close the door behind me. We both know I'll get over it.

Day 84

I'm walking fast, following the girl, Patsy, who knows that I'm after her. She's trying to get away, but I don't let her. I corner her inside the gym and say coldly that I want to talk with her. I lead her outside, and then I get in her face.

"I want you to stay away from Emily."

She makes protesting, innocent noises. She hasn't done anything to Emily. She doesn't know what I'm talking about. She's a thirteen-year-old girl the size of a grown woman, and I know she's had a very rough start to life. I don't care. I've been waiting for someone else to confront her, but no one is ever going to. She's trying to keep her defiant you-got-nothing-on-me face in place, but I can see that she's afraid. I must look really crazy. Good.

"You can lie to your mom," I say. "And you can lie to Edith, and to all the other kids, and anybody else you want, but don't lie to me." I move even closer, inches from her face. "Do you get me? I know you've been messing with Emily all year long. I want you to stay away from her."

"Okay." She's against the wall, looking even more scared, which makes me feel so good.

"If you so much as look at her, I'll hear about it. You get me?"

"Yes!" It's satisfying to see her tears.

"Good. Because I mean it. Stay away from her. Don't talk to her, don't talk about her, don't even think about her." And then I march back up into the school. When Patsy comes in a few minutes later, crying and asking to use the phone so she can call her mother, I'm standing in the hall telling another teacher what I've just done. The other teacher, looking troubled, tells Patsy to go ahead and use the phone.

"Right," I say brutally as the door closes after her. "Call your mother, and if she wants to talk with me, tell her to make an appointment. I'm really busy these days, but I'd make a special effort for her." I am completely out of control. I go to find Emily and tell her that Patsy probably won't be giving her any more grief. I drive off, ranting to the empty car.

Day 85

The implications of twenty kids coming to Heather's birthday party don't dawn on me for two days. When they do, I nearly panic. Just for starters, I'm the only one who can get Bruce in and out of the car, a process that takes at least five minutes. Eleven-year-olds can get into a lot of mischief in five minutes. Then there is the problem of navigating the wheelchair in the world, something I've only done once or twice until now. If something goes wrong, if he needs to go home, what am I going to do with all those kids? Twenty kids will show up, one or two at a time, outside the theatre. Someone has to be there to give them their tickets and tell them what to do. When the movie's over, they all have to go a half a mile down the road to the mall where the restaurant is. What if it's raining? They could walk, but do I want to turn twenty fifth-graders loose unsupervised along a six-lane road? No. Okay, so they'll need a ride, or at least a couple of chaperones. I get out the Plymouth phone book.

The first person I call is my friend Sue. She's the person who cleaned my refrigerator, the person who came to the hospital to bring me home when I was afraid to drive myself. The day after tomorrow? Sure, she can do that. Would it be good if her two teenagers came along to help? Yes, they're both free. No problem. This will be fun. We love birthday parties. I hang up and call our friend David. Of course, he'd be glad to. No problem.

Day 86: 4 am

We are insane. We are in our room, locked in a death struggle with spasms. I've pulled the queen-sized feather bed from beneath us, and I'm trying to wrestle it into a shape that will support his legs. Three nights ago I used a collection of pillows to prop whatever leg was spasming high in the air, and it was mercifully still for four straight hours. The tantalizing possibility of a repeat performance is driving me on and on. In my madness, I come to believe that the featherbed is purposely resisting. I punch it hopelessly, lift his knees, and stuff the space beneath them with great handfuls of the white monster. After a moment, the legs seize up like drawn fists.

"It worked once," I wail softly. "It worked before."

"Just let it be." His voice, from way up at the top of the bed, is resigned. "I'll just see if I can sleep through it."

"I can't sleep through it." This is true. I wake to the jerking of those legs just as easily as I once woke to nurse the girls. There is no sleeping through it. I think about going out to the couch, leaving him alone. No. "One more try." I set his leg over to one side, accidentally hooking the hose to the night bag with his knee, which causes the catheter deep inside him to pull. He grabs for it. "Sorry. Christ." I just sit there, dull and beaten. After a few minutes we notice that his legs are still. This is it. The position that will work tonight, this is it. I creep back to my pillow; he is already snoring.

Day 87: 6 pm

Inside the Old Country Buffet, the table is littered with birthday cards and confetti. Heather's friends are out of their seats, gathered around her chair to watch her open her presents. She's smiling and relaxed in a way I haven't seen her in months. Whatever else has fallen apart, she's managed to hold on to her gift for having a good time, and I am getting high from the sight of her happiness. Bruce is beside me in the wheelchair, game and here, trying.

David had to go with him to the buffet tables and ladle out the food he chose. Bruce couldn't cut his own chicken, or fix his own baked potato. He ate, though, and he's here, watching his girl turn eleven. What's more, he's at a party he helped to organize for her. Like so many moments, this one is—simultaneously—empty and overflowing.

Later, while our friends stand out in front of the mall to see that all the young guests get safely back to their parents, I load Bruce into the Prius. Just as he moves from the edge of the board to the car, his recalcitrant bowels make their move. There is not a thing we can do. When it seems to be over, he apologizes grimly, but I shake my head.

"Either it will become routine, or it will go away."

"Easy for you to say."

"You think?"

He is quiet. We're suddenly in the center of our dilemma. He's in this by accident, by necessity. I'm in it by choice. "No," he says finally. "Maybe not."

A person with spinal cord injury can exercise muscles above the injury site. Because [people with cervical injuries] do not have enough functioning muscles to engage in activities that can stimulate the cardiovascular and pulmonary system, they often spend 95% of their waking hours recumbent or sitting.

Dr. Wise Young

SEVENTEEN

Day 90: 11 am

Emily and I are driving away from school. I took her out of her afternoon classes last week, the day after I laid into Patsy. The other teachers have all come to me and said that they really, really hadn't been aware of what was happening, and that they certainly would have stepped in if they'd seen it. I think they don't believe me. It's okay. I'm not mad at anybody. But I don't trust Patsy, and I'm not letting Emily be on the grounds when I'm not here. So, every morning I teach, and Emily goes to her first couple of periods, and then we drive off together.

The school year is about to end anyway. Her grades are good; Patsy isn't coming back next year, and by then I might have more of a grip. The real reason I'm doing this is that I know I'm off my rocker. I can't be sure of anything. I don't trust my own judgment, so I'm trying not to take any chances. Besides, it's fun to leave with Emily. We sail down the street, calling triumphantly "See ya!" and stop at the latte stand. I buy her a raspberry and cream Italian soda, and then we go home.

Emily has turned out to be amazingly good at being with her dad. She lets me show her how to do the range of motion, and she's not grossed out to watch me take care of the business of the leg bags. She likes to be in our room while the unflappable Sarah is finishing her work for the day. She likes to fetch things for him. Now, she lies next to him, on my side of the bed, and tells him about her morning. Math. English.

There has been precious little to ask him about, but recently he had his first outpatient physical therapy session at Harborview, so they are having an actual conversation.

"Did you see Josh yesterday?

"No, he only works with people who are still in the hospital." He pulls thoughtfully at the skin under his nose in a gesture that is entirely his. "Poor souls."

"I'm glad you're here now," she says, lying on her side and gazing at him. "Were you in the gym?"

"They have a different one for outpatients. It's smaller, in the older part of the hospital."

She remembers. "By where RICU is?"

"That's right. It's on the fourth floor." He takes her hand to stop her from stroking him. Light touch makes his skin crawl, but all of us forget that. She lets him play with her fingers.

"Your hands are so soft, Daddy."

He doesn't like hearing this. "I know."

"What did you do in PT?"

"Same as usual. Tried to sit up. They measured all my muscles again." I have been putting laundry away during this conversation, but I stop at this news. He looks at me. "I'm stronger. I haven't done anything since I left the hospital, but almost every muscle group is stronger."

"Return, then." I mean that getting stronger without working out must be due to neurological "return"—better signals getting through the injured part of his cord.

"Yeah." He explains it to Emily. I ask him if he's been able to get any more appointments. "One this week," he says. "One the following week."

"So much for three times a week." Goddamn Harborview. First, they carefully train us to understand how crucial it is that he get back up there for regular PT sessions, and then, once he's out, he can't get into their damn schedule. If he goes once more this week and once next, that will make a grand total of three sessions in his entire first month at home. Six hours in thirty days. Why didn't they get all this arranged while he was sitting around up there? I close my dresser drawer a little too hard.

"They can't help it, Kate." Emily looks nervous. She's always had good radar, but lately she's fine-tuned herself to our most subtle signals. Usually, we aren't the kind of parents who fight in front of their kids. He softens his tone. "They're having staffing problems. There's nobody to schedule me with."

"Did you ask them about July?"

"It's even worse in July." Emily looks at me, gets out of our bed and goes downstairs. "A couple of their people are on vacation then."

"How nice for them."

Day 92

I have an email from Kris, my friend and supervisor at Plymouth. She writes that she's been thinking of me, and hopes I am finding ways to take care of myself. She prays for me. She also says that she has to think about next year ... do I have a sense of what I want to do about the Youth Forum?

Ah. Poor Kris, having to be the one to ask me this. My work at the church is, officially, two thirds of a part-time job. I'm charged with leading the teen-aged members of the congregation into something resembling an authentic spiritual life, hopefully centered around the teachings and practices of our particular faith. The way I do this is, I befriend them. Whenever a moment accidentally occurs in which they seem willing to hear me, I let them in on what I know about life and faith.

I also organize them to serve meals at local shelters, to lead worship in various ways, and to travel once a year in the hope of exposing them to the troubles other people face. Given the demographics of our church, these kids tend to lead sheltered lives. It's a great little job, and I have loved doing it. Three of these teenagers braved the grotesqueries of Harborview to sit with Bruce, so maybe something has gotten through. My crew of adult volunteers has been filling in with them since the accident; it's time now to figure out if I can come back.

I read the message again. There's a tone here that troubles me, a hesitancy that says Kris is not quite sure how to ask the question without causing me pain. She uses the phrase, "this chapter of your life." It's not the language of friends, not the way we talk to each other. I try to read between the lines. Is she hoping I'll bow out right now so she can get on with replacing me?

I go to talk with Bruce, who is parked at our kitchen table while he spoons oatmeal carefully up with his left hand. He's getting better at this, spilling less on his clothes and looking a lot less awkward. His right hand is going nowhere; the fingers are starting to curl themselves permanently toward his palm. I tell him about the email.

"So what's your thinking?" He's giving me a careful look.

"Depends on how it goes here." We both know that unless he gets a lot better by the fall, I can't add the church thing back into my schedule. I'm barely keeping my head above water now. "What do you think?"

He stares into the distance, then says, "Well, I have to be able to sit up."

It's so pathetic that I put my head on the table and laugh. "Right. That's key."

I go back to the computer and type in a reply. I'll be at the staff meeting in a couple of days. We can talk about it then.

Day 95: 10 am

I am in the sanctuary, sitting near the back where I hope no one will bother me. During this hour, the choir has one last practice for the 11 o'clock service, the church school is in session, and there is an educational adult forum upstairs in the reception hall. I only want to be somewhere undisturbed, but this is a busy place. Just now, to get here, I walked through several chatting groups of old friends, all of whom greeted me as if they knew me.

They don't. How could they? I know perfectly well that the problem is not in them, that they are trying to be kind, trying to help me. I feel like a stranger though, like a newcomer. I feel like an unknown person masquerading as me. Don't they see? The real Kate was married to Bruce, who was tall and had long, thick curling brown hair and a kind, quiet way about him. He was smart and funny and full of crazy plans. Now, he isn't like that at all, and I am transformed into this other Kate, who is—what?

Who is struggling not to be a tragic figure, and yet in this space, in my church, what happens is that I break open in all the fragile places. No. It's more like I dissolve. It's like whatever it is I have wrapped myself in dissolves here, so that all my sadnesses are hanging out in full view. And these people want to come up and touch them and inspect them, and there is no healing. Still, I have to come. The service has started, and I am surrounded by voices reciting in unison these words, printed in the order of worship: "There is a power in the universe forever on the side of those brave enough to trust it." I have to come. Where else could I go to find my way back home?

Day 97: 6 pm

Heather's team is about to play for the city-wide recreation league championship. I'm trying to navigate the wheelchair over the steep patch of grass and dirt between the parking lot and the smooth jogging track that surrounds the soccer field. The game has already started, and the Ladybugs are looking good. Along with most of her best friends, Heather has played for this little team since second grade. This is the last game of their last year together, and they want to win.

Now Bruce is alone in his wheelchair at the midfield line with his hands under a blanket, and I'm trying not to be afraid that a loose ball will hit him. He helped coach this team one year. He used to like to come help out at practices. He used to volunteer to be a lineman at the games. We know every single set of parents here; many of them have been making meals for us since he got hurt. No one knows what to say to him. I watch them move off gradually after a quick greeting. He just keeps his eyes on the game.

The girls are playing their heads off. The other team is good, probably better, but the Ladybugs do not give. Heather's friend Marie, in as the sweeper, makes a couple of brilliant moves that probably save the game. They're ahead by a goal, trying to hold on for the last ten minutes, but it could still go either way.

All the parents are checking watches, including me. Oh, let them win. Let something really good happen to her. Come on. Then the whistle blows and she runs away from her screaming friends, off the field and straight into my arms, soggy with sweat, laughing and crying. She bounds over to the wheelchair, where he is cheering out loud with everybody else, and I see them connect for one moment before she dashes back out to celebrate with her team. Thank you.

Day 98

Kris and I are in the hall outside my office. I know I look terrible. Bruce and I are still stuck in the stupid leg spasm problem, and I am more sleep-deprived than I've ever been. Emily nursed every two hours around the clock for the first three months of her life, and I was in better shape then. Kris is trying to be soothing, but I'm just weepy. Underneath that is irritation that she won't say what has to be said. She's going to have to replace me if things don't change soon.

She's questioning me in a very gentle way, asking for the details about why "this current chapter of my life" is so hard. I can't bear the tone of her voice—I have a sudden flash of Bruce twitching when someone strokes his skin. Stop it! I say that I don't know what's going to happen in two months. It has to be something because I can't keep going the way I am. She says, ever so gently, that she thinks I ought to let the YF go, and I muster the self control to say I'll let her know in a couple of days.

Everyone but us is upstairs at an end-of-year potluck lunch. She says she'll see me up there and leaves. I go into the staff bathroom, lock the door behind me, and cry. I can't even do my stupid little two-thirds-of-a-part-time job hanging out with kids I love. I'm losing every last thing that ever gave me a moment's pleasure. The death words are taking me over. No fair. I think of Bruce, sitting in that goddamn chair with his useless right hand, saying, "Well, I have to be able to sit up." Who am I to feel sorry for myself? Who am I to talk about what's fair?

It takes me a long, long time to get out of that bathroom.

Day 100: 7 am

I'm trying to wake up so I can get Heather off for her last day of fifth grade. Our nightly spasm wars are slowly but surely eroding my soul; try as I might to find rest and still get everything done, I can't. I can't make his legs be quiet. I can't sort the mail in time to pay the bills. I can't keep the house in order. I can't tell if I'm doing right by the girls. I can't make him well. I was brought up to believe in competence as the measure of worth. I was taught that I had to earn my place at the table by being good at everything. I am surely not any good at this. I suck at this. I'm tired, and I have to get up.

He turns his head a tiny bit toward me. "Hey." His left hand reaches across his body. "Give me your hand."

"What?"

"Gotta show you something." He looks positively mischievous. Could it be? He moves my hand under the quilt. Oh, dear God.

"Where'd you get that nice thing?"

"It was just there," he whispers. He has tears in his eyes, which is how I know that he's been afraid this moment would never come. I have tears in mine, too. I'm watching the prospect of a marriage without intercourse recede into the distance—some other unlucky people's fate, not ours.

241

Day 102

I'm beside Bruce in our bed, drinking my coffee and watching him try once more to sit up. From lying flat on his back, he can get halfway by pushing his elbows hard into the bed and using his shoulder muscles. Then he's propped up on his elbows, trying to push his forearms into the mattress so that his torso will rise. The bed is too soft. He grits his teeth and growls with the effort, but he still can't do it.

He flops back down. After a minute, he says, "If there was something right here to grab hold of, I think I could do it." He's patting the mattress near where his left hand lies.

I get up and look around the room. The chair. I roll it over and back it up snug next to our bed. I lock the wheels and stand there watching. This time he does it. He gets to his elbows, then uses the wheel of his chair for the hard surface he's been needing to push himself upright at last. He lies down immediately and does it again. "Voila," I say. "Man falls down. Man sits up. Happy Father's Day."

Day 103

Nights. They all start the same, with the sliding board transfer into bed, the undressing, the meds, still delivered through the stomach tube, the range of motion, the switching of leg bag for night bag, the fastening of the night-time boots. I often do these things in ten-minute segments, interspersed with quick trips out to be with the girls while they have a snack or watch television.

I try to arrange it so that when Bruce is comfortably settled and covered up, they're on their way to their rooms. They stop in for a visit then, climbing into my spot and sharing a little news. He seems more familiar lying down; sometimes even a little like his old self. After they say goodnight to him, I follow them upstairs and tuck them in their beds. Tonight, Heather doesn't want to be left alone.

"Stay!"

"You know I can't."

"I want you to." She grabs my arm and holds on, and then I do stay because this is not like her. She doesn't want to talk, or listen, or anything. She just doesn't want to be alone. Emily comes in to see what's taking so long.

"Heather doesn't want me to leave," I say. She's still holding firmly to my arm.

"I'll stay with her." Dear Emily. I expect Heather to say no, that's not what she wants, but she surprises me by agreeing. Emily goes off to get her pillow and a blanket, and when I leave them a few minutes later, she is lying on the floor beside Heather's bed, both of them reading.

I go downstairs, load the dishwasher, sweep the floor, and put Rocky outside. I find the cats and herd them to the family room for the night. I lock the house, climb past the lift, and cover the birdcages. Back in our room, I get the 3 am meds ready, and then finally crawl in beside him. One of the things he can't quite manage to do yet is read. In the old days, his night table was piled with reading material, and the floor next to where he sleeps was a mess. Now there's nothing on his night table except medicine, and his floor is clean.

So, I read. I'm reading Moby Dick out loud, three or four pages every night. It's a pure pleasure. Both of us have read this book before, but neither of us knew that it was meant to be heard. Melville's sentences are complicated, and his descriptive powers just knock us out. Plus, the book is funny. Ishmael is an astute, ironical presence in our room each night; I only wish I had enough juice in me to keep him with us longer than four pages. Tonight I read the part where Queequeg appears in Ishmael's bed, and we're both laughing.

When it's time to turn out the lights, we get nervous, but for a change his legs are still. When the alarm goes off four hours later, we've both been asleep for all that time. I turn on the little light I keep on the floor, go around to his side, and use the fat syringe to push meds into his stomach. As long as the tube is still there, it's easier than having him sit up to swallow. I take the long pillow out from behind him, so that he rolls onto his back.

He starts talking to me in his sleepy, sweet way about Queequeg, about the girls, about us. I crawl over and lie down on top of him, careful not to hurt him. The feel of his skin is balm to my own; helpless, I fall into my love for him, down and down until I am submerged. I hold his face in my two hands and whisper, "Come back to me."

"I'm trying. I'm trying so hard."

"I know." I tell him that no matter what, I choose him. He is still more man than any other three, put together.

"Thank you for saying that."

"It's true."

"Happy birthday."

"That's right ... Forty-nine. Seems like a good age so far." I put my head down on his chest, and after awhile I go back to my pillow and fall asleep again.

Day 104

We're back at Harborview for his first visit to Cathy, the nurse who'll be managing most of his outpatient care. She's sent us into a big examining room, where we're both falling asleep on the mat that covers an enormous low table. Last night was bad again; I'm not even trying to stay awake.

"You guys really do look tired."

She's here. This is the first time I've met her. I struggle to sit up, pushing my hair off my face. "We are." My mouth is dry. "We are tired."

"Hi, Bruce. Tell me about the spasms."

He's barely awake, so he lets me talk. I've been on the phone with Cathy so much that I already know exactly what her questions will be. Yes, we've been doing the range of motion exercises religiously. Sometimes muscles that don't get stretched will be more prone to spasticity. Yes, he's finished his latest course of antibiotics; no I haven't taken a urine sample in to be checked for bugs since last week. Sometimes spasticity is the body's way of saying it has an infection. Yes, I check all his skin every day, and no, he doesn't have any suspicious spots. Sometimes spasticity is a sign of pressure sores that have gone undetected.

"In other words, he's in perfect health," I say, aiming for lightness. "Maybe his spasticity is just a sign that he's really, really tired."

She smiles. She has a good smile, a good face. She's probably about my age, with curly dark hair and a certain alertness that I like. I want to be alert, like her. "We're going to solve this, don't worry. There are still a few drug combinations that you guys haven't tried."

As I push him back to the car, I look around at Harborview, a little surprised at how ugly it is. I realize that while I still had to come here twice a day, I couldn't let myself know how deeply I hated the sight of these halls. I know it now. It's noisy. It smells bad. The employees all look bored and the visitors all look freaked out. It's hell, and I'm going home.

Day 106

The first good thing about having my own therapist is that I get to go and see him all by myself. I'm not being anybody's driver or delivery person, not running anybody else's errand. I'm out of the house, and I'm alone with the radio for the whole half an hour that it takes to get to my new therapist's office. The second good thing is that his office is in Fremont, an interesting part of Seattle, just down the hill from the troll under the Aurora Bridge. All this, before I even get in the building.

His office itself is the third good thing. I'm sitting in a navy blue armchair next to a wide, low window, waiting for him to come back with a pitcher of water so we can begin. Whenever I want, I can look out to see the city and, since the day is clear, Mount Rainier. I can see the boat traffic gliding along Lake Union, and the tiny, colorful lines of cars on the freeways. The room is peaceful, but its message is not rest. Instead it seems to say, engage. Take up the work of your life. This thought comes to me, and I look around more carefully to see what it is that creates this feeling. Maybe it's the color: the walls are painted a warm shade of orange. Maybe it's the size: the room is small in a way that feels cozy instead of cramped. I notice that he hasn't set out boxes of Kleenex, which is something I hate—the evidence that they expect you to cry.

I don't cry. On this first day, I tell Michael about the accident. I tell him about the hospital, and about the time at home so far. I try to make him see who the four of us used to be, and who we are now. I describe every bit of it as clearly as I can, so that he'll know what he's in for. When I get to the part about going to Michigan, I almost cry, but then I look out at the view for a moment, and I can keep going. Michael sits in another chair, with a little Kleenex-less table between us. I have my shoes off and my feet curled under me, and so does he.

Michael himself is the fourth good thing. He is as tall as Bruce. He has the look of an attractive professor, the humorous kind, with a lively mind and a certain eagerness. He also, I can't help noticing, is wearing extremely expensive clothes that fit him perfectly. This makes me like him; he has a flaw. He's vain, and his taste is excellent. This morning, he is mostly a captivated listener. His posture, his stillness, his intelligent face all say: tell me. I do. The patient, interested quality of his listening makes it possible. When I'm finished and the hour is nearly gone, he almost blows it. It is, of course, a wrenching story, and the look on his face says that hearing it has made him sad. He's there in his chair, stunned with sadness, giving me a look that says, "Wow." This look is what will, finally, make me cry. No. I put up a hand.

"Don't do that." My voice has an edge. He composes himself instantly, and we are both quiet.

"Your story is very moving," he says in self defense after a few minutes go by. I make a dismissive gesture, but I don't answer him. I'm not interested in whether I've moved him, and I don't want him to be just another person who feels sorry for me. He asks me what it is I expect him to help me with.

This is the right question. I know exactly what I want from him. "I'm going to get through this," I say. "We all are. Bruce is going to get a lot better than he is, and the girls are going to make it. Somehow. But I don't want to just slog along—I don't want it to get me. I want to stay whole somehow, even while it's happening."

"What makes you think you're not staying whole?"

Another good question. Okay, well-dressed Michael, I'll tell you. "There's a girl at my daughter Emily's school, where I teach," I say. "She's got—a lot of problems. She was harassing Emily, like, saying mean things to her when no one else was around. Telling the other kids lies about her. Middle-school-girl stuff."

He nods. I'm talking very slowly. "I got fed up with it. Emily's vulnerable, and nobody was doing anything to stop this girl ... I got in her face and laid down the law."

"Sounds like she might have needed that."

"No, I know. I'm sure she did need it. But this is about me. I was really hard on her, and I liked it. I made her cry, and I enjoyed doing it. A lot." I can hardly breathe. I look out the window and wait. I'm shocked at how much it hurts to acknowledge this, but I have to. "That isn't who I am. I don't make kids cry. I teach them how to pray." I shift in my chair, setting my stocking feet on his carpet. "I want you to help me hold on to myself—not let me feel sorry for myself, not let me forget who I am." I give him a tiny little smile. "It would be good if I could keep my sense of humor, too."

He laughs at this, and it's a big, surprised, happy laugh, as if I've just given him a present. Maybe he's like me. Maybe he feels happier being with a person whose flaws are out there in the open. If so, this is the last good thing, and the best thing, about my new therapist.

Day 110

We're having company. Thomas and Helen are friends of friends from Portland; we were introduced to them while Bruce was still in rehab, and today they're coming to see us. Five years ago, Thomas caught a virus from an unknown source—they think it may have happened while they were traveling in Africa, but they can't be sure. The virus attacked his spinal cord and nearly killed him before they understood what had happened. He was partially paralyzed.

Thomas's walk is slow and a little awkward; he swings one leg forward from his hip as if his knee won't bend. Helen stays near while he climbs carefully up our two front steps. They've brought us fresh fruit and little packets of tea grown in their garden. When we met them in the hospital, they encouraged us to call if we needed to talk with them. We need to talk with them now. We talk and talk. They know so much that no one else but us knows; it's a huge relief to be understood, to be able to dispense with explanations. Our questions remind them of things they've forgotten, and this gives me hope that one day I'll be able to say, as Helen says about night spasms, "Oh, I do remember that. I haven't thought about that in so long ... that was really horrible. But it did go away."

They have very specific advice, all of it useful. We should be pushing to solve the spasm problem. We say that we are; we've just been on the phone with the clinic again, and Bruce's nurse has suggested a new combination of medications that might be the one. They say not to worry; they're sure it's solve-able, and I want to kneel and kiss their feet. This one problem has claimed so much of our energy that we haven't given thought to much else, but these kind people make it clear that we are only getting started.

Thomas is talking about physical therapy. They rented an apartment in the U District while he was doing his PT. Has Bruce been to the UW?

"I've had a couple of appointments at Harborview."

"When were you discharged?" Helen is looking troubled.

"Three weeks ago. They're having scheduling problems."

"That's outrageous. You're still getting return, right?" Bruce pushes his chair back and moves his legs to show them. Helen stands up to look. "You need to be seeing somebody." She says that Thomas went to PT every day.

I tell them that the people at Harborview have told us that the UW is just as overloaded. Do they know of anybody else? Thomas shakes his head. He doesn't, but we can't give up. "You can't do this without a good PT. I couldn't. No way." He asks Helen for a pen and writes down the name and number of his physical therapist at the UW. "I wouldn't be walking if it weren't for this guy."

I take the paper and set it next to the phone. Don't lose this. Helen is asking about our kids. Their kids were grown when Thomas was sick, so she didn't have the worry about what the crisis might do to them— at least not in the same way.

"I'm looking for a therapist for Heather." This makes all four of us be quiet. "She told me that sometimes right in the middle of the lunch line, or just alone on her way to the bus, she gets the same feeling she had on the mountain."

"Post traumatic stress."

"Yeah."

"What about you?" Helen is very still.

"Up and down." I tilt my palm, up and down.

"I took Paxil for three years," she says deliberately. "It saved me. I couldn't have managed without it."

I sigh. All during the time he was in the hospital, even on my worst days, I thought I was doing okay. I was secretly proud of this. I dismissed every suggestion that I might need antidepressants to get me through. I wasn't depressed; I was coping. Now—now I'm getting into trouble myself. "I should probably call somebody."

"It really does help. You don't feel like crying all the time, for one thing. There's just less of an edge."

Three years. She needed antidepressants for three years. "Was it hard to stop?"

"Not at all. When I didn't need it anymore, I didn't need it. It was no problem."

"I keep thinking that once we can sleep again, I'll be okay."

She shakes her head. "Why make it harder than it has to be?"

"I don't like to think of myself as needing drugs."

"Then don't think of it that way." She leans over toward me. "You're up against a big monster, Kate. You need everything you can get your hands on to help you. It's not about being strong now. It's about being smart."

These are the right words. She is not my mother, not my sister, not even my friend. She's been in my kitchen for forty-five minutes, and she knows everything about me.

Day 116

We're at the kitchen table with Dave and Mim, and it's time to talk about money. They came here to see how it is with us, now that some weeks have passed and a little of the dust has settled. They also came to get specific about how much help we need. Dave has a list, of course, and this time it's our budget. Bruce and I are naming, one by one, all the expenses normal to our household: mortgage, utilities, music lessons, groceries, gasoline, Emily's tuition ... no, we don't have any credit card debt. Yes, our cars are paid for. We do have insurance on the cars, and of course our private health insurance.

"That was really good, that you had that health insurance," Dave says, and a sort of sigh goes around the table.

He's not kidding. Bruce bought the policy in January, and we made a payment in February and another one in March. At the time, we were appalled at how much it cost, but by now that insurance company is into us for half a million dollars. If we'd been uninsured, we would have had to use up every bit of savings before qualifying for Medicaid. All the carefully saved college money, the retirement account, the cash reserve—we'd be broke.

Mim says that we have to include some fun things on the list. What about vacations? Dave writes down a number. She says we need some kind of budget for clothes; these are teenaged girls we're talking about. I exchange a small smile with her; she's raised three daughters and knows all about clothes budgets. I'm uncomfortable with this process, but resigned. I say that Heather is playing club soccer now, and tell them what that costs. Bruce and I look at each other, trying to remember if there's anything else.

Mim tells Dave to put in something for entertainment. What do we do? We go to the movies, sometimes. We go to Mariners' games when we can. We eat out once every couple of weeks. Dave comes up with a number and fills it in.

Then we move on to the abnormal expenses. Prescriptions. Bruce came home with a list of twelve different prescription drugs, all required. Insurance pays part of the cost, but what's left is still a pretty big sum. Sarah. We've decided this is going to be Sarah's last week, but none of her help was covered. Physical therapy, if we can ever get it arranged. Our insurance pays enough to cover about eight sessions per year … not even a month's worth. Therapists for our sanity. Bruce still has Fred, and now I have Michael. The girls will probably need to see someone as well, and none of it is covered. Dave writes all this down in his "abnormal expenses" column, estimating dollar amounts as he goes.

Then we have to go through our income. I tell them what I make at each of my part-time jobs. Bruce has income from a small disability policy, plus there is money from social security. No one mentions the possibility of him getting back to work. When everything is added up, we have enough income to support all the normal expenses, but nothing left for the abnormal ones. This is when they tell us that they've always had a fund set aside for a medical emergency. Really? Of course. They have seven adult children and ten grandchildren; odds are that one of those people would have some kind of a problem.

Mim looks apologetic, saying this, as if she's afraid I'll think they somehow caused this mess by planning for it. "Of course, we never dreamed it would be you two, or anything like this. We thought maybe one of the babies might be born with some kind of problem …"

Dave is nodding, assuring us that he and his finance guy thought through a crisis scenario a long time ago. And with that, he circles the number at the bottom of the abnormal expenses list. He says this is no problem at all. He says that when these bills come, I should send them on to him in Minnesota and let him take care of them. I'm sitting in my chair with my hands under my thighs, unable to think of a single thing to say. What could possibly be an appropriate response?

Mim says quietly, "We're very glad we're able to help you." I know this, of course, but it's still too much for me to take in. They're going to make sure we don't have to spend the college money. They'll let us pay them back if we ever can, but they're saying now not to worry. That's the message: just take care of yourselves and the girls. Get well, all of you. Here is love, freely given, in the form of a list with a number circled at the bottom. Bruce nods at me, and I say okay. Dave folds the list and tucks it into his front shirt pocket, and that is that.

Spectacular advances have been made in the past decade in rehabilitative therapies. For many years, rehabilitation focused on maximizing function that survived the injury ... most rehabilitative approaches assumed that there would be no further return of function. There has been a sea-shift of attitudes as people are beginning to realize that the brain and spinal cord are capable of remarkable recovery.

Dr. Wise Young

EIGHTEEN

Day 117

I wake up rested for the third straight day. The combination that works is Valium and Baclofen. When Bruce takes these specific pills in certain specific doses just at bedtime, his legs are quiet all night long. I lie in my spot, wondering if my sense of clarity is from rest or from Paxil, then decide that I don't care which it is. I feel like myself. Today Dave and Mim are going home, having removed a giant burden I hadn't even known I was carrying. Today, Bruce has a physical therapy appointment at the University of Washington.

The woman at Harborview who told me that the UW outpatient rehab clinic was overbooked didn't know what she was talking about. My only regret is that I took her word for it, and spent most of the last week on the phone trying to find an alternative to both of them. I contacted private agencies, sports medicine clinics, and every single number in the yellow pages with the words "physical therapy" in the ad. All in vain. With no place else to look, I called the UW.

The receptionist was named Don. When he said he could get Bruce in to see a PT right away for his initial diagnostic appointment, I was speechless.

"I heard that you wouldn't have any openings," I said when I could talk.

"Who told you that?"

"Someone at Harborview ..."

"Oh. Well, we do. What's your husband's condition?"

"C-6 spinal cord injury, uh, almost four months post. Incomplete."

"Yeah, we see lots of those. He got any movement?"

"Lots, actually. More in the left leg."

"Okay, well, bring him in tomorrow. If we can help him, we will."

Day 118

Bruce is going to see a physical therapist today, finally. He's going to be rested, and so am I. Dave and Mim are going back home because they've done what they can, and they can see that we're going to be all right. And there is more. This morning, I have another appointment with Michael. I'm going to go and be in the room that says, "Engage. Take up the work of your life." Okay. I get up and head for the shower.

3 pm

The University of Washington Medical Center feels different from the moment we approach the polished arc of glass that forms the entrance. I feel like one of those little cutout people architects use to give their models a sense of scale. This gleaming, subtly decorated building is perfectly sized for human beings. There are people everywhere, but no one is crowded, and the wheelchair is easy to maneuver. We find the right elevators and hit the button for the eighth floor.

The gym is much smaller and much busier than the one at Harborview. Here, there is room to move a wheelchair comfortably around, but not much more. The broad, empty dance floor room we're used to could hold three or four of this little one. Bruce's new PT is a broad-shouldered, blunt woman named Stacia. She directs him briskly over to a mat, half of which is being used by another PT/patient couple. I stand out of the way and watch.

She lets him stage the chair, set up the sliding board, and move himself onto the mat. She lets him put the board on the chair seat, unlock its brakes, and move it out of the way. She watches his every effort with critical, interested eyes. When he lifts his left leg up onto the mat without using his hands, her eyebrows go up. She puts a hand on his left thigh and asks him to flex the muscle.

"You got a lot here. That's great."

He has to use both hands to haul his right leg up. "Not here, though," he says.

"That's okay. Lie down for me." She puts him through a series of precisely described activities, making little comments as he performs. Good. Okay, can't do that. Try again. Very nice. So far, it's not very different from a PT session with Josh, except that her beeper is not calling her constantly away. She asks him to sit up, and he pops effortlessly off the mat.

"Wow!" I'm amazed. At home it seems to take a lot more effort.

She glances at me. "He doesn't do it that easy at home?"

"No way."

"Bruce," she says. "Your wife thinks you're doggin' it."

"Right," he says.

"No," she says to me. "I'm sure it is harder in your bed. This move is just a lot easier to do on a firm surface."

"It is," he agrees. He's sitting upright with both legs out straight in front of him, leaning back a little on his hands. He looks ready for anything. This is where the session becomes different from what happened at Harborview. Stacia sits down next to him on the edge of the blue mat. She says that he'll have to start working right away on strengthening his trunk. It doesn't matter how well your legs work if your middle is going to collapse every time you get vertical. He'll be getting a workout on his legs, too, of course. They'll want him to try electrical stimulation on some of the muscles that aren't firing. They'll want him to spend some of his sessions here in the standing frame, getting used to the feel of being on his feet.

I can't believe it. She's talking as if it's only a matter of time. Bruce is absolutely still.

"What's the matter?"

"You think I'll be able to walk?" he says.

"At Harborview they didn't talk about getting him on his feet," I tell her. "A couple of people said it might be possible, but they never got started on how."

"Well, it isn't going to be easy. It will depend on how well his muscles respond to all the ways we're going to find to torture them." She says that he's not as bad off as some people she's worked with. She says that she just saw a guy this morning whom she worked with a couple of years ago. "He went around Green Lake yesterday. Not fast, but he went around."

Green Lake is a local spot popular with joggers. The path is three miles long. I ask if she can guess how long it will take before he gets to his feet. I don't expect an answer; I've forgotten that we're not at Harborview.

Stacia thinks it over. She looks him up and down, calculating, then says, "Three months, probably, and he'll be standing in the parallel bars. Depends on how well his muscles respond. Maybe another couple of months after that before he can take a few steps." She flashes him a smile, and then her face is intent. "Seriously, this will be hard. You can't imagine how hard. You've got a lot of work ahead of you."

"I want to do it."

"Okay. Let me get Don in here to set up some appointments."

We leave with a whole new calendar: starting next week, he'll be up here for two hours every Monday, Wednesday, and Friday afternoon, for as long as it takes. We make our way out of the hospital and back to the Prius. I load him in, break down the chair, toss the pieces in the back seat, and get behind the wheel. We sit there looking at each other for a minute, and then he says, calm as grass, "I should call Jocelyn and see if she can help me find some rides here and back. You're not going to be wanting to do all this driving."

These practical words make me almost as happy as what Stacia said upstairs. Bruce is figuring out how to make this happen. He's going to manage his own transportation. He cares about whether I have too much to do. I think suddenly of the first morning, in the kitchen with Dave, when he was so matter of fact about what was happening. No tragic opera, no hysterics. This moment is the flip side of that record. No shouting with joy, no getting ahead of ourselves, just do what has to be done next. I put the car in gear and turn my head so he won't see my smile. Bruce is not Dave's son for nothing.

Day 119: July 4th, 2001

What our family is supposed to be doing on this night is going down to watch the fireworks at the park. There will be a brass band in striped jackets playing "Yankee Doodle Dandy" and "America the Beautiful." There will be a few thousand people sitting on blankets spread over the grass, eating popcorn from paper sacks and playing cards while they wait. There will be grandparents and babies and toddlers dancing to the music. There will be little possees of suburban teenagers with tasteful nose-piercings, roaming through the crowds and laughing, flexing their independence. It's an oddly touching celebration, unusual in our uptight suburban world, friendly and frankly corny. In our family, this event is a tradition.

This year, Heather is away at a week-long church camp for fifth and sixth-graders. Bruce is up in our room, waiting for me to help him with the ritual of getting into bed. Emily and I are in the kitchen, avoiding looking at the clock, which says it's time to leave for the park. We can't go. We can't bring Bruce, and we can't leave him alone for three hours, either. She's turning the pages of a Delia's catalogue she's already thumbed to death, pretending to care about the prices of pastel corduroy jeans.

I go upstairs. Bruce is in his wheelchair in the middle of the bedroom. I haul the stupid commode chair into position next to him, and let him help me set up the sliding board between the two chairs. With only a little assistance, he moves himself slowly across the gap and gets centered on the black bubble-cushion seat. I kneel and wrestle the footrests onto the frame. This simple task defeats me every single time I do it, night after night. When it comes to the footrests, I do everything wrong. I try to attach them to the wrong supports. I try to attach them backwards. I try to attach them to the wrong sides. I just hate this chair, and I can't seem to make peace with anything about it. In the bathroom, I push him into position over the toilet, then let him lift himself just enough for me to slip his pants out of the way.

"I think I'm going to take Emily down past the McCord's house to see if we can see the fireworks from the hill." I'm putting the glove on his hand.

"That's right, it's the fourth." He holds out one finger for the gel. "Good idea."

I leave the room to tell her to find some shoes so we can take Rocky out and try to watch the fireworks. When I get back, he's finished. I peel off the glove and throw it in the trash, then wheel the commode chair next to our bed, backing it into position. He rides with his hands in his lap in case I bump into anything. Once he's in bed and I've taken off his clothes, I can go.

The fireworks are visible. We stand for half an hour in the dark, watching them explode, small and silent, over the downtown Bellevue buildings in the distance. We talk about Heather, whom both of us have missed desperately all week, and about next year, when Daddy will be well enough to go to the park again. Rocky lies in the dirt at our feet with his face between his paws. He is the very image of patient forbearance. I point this out to Emily, who kneels to rub his ears.

"You don't care, do you Rocky?" she says. "You just want to be with your people." And then, without standing up, she looks at me and asks when Daddy will be better.

"No one knows. A lot of stuff is better." I'm thinking of the night spasms, which are quickly becoming a grim memory, and of the way he moved himself across the board earlier. I don't list the tiny increments of change I see, though, because I know that what she wants is not descriptions of muscle groups or neurological evidence. She wants her Dad, and whether he walks or not is hardly the point. "It will happen," I say. "He'll be himself again." Sometime.

Day 120

I am tired of spending every minute of every evening the same way: in the kitchen with Bruce and Emily, waiting for it to be bedtime. The days start slowly, proceed slowly, and end slowly. I'm stir crazy, and I know Bruce and Emily must be as sick of me as I am of them. We've got to do something. I pick up the phone and start calling people. "Can you come over and hang around with us? We're turning into the most boring people on the face of the earth—we need company." After a few calls, I have some dates lined up. My friend Sue says, after a pause, that her whole family will come over tonight. No, they're not doing anything. They'll bring a pie, would that be okay? Hell, yes.

We have a good time with them. They are Sue and Jim and Kristen and Kevin. Kristen just finished high school; she's been in my youth group for years. Kevin is going into ninth grade, and we've known him since he was a crabby toddler. Now he's funny and cool, a Bruce Willis look-alike. Jim and Kevin used to come up to Bruce's room in rehab and try to watch baseball on the TV's that were bolted too high for them to see comfortably.

Now they're sitting at our table, and even though—unbelievably—the sucky 2001 Texas Rangers are creaming the unbeatable Mariners, we are all relaxed and laughing. Sue is making funny faces to show how little she knows or cares about the infield fly rule. Kevin is talking about the movie *Rain Man*, which they rented and watched last night.

"Course I gotta have boxers," I say.

"Course we gotta go to K-Mart." The Mariners can't get anybody out in the fourth inning. The pitcher is giving up singles. He's hitting the batters. He's walking in runs. Alex Rodriguez, who played for us last year, hits a grand slam, which is the funniest thing we've ever seen. All nine Rangers have come around to score, and there is still nobody out.

After we eat the pie, it's suddenly nine o'clock—time for Bruce to get to bed. Sue's family is gathered in front of the refrigerator she once cleaned for me. We're talking about birthdays; these are the people who helped us on Heather's birthday in June. Kevin's birthday will be coming up next week, and then Kristen's. Sue says that all of their birthdays are in July, and she names three of the dates.

I'm leaning against our butcher block table, one hand on Bruce's shoulder. He's in his wheelchair in the middle of the group, looking up at everyone. "And what about you?" I say. "When's your birthday, Sue?"

She opens her mouth, takes a breath, and smiles. "Well." She gives me a little helpless shrug. "That would be today."

Her family stands around her, enjoying my expression, by the looks of them. After a moment, I ask what she was going to do tonight. What were her plans, before I called and said we needed company.

"We were going to go out to eat Mexican food."

"Oh, Sue."

"No, it's fine. It's really fine." She gives me a hug. I interrupted her family's plans for her on her birthday, and she wasn't even going to tell me. "I'll just go out to dinner another day. Actually—I think this is going to be one of my favorite birthdays, ever."

Day 122

Heather is home, pulling things out of her duffel bag and making a mess of the floor. Every single piece of clothing is thick with dust. Pine needles are tucked into every crease. Heather herself is tanned, smiling, and blonder than when she left. She's poking around deep in the bottom of the bag.

"Aha." She gets up and hands Bruce an object made of colored woven straw. It's about the size of a dessert plate, with flower petals built into the concentric circles that form its shape. "The other kids made dream catchers," she says. She's standing at a little distance from his chair, not quite looking at him.

"Is this for me?" He's admiring the workmanship.

"It's a spasm catcher. I made you a spasm catcher"

His mouth opens, and he reaches for her. She allows him to take her hand. He gives her a respectful little tug and says, very distinctly, "What a thoughtful, creative, original kid you are."

"Do you like it?" She moves one inch closer.

258

"I do. I love it. I'll hang it over my bed. The spasms have been gone for a few days now. Maybe it started working right away, even before you gave it to me."

They're both so calm. I'm across the room, stuffing her dirty things back in the duffel bag. I'm imagining Heather surrounded by kids making dream catchers in the craft room at camp. I'm seeing her privately decide what she's going to make instead.

Day 125

It is the worst time of day: mid afternoon. Emily and Heather have used up their interest in television, in books, in each other. Their friends are all gone somewhere. It's warm outside, and warm inside. The girls are drifting around the kitchen, casting furtive looks at Bruce, who has been downstairs with us for all of an hour. He's parked in his spot at the table with his empty oatmeal bowl pushed aside. The newspaper is spread out in front of him. His soft hands are covered by black leather half-gloves with padded palms; Heather calls these his "cool-dude-motorcycle-gloves." His right elbow is on the table and his head is propped up on that hand. He's dozing over the sports page. A long thread of drool hangs from his lip. I had thought that his daytime sleepiness was the result of the spasms, but not so. At the hospital, Bruce couldn't sleep, but here in our house he can't stay awake.

I get behind the chair and say, "You're going back to bed, Pal." I wheel him out and off we go.

When I get back to the kitchen, Emily is sitting with her knees up, looking out the sliding glass door at the empty deck. Heather stands in front of the window over the sink, flicking drops of water at a fly crawling along the sill. I put both hands on top of my head and sigh. We three have always loved our summers. For them, having a teacher-mom has been cool; I'm around every day, and when it's hot I can take them to the beach. We like to stay all afternoon. They like to play in the water, then come and find me reading on my blanket, then eat something from the snacks I've brought, then beg for quarters to buy a soda from the machine, then talk me into coming for a swim. We like to spend whole days this way, ending up all in a row on my blanket, talking silly and looking at the sun on the lake while we pick at the grass.

Now we are in the kitchen, listening to the refrigerator hum. I know what they want, and I know that they aren't going to ask for it. I could take them to the beach and leave them there, then come back and pick them up later, but of course that would be worse. That would only underline their loss. I also know they feel guilty for wishing they could have their lives back. What is their problem, after all, compared to his?

It is still not safe to leave Bruce alone. If he's down in the kitchen, he wouldn't be able to get back into bed, which he sometimes needs to do when his blood pressure suddenly drops. These are scary scenes. He'll be fine, then suddenly his face goes white and he calls, "Kate, I need to lie down!" and I scramble to get him horizontal before he faints. If we leave while he's in bed, he wouldn't be able to get himself to the bathroom in case his bowels suddenly wake up. We can't just go to the beach, but we can't stop knowing that we want to, either.

I decide to ask them something I've been thinking about. "Do you guys want to go to camp this year?"

Emily says immediately, "Yeah. Why wouldn't we?"

Heather gives her a look, then turns to me. "Do you think we can? I mean, do you think Daddy can?"

"I'm pretty sure he could," I say. "We'd have to bring all his stuff . . I could figure out that part. What I want to know is, do you guys want to go, even with Daddy like he is?" I'm trying to figure out how troubled they are by the idea of him being in public, in front of all their friends, the way he is at home: a wobbly, awkward, pale, exhausted, short-haired guy in a wheelchair who has a hard time eating with his left hand and falls asleep every ten minutes. A guy with a gurgling, disgusting cough. A guy with a bag of pee strapped permanently to his shin. They're middle-schoolers; it's not an easy time to have a parent so spectacularly different from everyone else's.

They understand this without my spelling it out. "I wouldn't care," Emily says stoutly, and I see that she means it. I love her so much for this I have to look away.

Heather is watching me, sad and thoughtful. "It would be good for him, wouldn't it?"

Yes. Camp is N-Sid-Sen, the scene of our family vacation every summer of their lives, except the time we had to miss it for a wedding. Both of them went to camp even as infants, Heather when she was six weeks old. It's seven hours from here by car, on Lake Coeur d'Alene in northern Idaho. Camp is our church people, usually over a hundred of them, gathered to hang out and play and sing together for a week, every year in the middle of July. Camp is not accessible.

"It would be great for him," I say.

"How could we do it? Would we have to stay in Spirit Lodge?"

I nod. Camp has twelve cabins scattered along bark-strewn paths no wheelchair could navigate. For years, we have been the lucky residents of Cabin 10, perched on the side of the hill near the dance pavilion. From its porch, Cabin 10 has a beautiful view of the lake. We can't stay there. We can't stay in any of the cabins, and not only because of the problem of getting him in and out. The cabins don't have plumbing. The lodge does.

Spirit Lodge is where the grandmas and grandpas stay. It's where the single people stay, or the people who are at camp for the first time and don't think they're going to like being in a cabin. It's a beautiful building, but it's more like a hotel than not. The lodge is camp for wimps, and it's where we'll have to stay if we go. I wait while they digest this idea, then I tell them they'd have their own room.

"That would be cool." I can see their little wheels turning. They could have their friends in. They could stay up late talking. They could sneak out for a look at the stars. They could snack all night without us telling them to brush their teeth.

I get out the church directory and find the number for camp. On the phone, I ask Randy if it's possible. Randy, the live-in manager of camp, knows our family well. He says he heard about the accident, and that he's been praying for us, and then he considers the question. There is a new ramp into Forrester, the beautiful timbered room in which all the meals are served. There is a ramp into the pavilion, the open-aired building where we gather in the evening for vespers. The entrance to Spirit Lodge is paved and level, so that would be easy.

"The bathrooms in Spirit are fine," he says. "The doors are extra wide, and there are hand rails. The showers are a problem." We talk this over. From what he says, Bruce will have to spend his week at camp without taking a shower. Who cares? We're going to camp. I call the church office and tell them to put us on the list.

After injury, the spinal cord can do its job while being connected to the brain by a fraction of the normal number of nerve fibers. In humans, it is known that 50 percent of the fibers suffice to preserve normal function in the lower body because people with the so-called Brown-Sequard syndrome ... can recover from paralysis almost fully.

Luba Vikhanski

NINETEEN

Day 127: 2 pm

We're back at Harborview, this time for Bruce's first visit with Dr. Barry Goldstein, who will be his attending physician. The nurse, Cathy, has Bruce drive his wheelchair up a short ramp that leads to a scale. I am standing across the room, looking at literature about spinal cord research.

"156 pounds," she says, and I turn around. She's walking away from the scale. He unlocks his brakes, rolls backwards, and suddenly the chair tips, wham, onto its back with him in it.

"Jesus!" I'm on my knees next to him, but he's okay. He's laughing. Cathy is trying to ask him something, but he's saying he's not hurt, and I'm practically yelling. "God damn it. All these weeks, I'm taking such good care of him, don't let him fall, check his skin, give him his meds, turn in the night, not a single problem, and then I bring him here and you guys let him dump over in his chair!" I'm making it sound funny. It isn't one bit funny, except that he thinks it is. Cathy goes out to get some help.

"That was such a rush!" he says happily. "Kate, it's okay. I felt myself going and I just automatically went into a little curl." He shows me. His head and shoulders are pulled in, and his arms are crossed in front of his chest. "See? I'm fine." He laughs again. "Wow, that was interesting!"

Adrenaline is still racing through my system. I just put my head down and wait, weak with relief. Another nurse comes in with Cathy. She assesses the situation, sees that it's all right, and then asks Bruce if he's ever directed anybody to help him get up again. This is one of the things Josh was going to have him practice.

"I know how to do it," Bruce says. "But I haven't had to, yet."

"Okay, go for it."

So, he does. The idea is to have the helper wiggle the chair into position, squarely lined up under him, flat on his back with his legs in the air. Then it's a question of whether the person trying to pick him up has enough muscles to tilt him forward. It turns out that I do. Once he's upright, Cathy runs him through a series of movements, just to be sure nothing is hurt. Amazingly, nothing is.

The exam with Dr. Goldstein begins when his resident comes in to do a preliminary workup. Dr. Burgess is a tiny woman with a cloud of dark, intense hair and sharp eyes behind enormous glasses. She goes over every inch of him, talking softly all the time, touching him with her child-sized hands. There is no hurry whatsoever. She asks him in detail about our situation and how he manages his day. He is independent in everything now, except for getting his feet into the pressure hose. He can transfer, sit up, roll over in bed, dress, undress, shave, shower and brush his teeth. He can use the computer, make himself something to eat, and take his own medications. Everything he does has to be carefully staged. Everything he does takes much longer than it once did, sometimes fifty times as long, but he does it independently.

"Except for the socks."

"Except for the socks," Bruce says. "And soon I'm going to start looking into what it will take to drive."

She wants to hear about the bowel program. He makes a face and I fold my arms. She waits. "It's variable," Bruce says finally. "I can't seem to find any kind of pattern, except maybe that my bowels only work when they feel like working. Lots of times it's at night, when I'm getting ready for bed."

"Do you still use"—she looks at her notes— "the suppositories?"

"I wasn't getting any 'results' from them," he says. "So I quit."

"Having accidents?"

"Some."

This monosyllabic response is a miracle of brevity. Since he got discharged, there have been a half a dozen times when he suddenly found himself sitting in shit, without warning, without any hope of getting to a bathroom. These incidents are the very worst thing about his life right now. The clinical way she's asking the questions doesn't begin to suggest how it is when he has to lie on our bed on a towel, enduring being cleaned up, saying he's sorry. I always tell him to forget it. I try to make jokes. You'd do it for me, I say, and he says that he would. We leave it at that, but it is hell for him.

She also wants to know about the Foley. "Foley" is the name of the inventor of the catheter that has one end currently lodged in Bruce's bladder. The other end is hooked to a slim hose made of tan rubber, which drains into the plastic bag I have secured to his leg with Velcro straps. Bruce is telling Dr. Burgess that he plans to learn to use "intermittent" catheters soon, maybe in August.

She folds her hands and asks him what the holdup is. Poor Bruce. He doesn't want to stick a red hose into his dick seven times a day. Does this really need to be said? She tells him that the urinary tract infection he has right now is very likely due to the Foley. He nods miserably. He knows he has to learn the other way, but he's not quite prepared to do it. Yet. I have been nursing a secret hope that when they take the Foley out, he will be able to pee. It could happen.

Now Dr. Burgess is sticking him with the safety pin. She does every section of his body, keeping a careful record as she goes. She takes a piece of metal like a screwdriver with a fat handle and tests to see if he can feel vibrations. I pay attention because this is a test I haven't seen before. He knows when the thing is vibrating if she touches it to either of his arms or his left knee. His stomach sensation is random; sometimes he feels it on his left, sometimes on his right. His left knee is good, but his left toes can't feel it. His right leg can't feel vibration anywhere.

His body is such a puzzle. His right leg can't feel vibrations, but it can feel pinpricks. His left leg is the other way around, and both legs can feel soft touch. All over his body, even on the parts that can't tell when they're being poked with a needle, he can feel fingertips brushing his skin.

Now he's sitting up on the edge of the mat, and she asks him to move his legs if he can. He swings his left foot back and forth easily, and she startles. "Wow! Is that in both legs, or just this one?" With a visible effort, he manages to move the right foot back and forth a few inches. She makes a note, murmuring to herself, and goes off to find Dr. Goldstein.

After forty-five minutes and a few hurried apologies from Cathy, Dr. Goldstein walks in, followed by Dr. Burgess. I like him at once; for some reason he makes me think of New York City, but I don't have time to figure out why. He's all over Bruce, repeating the tests Dr. Burgess has already done and adding another new one. He gets a spoon and runs cold water over it from the sink. He takes the cold spoon and touches Bruce's legs and feet with it. Hot or cold? I don't know what he's looking for, but he's obviously excited about something.

He sits down with one leg curled beneath him and tells Bruce that, based on his motor/sensation pattern of return, he has an unusual kind of injury. It's called Brown-Sequard Syndrome, after the physician who originally noticed its peculiarities. He explains that Brown-Sequard patients appear to have the damage to their spinal cords mostly confined to one half. He holds up his expressive hands to demonstrate.

"If you think of looking down on a cross-section of your cord," he forms a circle with his hands. "You can imagine the damage to it being mostly confined to one half—in your case, the right half." He makes a chopping motion so that his left hand has become a half-circle. He says that this kind of injury used to be seen in people who had been targeted by the mafia—the order given would be to slide a knife into the neck and sever half the victim's cord. Not to kill, but to paralyze. The fate that is worse than death.

Everyone in the room cringes at the very idea of someone being made paralyzed on purpose. Dr. Goldstein continues: "The thing that happened, though, was that some of these patients recovered very substantially. After a relatively short time, some of them even functioned nearly as well as they had before."

I am holding my breath.

"This is the kind of injury I think you have, Bruce. And the reason I think so is because of the pattern of your return. Look., your left side can move, but your right side can't. Your right side has much better sensation, though. Your right leg and foot can feel the pinprick. On the right side, you can distinguish hot and cold. But your motor return there is weak. The reverse is true with your left leg. It moves well, but doesn't feel nearly as well as the right.

"Your abdomen—I don't know. It's all mixed up, which tells me you're not a 'pure'—." He lifts his fingers in the gesture of quotation— "Not a 'pure' Brown-Sequard. But you do show a lot of the characteristics."

He's very intent, sitting next to Bruce on the blue mat, leaning forward with his legs crossed and his hands working. I'm across from them with my back against the wall, hugging myself. "What this means for you is that you have a better than average chance of getting out of that thing." He flicks a finger at the wheelchair. "We aren't sure what the mechanism is, but it appears that, over time, the damaged part of the Brown-Sequard cord has—like, sprouts, or buds—some people call them growth cones—which can eventually grow their way past the injury site, as long as they have some kind of guidance from the healthy neurons on the other side."

Bruce nods. I exhale. Holy shit.

"What this means for you is that there's a chance that," he pauses, looking around—"if you see something you want over there, you'll be able to just get out of the chair, walk over there and get it." Dr. Goldstein is gesturing at the far side of the examining room. "If I were you, I'd be busting my butt in physical therapy. Are you seeing the outpatient people here?"

"I just started going to the UW," Bruce tells him. "Three times a week."

Dr. Goldstein nods. "Good. Work hard there. You have a shot."

He stays with Bruce for another hour, discussing our present life, and the shape our life might take. The night spasms, the Foley, the stupid bowel. They talk at length about Bruce's right hand; Dr. Goldstein thinks maybe Bruce will want to think about Botox. The injections will relax the muscles that are making his fingers cramp, so that his other muscles won't have to work against the tightness. At one point, he asks Bruce to cough, and Bruce makes his wimpy, old-man chuff. There's a silence, and then the doctor says, "Well." He blinks a few times. "I'm kind of underwhelmed," he says, and all of us laugh much too hard.

When I leave the hospital to get the car, I walk deliberately through the halls that lead to the ER. I am remembering the night I spent here four months ago. I am remembering the hours I spent circling around and around these floors with my soul full of broken glass. I am walking with light steps , and I am shaking the dust of that night off my shoes as I go.

Day 130

We're just about to leave for Idaho, and I'm worried about what might happen to Bruce's skin on the long drive. He never sits for seven straight hours, not even in his wheelchair with the special, extra-forgiving, gel-filled seat cushion. I've tried to think through every moment of what happens during a week of camp and pack accordingly, but now that everything is crammed into the back of the van, I'm anxious.

"Do you think we could slide your seat cushion underneath you once you're in the van?" Bruce and I are in the driveway. The girls are already in the back seat, looking out at us with expressions that clearly say, "Let's go already!" Their seat looks like a nest of pillows and stuffed animals. I'm glad to see Bunny, who has slept in Emily's arms every night since she was two. In Heather's corner are her old baby blankets—the soft one made of quilted flannel and the cool one, a thin, transparent sheet of white satin.

"We could try," Bruce says. "It might make me too tall."

I set up the sliding board, brace myself, help him up into the front seat, and lift his feet in after him. He's right; his head is inches from the ceiling of the car. "Going to be close," I say. "Can you try to lift yourself up?" It takes five minutes of shoving and inching the cushion, but finally it's underneath him. He looks absurdly tall, but his head still clears the ceiling by a sixteenth of an inch. "Excellent." I'm sweating and happy. "Let's go to camp."

Day 131

It is vespers, the worship service we have every evening between dinner and bedtime. The whole camp is gathered in the elegant, polished structure known as the dance pavilion. It has a built-in bench along the side that overlooks Lake Coeur d'Alene, which is where I am sitting with the girls; Bruce is in front of us in his chair, looking cold with his hands tucked into his sleeves. The floor around him is crowded with parents holding babies and toddlers in their laps. I watch them, remembering the challenge of keeping those squirming bodies still for this twenty-minute service.

We're about to sing a song called "Bring Many Names." The verses are all about expanding the possibilities of who God might be. There are verses for old, aching God, and strong mother God, and young, growing God. The melody is yearning, and because it's a song our congregation sings often, we know it well. I give Heather a nudge. "Sit in Daddy's lap," I whisper.

Her eyebrows go up. "Can I?"

"He'd like it."

She gets up and goes to him. We're singing the verse about the warm, father God ... she climbs on his legs and backs herself up until she's leaning against him. She takes his hands and pulls his two arms tight around her own waist, and then his eyes close and I see them both sigh.

Day 133

In the kitchen at Spirit Lodge are three deep, stainless steel sinks set in front of windows with a view of the lake. I'm using them to wash and rinse the urinary supplies—a job that has been mine since we let Sarah go. It's a job which must be done every single day, and it's a job I deeply hate. I try to be philosophical. I count the seconds it takes to do one leg bag. Set up the funnel at the top, close the spigot at the bottom, fill slowly to rinse. Fifteen seconds. Open the spigot and allow it to empty. Twenty seconds. Close the spigot and use the funnel to put in soap and vinegar, then fill with water. Rinse three times. Start on the night bag: same steps, only they take longer because it's bigger. Okay, the whole sequence takes seven minutes.

Am I such a bitch that I can't spare seven minutes a day? Am I such a martyr that I can't do this simple task in front of this glorious, shimmering sunset without feeling sorry for myself? If I do it carelessly, the possibility of him getting an infection is high. It's better to be Zen about it. Pay attention, get the details right, and let the meaning fend for itself. My friend Nancy wanders in to get something out of the refrigerator. She comes over to watch, puts a hand on my shoulder.

"So, how's it going?"

I hold up the leg bag to let the soapy water run into the sink. "Pretty well, actually."

"Is everything working all right for you guys? Your room ... ?" She seems not to be sure how much she wants to know.

I glance at her, suddenly curious. "What does this look like from the outside?" By "this," I mean the whole thing: the wheelchair, the disability, the ill, twisted, debilitated look of him, the idea of us being here at all with kids in these circumstances. She understands me.

"It looks hard," she says.

"It is harder than being at home," I admit. "But not very much." I'm adding the vinegar to the funnel for the third rinse. "What's hard is being around everybody who isn't having to deal with it, and not feeling jealous."

"Well, anybody would feel that way, Kate." Nancy has a round, softly wrinkled face, a mom's face. Frowning, she watches me slosh the vinegar and water around.

"I know," I say. "But that's also what's good—being around regular people—being with all of you, especially!—and not being stuck at home. Or at the hospital."

"Well, everyone is so glad you decided to come. How is his—is he ... getting any better?" Her voice is delicate; she's afraid of the answer.

Ah. This is what everyone really wants to know. Is he ever going to walk again? In so many ways, it is still beside the point. I sigh and tell her about our visit with Dr. Goldstein last week. I tell her about going up to the UW to meet Stacia, and how Stacia predicted that he would probably be able to stand up in the parallel bars by Halloween. She's thrilled at this news, and so am I, in fact. Just telling her, I'm excited and hopeful all over again. I still have to wash the leg bags, though.

I still have to go in and get the girls settled for the night, trying to see in their eyes if this is hurting them as it is hurting me. I still have to walk the paths through the camp in the daytime, seeing our friends chasing their kids down to the field behind the cove for an afternoon playing baseball. I still have to catch sight of my friend Mimi, coming innocently down the steps of Cabin 10, not even knowing that her family's carefree presence there is a blade in my heart. I still have to wake up when our alarm goes off at three, help Bruce turn over, and lie there listening to his uneven, rattling breath. I still have to come around the corner and see my friend Kris walking with her husband, their arms around each other's waists, laughing together over a private joke, on their way to bed.

In so many ways, I'm just as isolated as he is. In the mornings, when the rest of the camp is down at the rock beach for morning worship, Bruce is sitting high above them in his wheelchair on the wooden porch of Forrester Lodge. If we started getting ready in the middle of breakfast, we would still not make it to that beach until the very end of the very last song. It would take three or four of the men to help us move him, and he would still have to sit in his chair, excluded and alone while the rest of the group sat crowded onto a tight series of log benches.

When I go to that worship, my mind is up on the porch with him. When I skip it, my mind is down by the water with our kids. I'm nowhere. But is he ... getting better? He is. Am I such a fool that I don't know how to be grateful for it? Yes. Sometimes I am.

Day 135

It is dusk on the last night of camp. Heather and I are standing by the basketball court next to our van. The whole camp is down at the rock beach, in front of the little morning worship place. Bruce is with them, in his chair. I drove him this far, and then a group of the men lifted his chair and carried him out near the fire pit so he could stay warm and watch the kids launch their boats. On the last night of camp, the tradition is for each kid to bring a boat they've assembled from scraps of lumber and flowers and driftwood and branches. Each boat is fitted with a tea-candle, and each child lights their candle, then wades out into the lake for the launch.

We can hear them splashing and calling to their parents. Some are crying; Heather smiles a sad little smile over this. She has not once in ten years of boat-launches been able to send her creation out to float away. Every single year so far, she's begun bravely and then collapsed in sobs, until Bruce or I give her permission to wade out to get it. At home, there is a collection of these treasures that I don't have a clue what to do with. This year, she's told me already, she's not even going to try. The boat she made is safely stored in her room at the lodge. She looks like she wants to say something.

"You okay?" I lean against the van, inviting her to stand beside me. Heather always has to have her important conversations sideways.

"I was thinking about Daddy."

"Yeah?" We can see him through the trees, in his chair by the edge of the campfire.

"It's like—there's the old Daddy, and the hospital Daddy, and the Daddy at home." He has his harmonica bag out, and he's digging in it with his left hand. "And now the camp Daddy."

"He's been a little more like the old Daddy here." She doesn't answer me. "I think."

"I know. I just keep wondering what he's going to be like at home again."

We start walking toward the water and the campfire. I tell her that I guess we're about to find out, and against the voices of our friends, the plaintive sound of his music rises to meet us. It is too soft, too hesitant, but it is definitely his sound.

Day 145

I drive everywhere now. I drive Bruce to his PT appointments at the University of Washington every Monday, Wednesday, and Friday. When we get there, I put his wheelchair together, help him into it, and let him push himself into the hospital. Someone else, someone Jocelyn has lined up, comes to get him two hours later and bring him home. This is an enormous favor to us; it saves him from having to endure hours riding the accessible Metro bus, and it makes me available to the girls.

I'm standing now in the turnaround outside the entrance, next to his assembled chair. I'm waiting for him to unbuckle his seatbelt and lean over so I can put the sliding board under his butt. He sits with his black-gloved hands in his lap, staring out the window, and suddenly I want to scream. "Move! Undo your fucking seatbelt, goddammit! I have to go home and get Heather to soccer, and she's going to be late! Get out of the car!" He just keeps staring straight ahead, until I say his name. Then he reaches calmly, slowly, to unfasten his seatbelt.

An hour later, I'm trying to get a reluctant Heather to put on her shin guards. Her face says she'd rather forget the whole thing, which would in some ways be fine with me. One less place to drive to, and besides, premier soccer is hard. The practices are twice as long and twice as often as she's used to, plus she's never played in the summer before, and it's hot. The girls on her new team all know each other and don't seem one bit interested in her. They're a good team, aggressive and fast, and I know she feels second-rate.

"You can quit, you know." I can't figure out how to help her, except to give her permission to just not do this if it's too hard.

She says she doesn't want to quit, then goes forlornly to get her ball. In the car, we're both quiet. The traffic is building. Emily is at home alone, again. When we get back, I'll have to hurry to make some food for everybody.

"I had this weird dream last night," Heather says.

"Yeah?" I'm looking past her, waiting for some polite driver to let me change lanes.

"I was in the water at camp, way far out in the middle of the lake. There was, like, this big storm, with huge waves."

Finally. I get in the lane I need, just in time, and head east. "You were swimming?"

She nods. "Me and some other kids from church."

Good. I don't know why, but I think it's good that she wasn't alone. "Uh huh."

"And I was scared because the waves were so big that I couldn't see the shore enough to know which way to swim." She tilts her head and shoots me a glance. Heather knows that dreams can be clues, and she obviously knows this was an important dream. "I was, like, afraid to swim in any direction because I might be going away from the shore."

"What did you do?"

"I don't know. I don't think I did anything. I finally just got washed up, and I landed on the beach by camp ... there were some grownups there, but they weren't the people from our church. Not anybody I knew."

"Did they take care of you?"

"I don't remember."

At the soccer field, I sit in the car and wait for the practice to be over, trying to nap. I notice that nobody greets her when she lopes onto the field, kicking her ball in front of her. I have a lick of hot rage at her team. Self-absorbed twits! Would it kill them to be a little nice? Tomorrow she has her first appointment with the therapist I've hired—someone Michael recommended. He didn't have any contacts on the Eastside, so it will be another trip to Seattle, but if the woman is good, I won't care.

I shift in my seat, and all at once a wave of panic rises in me. Please, God. Let it be over. Deliver us from this evil. I breathe slowly, in and out, trying to talk myself into ordinary thought. I order myself to remember all those Harborview PT times when it seemed like nothing changed and nothing ever would—and then suddenly something new would happen ... a new strength, a longer endurance session, getting the legs up, the unassisted transfer. Coughing. Remember when he needed help coughing? Remember room air? Standing will be like that, I tell myself. Impossible. Then, triumphantly, done. Then excruciating, then just hard, then routine. Oh, God, let it be so. This ever-so-incremental repairing of a body compromised to the edge of the grave is draining us all to dust.

It isn't working. I'm breathing fast and sweat is standing out on my face. I give up and simply pray. Jesus, protect us. I am so afraid.

In 1998, it was clear that embryonic stem cells are pluripotent. In 1999, John McDonald published the first paper indicating that mouse embryonic stem cell transplants into the contused spinal cords of rats two weeks after injury improved functional recovery. The field was poised to take off. In 2000, it was shut down by President Bush, who then took a year to announce his decision to fund human embryonic stem cell derived before August 2001, effectively slowing funding for human embryonic stem cell research to a trickle.

Dr. Wise Young

277

TWENTY

Day 146

Heather is explaining to her new therapist what happened on the mountain. She is sitting, Indian style, on the couch behind me; I am on the floor with my back to her. Alice is across from us, one slim, high-booted leg crossed over the other. Heather describes the way everybody's skis lined up in the snow. Daddy's were the longest, and then all the ski-patroller-dudes', and then mine were the shortest. She says they were all wearing red vests. Her voice is clear but a little high, as if delivering these details makes her breathless. It makes me breathless.

I've never heard this story. At one point, Heather reaches down to take my face in her hands. She tips my head up towards her and bends over to look into my eyes, so that she can see if it is okay to say these things. I make my eyes communicate, "Keep talking, Honey," but I am deep in shame that I haven't ever asked her how it was. Why did I not let her tell me this? I had always pictured them on the mountain with just Jill and Dr. Huseby and maybe one other guy. Now she's describing a whole crowd of people working on Bruce while she stood by in her ski gear, terrified that he was going to die right there in front of her.

"Then we went to this office place, and Jill helped me fill out a form."

Alice's dark eyes are moving back and forth between the two of us. She has black hair that falls in languorous curls all the way to her waist, and her clothes complement her lean body beautifully. I'm sitting on the floor with my graying, grown-out perm and my second-hand-store jeans, listening to my daughter tell Alice the story of how it was to see her dad break his neck. I understand that coming here was a good decision.

Heather needs a place to talk about things where she won't have to be worried about protecting me. She needs to be able to be sad without knowing that her sorrow is adding to mine. She also, surely, needs to be

278

allowed to hate me for not being able to make this right, and she needs to know that I won't find out and hate her back. If this Alice who is now looking at me so speculatively can make a space for any of that to happen, then more power to her. No, all power to her.

6 pm

Bruce and I have been in our bedroom for an hour with the door closed. He is still struggling with his disruptive, unpredictable bowels. It is almost dinner time, and I'm wondering what I might have in the cupboards when Emily knocks softly on our door. Can we come down now? They have a surprise. We are required to go out into the garage to receive it properly. Okay. He rides the lift down, and then we cross the wide door into the garage.

Emily closes the door in our faces, then opens it immediately. She's holding a paper sign. In green magic marker script are the words: Café Italy. She scotch-tapes her sign to the door, then guides us into the house and toward the deck. "Right this way, please." She's very solemn, in the way of a girl who might get a killer attack of the giggles any minute.

I open the sliding glass door all the way, tip the wheelchair back to get it over the sill, and we are outside. They've moved our picnic table to the very end of the deck, so that we're far from the kitchen, out under the soaring fir trees in the back yard. It's a peaceful, warm evening. The picnic table has a white flannel sheet on it, and there is a vase of flowers from the garden in the center. Our places are set with the white china we got for our wedding; we even have cloth napkins. Bruce wheels up to one end of the table, but it's all wrong. The footrests stick out so far that he can't get under the table. He won't be able to reach his food. I figure out a way to extend the end of the table with a spare piece of plywood, anchoring it with loose bricks so that he can roll comfortably underneath. I am efficient and casual, laughing. I am remembering when he went out and bought this table and assembled it, the same year Emily was born.

It's just a cheap wooden table, with two benches attached on either side. There is barely enough room for four plates, and it is so rickety that if any two of us sit on the same side, we might just tip it over. Once he and I are settled, we admire the view, thank them for arranging this great private room, and then get on with ordering our dinner.

279

Heather is our waitress. She hands us their official Café Italy menus, printed off the computer and glued to custom-cut pieces of cardboard. There are two appetizers and six main courses, all pasta. Emily loves pasta. Heather wants to take our drink order. Yes, we'd love some water right now. She's offering me a latte. Dear God, yes. I would love a latte.

"Wait! Do you know how to make that?"

She rolls her eyes. "Yes, Mom!"

Twenty minutes later, we're eating. We both have a salad (crisp, green leaves tossed with tomatoes in a dressing of our choice), and I choose the course of the day (soft, spirally pasta, sauce and parmesan cheese on request). Heather comes out to ask if everything is okay. We tell her that everything is lovely. It's perfect.

She inspects our plates to see if we're really eating, and then goes away looking satisfied. Five minutes later, she's back again.

"Uh, would you like anything else? A refill on your, uh, salad?"

To her obvious relief, Bruce says he would like a little more salad. The girls are very frustrated at how slowly and how little we are eating. They watch us through the big kitchen windows until we wave them out. They can't help themselves. They come and sit down, unable to resist describing how they thought of it, unable to stop asking if everything is really okay. It is, we say. It is really, really good.

Day 155: August 9th, 2001

Today is our fifteenth wedding anniversary, and it is much too warm to cook. In the hospital I used to worry about days like this one. Bruce's body doesn't regulate its own temperature very well because he no longer sweats below his neck. I don't feel like cooking anyway. I've bought us a salmon quiche and made a dark green salad with mushrooms and vine-ripened tomatoes. Emily is here with us; Heather is off at another camp, her fourth trip away from home without us since last spring. Our plan is to eat and then take Rocky to the park for a swim, but right now we're listening to the president.

George W. Bush is on television, finally announcing his decision about whether or not he's going to let government money pay for stem cell research, and we're in the kitchen, listening carefully. Bruce has his chair parked right up against the counter where the television sits. Emily wants to know what stem cells are.

I put my hand on her arm. "Just a minute, I want to hear what he says." W is sitting in an easy chair upholstered in a pattern of giant flowers, wearing a suit and tie, with his hands folded in his lap. Behind him is an expanse of glass with a view of his ranch; he's in Texas, taking a vacation. He talks for a few minutes about the background of the debate, and I honestly can't tell which direction he's heading. I hear the word "ethical" a few times, which probably isn't good news. Then he says that scientists believe stem cells could help people with Parkinson's, people with juvenile diabetes, people with spinal cord injuries.

Emily looks up at me and starts to say something, but this time Bruce shushes her. W is still giving me hope. He's saying that the United States is a leader in science and medicine. Then it's back to ethics. Uh, oh. Now he's talking about an ethicist who told him these clusters of cells are the same as me and him. He wraps it up a few minutes later. There exist sixty lines of stem cells. The government can spend money on these, but not on any new ones. W has prayed about this a lot, and he hopes it's a good decision. Bruce clicks the television off and spins his wheelchair away.

"Fucker."

"What did Bush say?" Emily doesn't get it.

Bruce stops at the door to the dining room and turns his chair around again. "Stem cells are cells that neurologists think can be made to grow into other kinds of cells," he says. "Like nerve cells. The kind I don't have enough of. It's going to take them a long time—it was already going to take them a long time to figure out how. Now he's basically stopped them."

"Why?"

"Because he doesn't want to piss off the people who think abortion is murder. Goddamn him." He turns around and rolls over to the computer desk, where he'll get online and listen to the SCI discussion group hash this one over.

Emily and I clear the table and get it ready for the anniversary dinner. I keep glancing at the dark screen on our little kitchen television. W is back there somewhere, shrugging out of his suit and tie, unbuttoning his dress shirt, all ten of his fingers effortlessly working. He's changing into jeans, maybe. He's about to go out and enjoy his ranch, where the heat won't bother him one bit. He can sweat all he wants. Maybe he'll even go for an evening jog.

I hand Emily the china and silverware. She looks a little frightened. How mad is Daddy? "It sucks," I tell her. "But we knew Bush would probably do that."

At Newcastle Beach Park there is an accessible sidewalk a couple of hundred yards long that ends at a dock with a view across Lake Washington toward Seattle. We're sitting on a bench—at least, I'm sitting on a bench. Bruce is in the chair parked next to me. Emily is down in the water at the place we call "the secret beach," throwing a stick in the water for Rocky and then letting him beat her to it. There's a lot of happy splashing. I watch them and think about the day a month ago when Helen and Thomas came to visit us—the day she told me about Paxil.

She said that Thomas's illness had made them old. Has this injury made us old? It's made us different. Uninjured, Bruce would be waist-deep in that water, tossing Emily into the lake and letting her dunk him. He would be swimming out deep, relishing his strength. He would be laughing at the dog, paddling desperately to keep up. Instead he's sitting here like his own great grandpa, twisted and weak, and he cannot even get his toes wet.

We stay quiet for a long time, listening to Emily laughing, and then something changes. It's as if we have been in a room that was too dim, and one of us got up and turned on a light. We talk softly. He's telling me that I need to come up to the UW and watch his workout so that I can learn how to help him do some of his exercises at home.

"Stacia says I have to work on my trunk, like, every day." He shows me. With his arms crossed over his chest and his gloved hands on his shoulders, he slowly leans forward over his own lap, then straightens up again.

"Is that hard to do?" I try it myself, feeling which muscles are working. Abs. Thank God he has abs.

"Yeah." He's bent over on his fourth one. "After it gets too easy, I'll have to hold a phone book against my chest and do it that way."

At home again, we get out the wedding album we've never bothered to assemble. It's still in pieces in its cream-colored box, just as the professional photographer handed it to us fifteen years ago. Emily spends a long time looking at the formal pictures of us on our wedding day—her own parents with their strange eighties haircuts, posed and smiling. We show her the pictures from the famous floating reception. It was a boat cruise around Lake Washington; the temperature that day was in the nineties, too.

There we are, out of our wedding clothes and into our bathing suits, feeding each other cake. I tell Emily about the toast her Uncle Paul made, and about how delighted her Grandpa Dave was when he realized we really did mean for the guests to dive off the boat if they felt like it. Bruce asks me if I remember the name of the boat.

Of course. "It was The Viking Dream," I say, and we smile.

Day 159

Heather's game is well underway by the time I get the minivan nudged into one of the three handicapped parking spaces. We're at the Northwest soccer fields in Bellingham, a hundred miles from home, and it's about a hundred degrees in the shade—or it would be if there were any shade. Emily is already complaining. I tell her to be grateful she doesn't have to play soccer. There are a dozen fields; hopefully the game will be in one close to the parking lot so I don't have to push the chair across a half a mile of grass. I'm standing behind the chair, watching while Bruce gets himself slowly out of the van. Feet out and onto the ground, lean over and set one hand on the seat ... he's okay. I turn away, shading my eyes to search for the team in red jerseys and black socks.

"Look at this."

He's half-standing. He's got himself braced against the car door, halfway to his feet. "Dude."

He looks down at himself for a long moment, then plops into the chair. "That's the first time I've believed it," he says. "That I'm actually going to be able to get on my feet." His eyes are bright. "It actually seems possible."

When we stop for dinner on the way home, he does it again, so Heather can see. Inside the restaurant, the hostess leads us to a table. Bruce looks longingly at a booth.

"Could we sit there?"

The waitress is confused. "Sure," she says.

283

Bruce drives himself over and sets his brakes. He pushes on the bench seat of the booth, which looks mighty low and spongy to me. He gives me a shrug. "What's the worst thing that can happen?"

You could fall on the floor. "Go for it." The girls are looking as if they want us to stop making a scene. He sets his arms, lifts his body off the seat cushion, and swings into the booth. Heather crawls under the table and up onto the seat next to him. Emily slides in across from them, and I take the wheelchair and roll it all the way across the room, next to a coat rack. It could belong to anybody.

In the booth, Bruce is slumped. His hands are in their black half-gloves. His hair is funky because it's so much trouble to shower. He's still ridiculously skinny. He's looking great.

Day 165: 4 am

We are in our bed. If you look down on us from above, you see him on the right, me on the left. He is facing me, propped up about forty degrees with a long green pillow—a pillow I tucked in behind him an hour ago. I gave him this body pillow for a long past birthday, but he never used it, and it became part of the family room things, kept there for company and TV watching. Now it's perfect for stuffing behind him.

At three, this is what happens. His CD alarm goes off. It's set to play the 7th track of Abraxas, a haunting melody called Samba Pa Ti. I like to picture Carlos Santana bent over his guitar, his strong fingers making this quiet music for us, for our private nighttime shadow play. I'm not aware of waking up, but somehow just moving with the first wistful bars. My job is to roll my husband from his back to his side and get the long pillow stuffed beneath him so that he doesn't roll back.

Without opening my eyes, I reach for the pillow where I've staged it on the floor next to me. I haul it up and then, kneeling over him, lay it along the edge of the bed. It is the perfect length; it goes from his shoulders to his knees. We don't speak, and I try to keep my eyes closed. Bruce is lying on a three-foot-square pad with a quilted top and a moisture-proof underside, made to protect our mattress in case of accidents. It also works well as a tool to help tip him. I reach across his body, roll up the edge of the pad, and grab it firmly with both hands. I am kneeling crosswise over his stomach. If his left arm is in the way, I lift it and set it across his chest.

I say, very softly, "Ready, go!" or "1-2-3," or, sometimes, if he seems to be sleeping, nothing at all. I pull hard on the pad so that he rolls toward me to face my thighs. I lean over and hold him there with one arm while I push the waiting pillow into the space behind his back, stuffing it hard at the shoulders and his butt, trying to do it smoothly and gently and firmly. Then I unroll the pad over the green pillow and let him fall back against it. I cover his upper body with the sheet and comforter.

Next I take an ordinary white pillow, also ready on the floor at my side of the bed, and place it lengthwise behind his legs. I lift his left leg and arrange the pillow between his knees, feeling in the dark for the catheter tube that leads to a two-liter plastic bag hooked over the end of our bed. I make sure the hose isn't caught on anything, then cover his legs and feet. With my eyes still closed, I feel around to be sure his toes aren't exposed. It's exactly like when the girls were infants, and I had to nurse them in the night. I would do it without opening my eyes in just this way, fighting to stay asleep.

Usually, I can't tell how much this process wakes him up. We're silent through the whole ritual, now so routine that I can easily finish it before the end of the song. I swing my legs over the bed and go in the dark to the bathroom. I turn off the music and climb back in next to him. "Okay?"

He says "Yeah, thank you." Sometimes his left hand comes across to find me, and we fall asleep again like that, his odd, silky fingers holding mine. Sometimes, like now, I'm awake in spite of my best efforts not to be, and I lie there thinking of my secret failures and worries.

I've lost my check card. What if someone has it and is using it to clean out our checking account? I haven't paid the bills, and it's the middle of the month. What if they cancel our health insurance? Why do my breasts hurt so much this month? What if I get cancer? I should schedule a mammogram. I need to go to the dentist. I don't want to; I hate going to the dentist. But there's a tiny brown spot on one of my front teeth, which looks like a stuck piece of food, but isn't. I need to go to the dentist.

I wonder where my check card is?

Sometimes I pray. I lie still and repeat: "In quietness and trust is my strength." until I feel myself go down into it, and once in a while I feel Jesus nearby—a steady change in the inner atmosphere, like an awareness that someone is awake with me. Beside me, Bruce breathes his quick, hard, uneven breaths—not the rhythm of sleep, and yet he is asleep, and then so am I.

Day 167

Harborview is still a rough place. Outside the ER, a black guy with a huge chest, massive arms and no legs at all sits smoking and talking with a skinny white guy dressed in the blue and white striped patient's pants and jacket. Inside, in the hall leading to radiology, a woman in a cheap sweater walks past us, crying. Bruce is here for his six-month-post X-Rays. We have to get them done here, then deliver them to the surgeon who operated on his neck last spring.

A man with some kind of mental disorder shouts for twenty minutes into a hospital phone mounted on the wall ten feet from where we sit in the radiology waiting room. It sounds as if there's no one on the other end of the line. It's early afternoon, and the ceiling-mounted televisions are playing soap operas. Half a dozen people are slumped in rows of chairs, ignoring the tube, and also ignoring the view of Elliott Bay behind them. The chairs are arranged to face a central desk area, where young women of various ethnicities answer phones and type at keyboards and look into computer monitors.

Bruce and I sit at the window, he in his chair facing the view, I leaning on the sill. There's a fire on one of the piers, behind the new Seahawks stadium. We can't see flames, but the smoke is impressive. After forty-five minutes, they take Bruce back to the X-ray rooms. Alone, I watch a medevac helicopter angle down onto one of the three landing pads just below. An ambulance backs up to the gate, lights flashing, and the driver gets out and leans against the back door.

For ten minutes, the helicopter crew moves mysteriously around, climbing half in, then back out, moving to the opposite side, bracing themselves and leaning hard through the doors. They wear bright blue jumpsuits. Everyone at Harborview is color-coded: the transport workers in dark green, the nurses in dusty blue, the cleaning crews in dark purple, the volunteers in pink. Just as the patient—a long white bundle with no visible face—is pulled on a stretcher from the helicopter, Bruce wheels silently up next to me. We watch as they slide the bundle into the waiting ambulance for the hundred-yard ride into the ER bay.

"Poor soul," he says.

We roll down the hall, out the ER doors, and across 9th Avenue. Dr. West's office is in an old three-story building two blocks away. I push the chair carefully down the broken sidewalk next to the parking lot where I had a space for most of the spring. Bruce holds the flat blue folder with his X-Rays in his lap and watches for bumps, of which there are plenty. It isn't raining, but everything is damp and cool.

Dr. West's office is on the third floor of a building that used to house lawyers—apparently not the super-rich kind. The offices are tiny, and the halls barely wide enough for the chair. The front entrance is locked for security, but when we are buzzed in, we find that we can't fit the chair through our half of the double door. A woman sitting just inside gets up to help, unhooking the high and low deadbolts on the locked half, then holding it so that Bruce's chair can get in over the sill.

Carpet. We're both thinking the same thing, and it's the same thing we thought three months ago, on our first experience here, when he was a brand new outpatient. Why would neurosurgeons choose to see their patients in a barely accessible building like this?

Our wait this time lasts an hour and a half. We read magazines, he the very same issue of Skiing that he read last time, though with less irony and more interest. I have a new Cosmo with a column about embarrassing "love moments." I laugh out loud and show him a woman's confession that she lost her gum in her partner's pubic hair, then left it there because she was too ashamed to tell him.

The nurse/receptionist takes us up a miniscule elevator, down a narrow hall, and into the room where we'll talk to the neurosurgeon. Dr. West is on the short side, and his presence in the room is somehow animal. I study him, trying to decide what gives me this impression, then decide that he is ultra-alert, like a predator. His eyes are wide behind glasses, his posture relaxed but very ready. Bruce sits in his wheelchair; I'm squeezed into a corner next to him. Dr. West leans against the high exam table that Bruce can't get on and asks the usual questions.

Sensation? Movement? Really. It's obvious that he's surprised, in spite of a carefully kept professional stance. He rolls up Bruce's pant legs and gets down to do the hot/cold sensation test himself. When he straightens up again, he's scratching his head a little. Bruce shows off his quads and his abs; they talk about Brown-Sequard Syndrome. Dr.

West shrugs, dismissive, and I know he doesn't think that's a sufficient answer.

This is the man whose hands were in Bruce's neck. He saw the cord itself. He picked out the broken shards of vertebrae. He can't explain why Bruce has any movement or sensation at all; according to the numbers, he shouldn't. Dr. West tells us finally that sometimes it just happens. Some people are off the charts, out of the statistical range. As we're getting ready to leave, he says that he wants to see a new set of X-rays in six months.

I smile at him. That will be in March. Bruce will be able to get out of the chair. "Then you'll see how tall he is," I say.

He gives me a look that says I shouldn't be so sure. I don't care. Before we leave, Bruce thanks him seriously for doing such a great job on his neck; Dr. West just keeps looking down at him as if he's trying to figure something out. Back in the car, we're both laughing.

They always say time changes things, but you actually
have to change them yourself.

Andy Warhol

TWENTY-ONE

Day 170

"You really think I could do it?"

"Of course." We're in our room, doing the nightly range of motion. He's flat on his back, and I'm holding his right knee up against his chest and counting slowly to twenty. "Once you lose the catheter, the only thing you need help with is your socks." I bring his thigh to a ninety degree angle from his body, then slowly straighten his leg so that his foot is high in the air.

"You could go a little further with that."

"Like this?" I push his leg past ninety degrees, he nods, and I start the count in my head. Bruce is thinking about whether or not it's possible to go to Peoria, Illinois next month. A friend of his from Vermont College is the director of the Peoria Arts Guild, and she's putting together a fair. When she asked him in July if he could come up with a video projection piece, he told her he didn't think he'd be able to travel. Now, it seems possible. Maybe possible.

"I'd have to call her and describe exactly what help I need." He sighs with pleasure as I bend his leg again, this time to stretch his hip muscles.

"I love it when I do something that makes you go 'ahhhh'."

"It just feels so good." He closes his eyes and says again, "You really think I could do it?"

"You went to Paris alone. You went to Budapest. London, lots of times. This is Peoria. Of course you can do it. You need a driver, and somebody to put your socks on your feet. The only real problem is this." I release his leg, lay it out flat, and touch the Foley tube.

He sighs. "I guess it's the motivation I need to finally get rid of it."

"Then that's a good thing. You should do it."

"I'll call tomorrow. And make an appointment to practice peeing."

I restrain myself from dancing around the room. No more leg bags!

Day 173

This is my day to learn the new physical therapy routines. We're up in the gym on the eighth floor of the UW Medical Center, and Stacia is using a Velcro strap to fasten a three-pound weight to Bruce's left ankle. Lying flat on his half of the big square mat with his right leg straight, he slides his left heel towards himself so that his knee rises slowly upward. He's got his eyes closed and it's obvious that this is hard work, but he can do it. A full set of fifteen, and then same movement on the right side, this time with no weight attached. Even without the extra weight, his right leg couldn't do this without her two hands helping him, one to slide his foot back and the other to keep his knee from flopping over. I ask how much she's pushing.

She looks over one shoulder at me. "I'm doing most of the work on this side, but it's still important to do all the reps."

She makes conversation as they go. Is our daughter still playing soccer? Yes. How's her team doing? Great, they're a fierce group. What does she play? Outside mid. Is she fast? Very. Okay, done with two sets of fifteen knee lifts. Now, still lying flat, he slides his straight left leg out and then brings it back. Again, it's hard work, but do-able. On the right side, Stacia pulls his leg out and he drags it back in. For the second set of fifteen, she reduces the three-pound weight to two pounds. He's getting tired, but he's determined. His whole trunk from hips to shoulders is rigid with the effort.

"Nice job," is Stacia's comment, delivered briskly. Two sets.

Then he tries a straight leg raise, with her hand under his left heel and his knee straight. No weights. With her help, he lifts his foot about eighteen inches into the air, then slowly lowers it.

"Not bad," she says. "You're going to be one of our first customers for the LiteGait."

I move around so I can see her face. "The what?"

"It's a machine that will hold his weight suspended over a treadmill, so that he can practice walking without having to worry about falling or even bearing his own weight."

Bruce finishes his fifteenth rep and gasps.

She tells him to take a break and goes on. "This is new—a therapy they've been experimenting with in Germany. Apparently it works even for some folks who don't have as much return as what you have. I think it's going to be really good for you—you and lots of other people." She tells us that the majority of people she sees now are "incomplete," meaning they have at least partial return of sensation or movement.

"Why is that?"

"MP," says Bruce.

Stacia nods. "Methylprednisolone. It's a steroid they started giving people about ten years ago. Before that, almost everybody was pretty complete, and there wasn't all that much we could do. Now, the majority of people have at least something to work with."

"I got it," Bruce says. Stacia is lifting his knees and setting herself up to hold them upright together while he tries some crunches. She calls a helper over to hold his head, directing him to fold his hands across chest and just concentrate on lifting his shoulders off the mat.

"You got the steroid?" I say. This is the first I've heard of it.

"He got it in the helicopter," Stacia says. "I read his chart. Do these in sets of ten, three if you can." She watches him critically. His shoulders lift a bare inch, and he's grimacing with the effort. She asks a second helper to hold his knees up so she can lay a hand on his belly to feel his abs working. She smiles at him, congratulatory. "You got abs," she says. "Upper and lower. Two sets of ten of these, every other day." She looks back at me. "They have to give the MP in the first few hours. It stops the soft tissue around the cord from swelling up and doing more damage to the nerve cells."

Now she sets a padded wedge under his knees. With the three-pound weight strapped on again, he lifts his left foot into the air. His body goes tense with every exertion, his wrists curling back as if they could help pull his foot up.

"Think you can do anything on the other side?" Stacia is merciless.

"I'll try," he says.

We all get excited to see his right foot lift itself away from the wedge. "Two sets of fifteen," she says. "You need those hip extensors to hold you up when you're standing." She glances at me, sly. "They're also the muscles that make the hips move forward."

Like to pump. "Oh, those," I say. "Work those, dear. You're gonna need 'em."

Stacia laughs, but Bruce, teeth gritted, ignores me. He makes it all the way through the second set of fifteen.

Last is the NuStep, which is a seat mounted on a little white stand. There are long levers like gearshifts, and a pair of pedals. His job is to work the pedals so that his feet go up and down like on a seated stair-stepper. He uses the arm levers to help out the feet, in an opposing motion that looks vaguely like cross-country skiing. He loves this machine, I can see right away. He has to have his limp right hand strapped to its lever. He has to be buckled in, and someone has to stand by in case he starts to fall off. It's real exercise, though—it's his whole body engaged in something, all his limbs moving under their own power. I could watch him do this for hours.

That night at home, he gets on the phone and calls his friend in Peoria. Yes, he'll be there for the fair. He'll buy the tickets tomorrow.

Day 178

I'm getting nervous. Last week, I sent a secret broadcast to the Great Big List inviting anybody who felt like making an appearance to come help us celebrate Bruce's birthday. This means we're about to have a party without any idea how many people to expect. The girls and I have made him a banana cream pie; as far as he knows, eating that is going to be the extent of this year's celebration. He's parked in front of the computer, looking a little weary. I walk over and stand where he can see me, next to the lift.

"Uh, Bruce dear." When he and I use this phrasing, it usually means we're about to say something the other one doesn't necessarily want to hear. (Kate dear, you left the house unlocked again ... Bruce dear, you forgot to pay the mortgage.)

He looks up at me, wary. His eyes are droopy, and he needs a shower. I should have warned him earlier. "Yeah?"

"There's a possibility that we might be having some company tonight." Suddenly I feel completely happy. I've surprised him!

He's smiling a little. "Really."

I explain about the broadcast. "So, basically, I've invited a couple of hundred people ... but I don't have a clue who's going to show up."

"Okaaay." He backs away from the desk and navigates his way around me. "Guess I better get presentable."

Two hours later, the house is full of people—or rather, the kitchen is full of people. This happens every time we have a party; no matter what I do to make the rest of the house inviting, we all end up crammed into the kitchen. Bruce is in his chair, so surrounded by our friends that he can't move. Both the butcher block counter and the table are loaded with food they've brought, and the noise level is ridiculous.

It's completely wonderful.

Day 188: September 11th, 2001

My morning routine begins at night. The last thing I do before going up to bed is make myself a thermos of strong coffee. When the alarm goes off, I take it with me into the shower, along with my radio. The radio is tuned to the local NPR station so I can catch the Morning Edition while I shower and down my first cup. I'm standing under the water, listening to Scott Simon say that—it's unbelievable, but—the twin towers are—just gone.

I think it's some kind of hoax, but right after that he says that another plane has apparently crashed into the Pentagon. Someone has crashed an airplane into the Pentagon? And the World Trade Center is gone? I shout for Bruce to wake up and turn on his radio. I dry myself, throw on a bathrobe, and go down to the kitchen, where the girls are eating their cereal. I tune the television to CNN, and there it is. An airplane heads straight at the slender black tower and erupts into flame. The girls put their hands to their mouths, and so do I.

It happens that this is the day he is scheduled to lose the Foley catheter. A friend will pick him up at our house and take him to Harborview, and I'll meet him there after my classes. I put his socks on his feet, hook up the leg bag for the last time, find him some clothes, and rush off to drive the carpool. My students, I can see, don't yet understand that this is a day they will remember all their lives. We don't get a lot of math done.

The hospital is under heavy guard. There's a security checkpoint at the main entrance; I stand in line with everyone else to wait while they go through my bag. I have to tell them why I'm here, and they have to call upstairs to make sure I'm legitimate. Harborview is a trauma center; they're trying to be prepared for God knows what. Inside, it's much quieter than usual.

Upstairs in an outpatient rehab room, Bruce is sitting in his chair, drinking glass after glass of water. The Foley is out, and now he's going to fill his bladder and see if, by some miracle, he can empty it in the usual way. His nurse, Cathy, keeps coming in and out of the room to see what's happening. He's got a jug between his legs, ready to go.

"Do you feel like you're full?"

"Oh, yeah." Good. It's good that he can feel it. That was my first worry.

She quirks her mouth. "Couple more minutes, okay? Here, maybe this will help." She walks over to the little hand-washing sink and turns on the water.

Bruce closes his eyes to concentrate, and I say "psssssssssss." Two minutes pass. Nothing. Shit. Cathy turns off the water and gets out a pair of disposable gloves. The new system will involve a narrow, flexible hose about sixteen inches long. Its color is deep, dusty pink, and it's about the thickness of an ordinary electrical cord. Cathy shows him how to apply some numbing lubricant, and then she watches him slide the narrow end of the hose slowly into himself. In a few seconds, the plastic jug between his legs starts to fill. When it seems to be done, he pulls out the hose, and she takes it from him and drops it in the trash. He looks a little green.

She lifts the jug from his lap and holds it up to see how much there was. "Six hundred and fifty milliliters. That's a lot fuller than you want to be. A person will usually start to feel the need to go at, oh, about three or four hundred." She explains that if he doesn't do this to himself every few hours, his bladder will overfill and either leak out onto his clothes or back up into his kidneys. Terrific.

"What about at night?" He's fastening his pants.

"Then, too. A lot of people do it once, whenever they turn over, and that seems to be enough. Depends on how much you drink, and when." She recommends he cath at 11 pm, 3 am, and 7 am. Also, every afternoon he should put his feet up for an hour or so; it will keep fluids from pooling in his feet. She hands me a stack of hoses, each one wrapped in its own cellophane package. "The package says not to re-use these, but they're kind of expensive, so you'll probably want to. Here's instructions—be careful how you wash them if you don't want to keep getting urinary tract infections." Tell it to Bruce, I think, taking the paper from her. He's going to wash them, not me. Cathy points to the number we should call when he needs more.

I ask him if it hurt.

"No," he says. "It's a little weird, but it doesn't hurt."

Cathy says that for most people, it's not a big deal at all. She tells us about how casually some guys treat their catheters. "I had one guy come in here with it folded over and tucked inside his sock. I was like, get a lot of urinary tract infections?" She shakes her head.

I'm trying to be patient with this conversation, but all I really want to do now is get the hell out of the hospital. Everyone here is nonchalantly certain that the disabilities he has at any given moment are permanent. "We're going to measure you today for your permanent wheelchair ... your right hand is paralyzed because of damage to your cord; it will never move again ... I just think he's always going to have a lot of spasticity ... you'll never be symmetrical again ... you'll need to order a lot of these catheters because your bladder is never going to work normally again ... I was thinking he goes home a complete quad."

I know these comments are based on the experience of years and years, and I know these people are trying to help us deal with what's in front of us now. I also know that, at least in Bruce's case, they've been wrong again and again. His blessed, stubborn body is still changing. Every hour of his life is an exercise in persistence; every hour of mine is a labor of faith. I push him out of the hospital, wondering when the day will come that we have to admit that now, finally, he's really done, and, until there is a cure, he's not ever going to get any better. We roll past the security checkpoints and head for home.

Day 201

Driving down our street after school, I'm always anxious. Bruce is never up when I leave the house; usually he's not even awake. What if he's fallen trying to get into his chair? What if I walk in and find him with a broken arm or something, lying on the hardwood floor, unable to move himself? What if he's hit his head? So far, he's always fine. Today, I find him parked in front of the computer next to the lift, laughing.

"These guys are hilarious," he says. "I asked them what I should know about flying, and look." He backs up the wheelchair so I can see the screen.

"Is this that spinal cord injury site?" Bruce has been spending a lot of time at this desk, logged onto something called CareCure.

On the screen is his question: "This coming week I'm taking my first airline flight since becoming wheel-chair bound ... I'm wondering if any of you have any words of advice." He shows me how to scroll through the answers. One guy says that he often gets upgraded to first class. He describes how airline employees will get Bruce into his seat, and recommends that he use his chair cushion if the flight is long. Further down, someone else jumps in with a question of his own.

"How do you handle your cath problems while you're in flight?

The reply to this post is what Bruce was laughing at. "Some guys put a blanket over themselves—not very inconspicuous—but still keeps people from seeing ya wrestling the one-eyed snake. They'll probably assume you're jerkin' off, but oh well."

"Wrestling the one-eyed snake," I say appreciatively. "That is good. Who are these guys?"

"People with spinal cord injuries. This is Dr. Wise Young's site."

"The guy who was in Time?" Bruce's dad sent him an article about a spinal cord injury scientist; I haven't read it yet.

"Yeah." I move aside, and Bruce wheels back into place and starts clicking through some screens. He twists his head to look at me. "He's the one who did the research on that steroid they gave me. MP."

"Really." I remember Stacia telling us that most of the injuries she sees now are incomplete because of MP. "So, what do you mean, it's his site? Does he write to people on it?"

"All the time. Look, there's a forum for you ... you won't like the name, though." He's moved to a page titled, "Caregivers."

I make a face. We've had this conversation before. I'm not a caregiver. I'm married to a temporarily disabled guy; that's my attitude. I'm a partner, up against a particular face of this monster, but I'm definitely not a caregiver. If I were, it would mean something about Bruce—something we both still refuse to accept.

"What else is on here?"

He shows me. He put up his question on a forum called "Life." He scrolls to "Care" and "Pain," and another called "Cure."

"Whoa, there." I put my hand on the mouse. "Cure?"

On the "Cure" pages, he moves the mouse through a list of topics. "Australia Neuroscience Conference, Neuroimmunophilin Ligand Program, Fibrous Adhesions," I read out loud. "Good grief."

"They're working on it, though" he says. "There's some good stuff here."

I see that many of the topics have been put up by Wise Young himself. "Do they have a timeline? For a cure?"

Bruce says that he's just getting started reading it, but from what he can tell, they're still a ways off.

"Years?"

He shrugs. "Maybe. They have a lot of leads, and it's complicated. Plus, no stem cell research, at least here."

Bruce is only forty-six. "You'll still have a lot of skiing left in you."

"We'll see."

Day 203

For days, rain has been pounding down in sheets. This morning there was water coming through the light fixtures in the kitchen ceiling. The roof is leaking. Bruce and I saw it just as we were leaving for his physical therapy session.

"I thought you were going to call a roofer." He was going to call a roofer last year. He was going to call a roofer all summer. He ought to be able to make a damn phone call, but he didn't, and now our roof is leaking. Our ceiling is going to fall in under all this fucking rain, and then I'm going to have to clean up the mess.

"I will."

"When?" I pull onto the freeway again.

"What is your problem?" He's pissed. He's pissed?

"My problem," I say through my teeth, "is you didn't call somebody to fix the roof. And it's pouring and I don't want the ceiling to fall in."

"The ceiling isn't going to fall in. I'll call them later."

After I drop him at the UW, I drive on to see my therapist, where I rage for ten straight minutes about the injustice of having to do everything, including find somebody to fix the roof.

Michael isn't sympathetic at all. "What would happen if you didn't?"

Has he not been listening? Does he not get the picture? "If the ceiling falls in, it will cost a lot to fix, and I'll have another big mess to clean up."

"Why will you have to clean it up?" He's sitting there in his hundred-dollar sweater, not evenly remotely getting it.

"Because Bruce can't." Dummy.

"He could find someone else to help him."

I think about this. "I suppose he could. But it would be all over my kitchen. I'd have to live with it."

"Then you have to decide which you'd rather do: keep being mad because you think you have to do everything, or find out what happens if you don't."

Michael really does enjoy this. His smile is eight inches wide, but his eyes are dead serious. Take up the work of your life, says the room. Not the work of someone else's life. Okay, I'll try.

And yet. It's now six-thirty on Wednesday night, and we have to go to choir. I'm sick and tired of sitting in the messy, stop-and-go traffic, but I'm still the only driver. I have to keep taking all of them wherever they have to go. Just before we head out the door to choir, Bruce says he wants to come along. Dear God.

Okay. Now that he uses the dark pink hoses, he has to be careful not to leave the house without emptying his bladder. I push him onto the lift so he can go upstairs and use our bathroom; it's the only one in the house he can get into. Then we wait. The girls are going to be late. It's already dark, and I'm irritated all over again. I'm sick of being late. I don't want to drive anywhere. Ever since school started, all I've done is drive. I want to stay home, all alone, and let him drive. I don't want to take Heather to a therapist, ever again. I don't want to feel like a single parent who is overstressed and unable to cope. I'm sick of this, already. When he comes down on the lift, I wait silently while he gets into the car. I take the chair apart and stash the pieces in the trunk, then put the frame in the back seat.

Heather gives it a shove. "Move over, Jack." Jack is our name for the chair. He rides between the girls, who stare out their windows while I steer us out of the neighborhood one more time. At church, Emily and Heather run into the building. I park the car, assemble the chair, and push him up the long ramp from the parking garage. We go into the sanctuary, where we are alone, and suddenly it's all right. The quiet soothes me, and the rage in my head dies away. After awhile, I can even see how much Bruce needed to be here.

The NIH tried to compromise and developed the
consensus of obtaining stem cells from fertilized eggs
from fertility clinics. These are eggs ... that would be
thrown away. This consensus was reached after
extensive discussions and participation by consumers,
religious leaders, philosophers and ethicists. That
solution turned out to be unacceptable.

Dr. Wise Young

TWENTY-TWO

Day 207

Bruce is in Peoria. He's calling me on the phone from Peoria, Illinois, and his voice is full of life and excitement. I can't believe it; he sounds exactly like he always has. He sounds like he has not sounded since March 6th, when he kissed me goodbye before going to take Heather skiing. Yesterday morning, I left him at the new security checkpoint at the airport. He had to let them go over his whole wheelchair with the wand. He had checked a duffel bag full of whatever we guessed he couldn't do without, and he had supplies of pills and catheters in his carry on. I stood in the terminal watching him wheel himself away, praying that he could pull this off.

And now he has. He's telling me about his evening. He went downtown to project his famous blue eye on the federal building in Peoria. It's white, he says happily, a perfect site. The blue eye was looking good, huge, about thirty feet wide. The eye is actually Bruce's— it's an image of his own eye in extreme close-up, which looks wonderfully strange when projected, giant-size, on the side of a building.

"So, across the street there's this strip joint called 'Big Al's'—"

"Big Al's?" What a great name.

"Yeah, and so apparently some drunk in there saw the eye and called the cops." He sounds so happy.

"Did they come and bust you?" I'm standing by the sink, looking at my own reflection in the window. I can't get over how much he sounds like his old self.

"Well, this policewoman did come and talk to me. I convinced her I was harmless—"

"A crackpot, but harmless—"

"Exactly. And so after about ten minutes, she went across to Big Al's to tell them I wasn't some crazy terrorist with a projector."

"Just a crazy person with a projector."

"It was so cool."

I really could listen to this happy voice all night long. I tell him that hearing him right now is like being sent suddenly back to before the accident. "You sound like you used to."

"I feel like I used to."

"And everything else is okay?"

"It's fine. Everything has worked out fine."

"Except you scared the bejeezus out of some poor drunk."

"Big Al's," he says. "That was so cool."

Day 212

I astonish myself. I am, it turns out, still capable of feeling mortified by the "flaws" in my own body. I still worry about whether my thighs are acceptable; I still stress over what the magazines call "problem areas." Bruce is still required to reassure me about my desirability and worthiness as a partner. The irony of this does not lessen its power one bit. Even in bed with my underweight, partially functioning, beloved husband, I can locate a specific place in my head that is hoping he hasn't noticed all the things that are wrong with me.

Day 227

I am doing what Bruce cannot: taking a break from all of it. A lot of my friends from church are on the Kitsap Peninsula this weekend for the women's retreat; they assumed I would want to come and wanted to help me get there, but no. I wasn't even tempted. The last thing I want is to be among people who know me. I have no desire to talk to anyone about anything. The country has been at war in Afghanistan for the last two weeks. I don't want to discuss it. People are getting poisoned with anthrax, delivered in their mail. I have nothing to say. I spent last night, silent, in downtown Seattle at the Pioneer Square Hotel, and I'll be there again tonight. I'm on a Kate Retreat.

Until tomorrow, I'm not looking out for anyone, not anticipating anyone's needs, not having to know who is unhappy. I'm not driving anywhere. I'm in a restaurant right now, eating a green salad very slowly. There is a television on one table, tuned to Game 3 of the American League Championship Series. The Mariners are playing the Yankees, looking for their first trip to the world series. I've slipped through a hole into the normal world.

This is what Bruce can't do. He can't ever get out of his body. He goes to sleep in it, wakes up in it, struggles every minute to find some tiny new improvement.

In physical therapy now, he stands in the parallel bars. He has to be lifted to his feet. He has to support his weight with his arms, and he needs two trained helpers to stand by in case he crumples. Stacia called it exactly right—by the end of this month he will be able to take a few steps. They've measured him for a custom-fit, full-length leg brace, which will keep his right leg from collapsing when he tries to put weight on it. He should have it in December.

The Mariners have won, 14-3, but it isn't looking good. They finished the regular season with a record 116 wins, but something happened to them after September 11th. They aren't the same team; the air has gone out of them. I pay for my food and step out, anonymous, into the cool, damp sidewalks of downtown Seattle. It's an easy walk back to the hotel. My tiny single room is on the third floor of this funky old brick building. My bed is wide and comfortable; I lie on my back, listening to the traffic and thinking of nothing.

Day 235

We're getting good at figuring out how to get Bruce in and out of places that shouldn't be accessible. Our friends Christine and Dale have invited us to dinner; they have a back door with no steps, but it isn't wide enough for the wheelchair. After scratching our heads for a few minutes, we set up a straight-backed chair just outside the door. He transfers himself onto that, and I take the wheelchair apart and pass the pieces into the house. I climb over him, go in the house, and assemble the chair again. I angle it in the doorway, close to the edge of the chair he's on, and he lifts himself across the gap. He's in.

Dinner is lasagna. The girls and I tell the story, rolling our eyes, about how much lasagna we got last spring when people first started bringing us meals. Christine's lasagna is delicious, and it's delicious to be eating it with these kind, interesting people. I sip red wine and wonder what it is about their attitude that makes his disability irrelevant.

They're not afraid to talk about it, and they don't pity us, but it's more than that. They act as if we've moved into a new house with a variety of knotty but fixable problems—and as if the house and its problems are beside the point. The fact that it's us in the house is what matters to them. At their dining room table, I remember who we are. After dessert, when someone puts on the old Led Zeppelin recording of "Stairway to Heaven," I get up and dance, alone, in the darkened living room.

Day 237

The sauna at our local pool is one of my favorite places, but for months I've been afraid to come here. All last year, Bruce and I used this wooden room as a kind of untangling space; whenever we needed to be alone together, we would come here. He would sit against that wall, facing me and rubbing my feet. We would stay in as long as we could take the heat, then go outside to sit together on a painted red bench, our skin steaming in the cool, damp air. Bruce was better at the sauna than I was; by the end of a session, I'd be down on the floor staying cool while he still sat on the highest bench, saying "ahhhh." We came here on the sixth of March, the night before the accident, and I haven't been back since.

In this room, I can remember what he used to be like because in here, I've only seen him well. Do I have to give up saunas because his body can't sweat anymore? Do I want to find a way to do this alone? I'm trying. I'm here, and the dry heat still feels so good. I miss him. I miss him.

I'm sitting in the wheelchair. The gel-filled seat cushion is too long for my thighs, and my feet dangle several inches above the little shelf where his feet sit. The chair back is vertical; it reaches exactly to my waistline. I navigate the doorway into the kitchen, turn awkwardly and open the refrigerator. I can't reach anything in the back of the shelves, and I can't even see what's in the freezer. I push myself carefully around the room, trying to imagine how it would feel to know that I couldn't stand up.

Day 242

Heather and I are sitting side by side in the second row of chairs at the front of the sanctuary. We're sleepy because last night we had our first singing party since last winter, and it was midnight before everyone went home. The singing party goes like this: we send an open invitation to as many people as we can think of. We encourage them to bring instruments, music, friends, kids, grandparents, whatever. We don't know or care who will come, but someone always does. Once we had twice as many people as could fit into the living room; another time only a few families could make it.

Last night was a medium-sized party. Jocelyn came with her husband and their twin boys. Bill made it a point to look over his ramp handiwork before going up to play his mouth organ. Five or six of the kids from my youth group took over the kitchen table during the potluck part of the evening, and when it was time to sing, they managed to look comfortable lolling on the hardwood floor. Stan's fingers still remembered all the Beatle songs, and later Bruce, sitting in his wheelchair, played the sweet blue hell out of his harmonica while I sang Dylan's "You Ain't Goin' Nowhere."

Right now, many of the people who were at last night's party are facing us from the tiered seating area that belongs to the choir. Bruce's rightful place is up in the back, with the basses, but he can't get to that row. He's sitting instead in the center of the women, with the altos to his right and the sopranos to his left. The robes are multicolored, in a blue-purple-green palette. Bruce's robe is lavender; they had to have it specially made because he is so much taller than everyone else. He has a music stand in front of his wheelchair. I'm hoping this won't be one of the times he falls asleep when the sermon starts.

Tony has just returned from a six-month-long sabbatical leave, which means that I've scarcely seen him since the night of the accident. His last pastoral duty before he started his vacation was to stop in to say hello to Bruce, way back in rehab. He's talking now about September 11th.

"I honor the human impulse and courage of a 'return to normal'. And yet I know, as you do, that we cannot really return to normal. We cannot go back to September 10th."

Heather, who has been leaning against my shoulder and letting me play with her fingers, pulls my collar so she can whisper in my ear. "We can't go back to March 6th," she says.

We exchange a look. "I know," I say. I've been nauseated for weeks, listening to people in Seattle talk about how dramatically their whole lives have been changed. For most of them, it's simply not true. Their lives haven't changed. They don't even know what that means. Heather's weight against me is a sort of anchor; I come back to the sermon. Tony is saying that our sense of invincibility and invulnerability has been shattered. He goes on in this vein for a few minutes. He's saying that we've entered a torn place—a season of hurt and anguish.

"This is not an easy place to be," he tells us. "But most who have been in these places later report that it was also a holy place, a transforming place."

She shifts against me again, and whispers, "Before Daddy's accident I wouldn't have known what he's talking about." I whisper back that I sometimes think our family got, like, a six-month head start on everybody else in America. She thinks this over, then asks if I think that was a good thing or a bad thing.

Tony has finished the sermon and gone back to his seat beside the lectern. The choir rises as one to stand, except for Bruce, stranded in his chair. "I don't know," I tell her. "It's just what we got."

Day 247

Our friend Kathy pulls in with Bruce in the front seat of her car, fresh from rehab. I've been watching for them; most of the people who give him rides in the daytime are women, and they tend to have trouble with the wheelchair assembly. Kathy probably needs to hurry, anyway. She lives all the way out on the far end of Bainbridge Island. This trip already took up most of her afternoon, and she still has to drive back to Seattle, get in line for the ferry, and make her way home.

She's cheerful and warm, a brisk, elegant woman with clear brown eyes and an easy smile. When Bruce is back in his chair, he looks up and thanks her for the ride. She brushes him off, saying that it's a privilege to be allowed to help. A lot of our friends use language like this, as if our predicament has given them something they didn't know they wanted.

Bruce tugs at my arm. "Hey. I took ten steps today," he says quietly.

"You did? In the parallel bars?"

He nods. "Most of my weight was on my legs, too." As usual, his restraint requires me to be casual. I also know that taking ten measly steps after four months of PT torture is only a kind of checkpoint—not the victory he's working toward and waiting for. Still ... the day is going to come when I can look up at him. I say goodbye to Kathy, who gives me a quick hug.

"It's so good to see you smiling," she says.

It's good to be smiling—in a casual, Norwegian, restrained way, of course.

Day 258

Bruce has successfully navigated the labyrinth of bureaucracies that stood in the way of his ability to drive our van. The first problem was that he no longer had a valid driver's license; it expired on his birthday a couple of months ago. The second problem was that without a license, he couldn't legally take the expensive specialized training required by the state to get a restricted license. The third problem was to find out whether it was possible to have adaptive equipment installed in our van, and if so, who was qualified to do the work. The fourth problem was to get a doctor to recommend him for the expensive specialized training, once he had convinced the driver's license people to issue him a special, limited learner's permit.

A week from today, he's finally going to get the expensive specialized training. The week after that, "Rich's Mobility Service" is going to put hand controls into our old minivan. Once that's done and he's practiced a bit, he can go back to the driver's license people and take a road test. Then, Bruce will be street legal. There is still one more hurdle, though. The whole point of driving is to be able to go places all alone, which means he has to figure out how to load and unload the wheelchair by himself. He still can't stand up without trained assistants, so he has to be able to deal with the chair while seated in the van, using only his left hand.

This is why I'm standing in our driveway in the gathering dark, holding an umbrella. Bruce has decided he's going to solve this one now, tonight, and he doesn't care how long it takes. He has transferred himself into the driver's seat, and is sitting behind the wheel for the first time in more than eight months. I'm shivering, trying to keep the wheelchair dry. The umbrella isn't big enough to cover both me and the chair, so my back is getting wet. I'm also wishing I'd thought to put some gloves on. Bruce, on the other hand, has apparently recovered his famous ability to ignore cold. He hooks his right arm through the gap in the steering wheel and leans over. He grabs the strap at the front of the seat cushion and rips its Velcro fastener free, then pulls the cushion into the van and sets it on the floor in front of the passenger seat.

The seat back is next; pulling a cord strung behind it will release the catch that holds it upright. Still keeping his right arm threaded through the steering wheel, Bruce reaches out and muscles the chair around to feel for the cord. The seat back flops neatly forward. Now the job is to remove the wheels. In the center of each wheel is a metal disc which, when pushed in, frees the wheel from the frame of the chair.

"You have to unlock the brakes first," I say. It's very hard not to reach over and push the chair frame into a better position for him, and not only because I want him to hurry up so I can go inside and get warm. It's the same complicated feeling I have when I watch him struggle with any other task: a twist of impatience, pride, sadness, fury, and love.

"Thank you." He flicks up the lock and takes off one wheel. The frame on that side makes a dull clunk as the chair tips over and hits the driveway. He hauls the wheel up over his lap and sets it behind the passenger seat. When the other wheel is off and in the van, it's time for the hard part. The frame of the chair does not collapse; it's a roughly rectangular box made of welded aluminum pipes, and it weighs about thirty pounds. How the hell is he going to lift this bulky thing up into his lap? And if he somehow manages to get it up there, will there be room to pass it over between his body and the steering wheel?

Bruce doesn't know, either. Grunting with effort, he tries three different tacks, and each time has to stop and lower it back down again.

"Can I just help you lift it so we can see if there's even room to get it through?"

He's taking a break. He answers me with his forehead resting against the top of the steering wheel. "Yeah. Just give me a minute."

We try for ten minutes before we hit just the right orientation. The driver's seat in the van has to be all the way back, and its back has to be all the way lowered. The wheelie bars on the chair have to be turned inward. The steering wheel has to be adjusted all the way down. The frame has to go in front first, and when all is adjusted just so and Bruce is leaning back as far as he can, it will fit.

He's got the frame in his lap. He's painfully inching it past his nose, using what grip he's got in his right hand to settle it, finally, into the passenger seat.

"Yay." So, it can be done.

He looks at me. "Now I have to put it back together."

Jesus Christ! It's going to be another forty-five minutes before I can go in and start dinner. Okay. I settle myself down. He has to be able to drive. He has to be able to go places alone whenever he wants. He's got the frame back out of the van, and he's struggling to find the hole where the long bolt on the wheel has to go. It's raining harder and there's enough wind to move the leaves around in the front yard. I have a sudden strong sense of déja vu; where have I seen this before?

I stamp my feet to get some feeling back in my toes, and it comes to me. This is how it was when Bruce was trying to get the four of us organized to go night skiing. Cold, usually raining, and dark. Our driveway the scene of his absolutely mulish determination toward the goal—then, to get us and all our scattered gear collected and up to the mountains. Now, to load and unload the goddamned chair. Cold, wet, and physical misery are irrelevant. It used to take him two hours to find all the skis, poles, boots, neck-gators, gloves, ski socks, hats, passes, goggles, jackets, snow pants, and long underwear. He usually had to throw at least one fit along the way. I used to wonder if it was really worth it—all that effort just for a few hours on skis. I watch him lower himself, at last, out of the driver's seat and into the chair, and sure enough. The look of perverse satisfaction on his face is utterly familiar. He's still the same man.

In 1995, Werner, et al in Germany reported that they were able to restore functional locomotion in as many as 40% of people who had never walked after spinal cord injury. They did this by intensive locomotor training by placing people in harness supports and walking them for hours on treadmills. ... this approach was initially greeted with skepticism by many people ...

Dr. Wise Young

TWENTY-THREE

Day 272

We're breaking the law—well, Bruce is breaking the law. He's three cars ahead of me, heading south on the interstate in pouring rain. He's driving our creaky old Dodge Caravan at sixty miles an hour, in rush hour traffic, and he doesn't have a license. His wheelchair is in the back of the van, where I tossed it twenty minutes ago. His left hand is doing all the tricky work. The guys at Rich's New Mobility have installed a mechanical attachment to the brake and gas pedals; the business end looks like the grip on a bicycle handle. Conveniently positioned just above his left knee when he's in the driver's seat, this gizmo makes his numb right foot irrelevant. Pushing it forward steps on the brakes, and pushing it down works the gas. His right hand is set into a tri-pin mounted on the steering wheel, which makes it possible to steer even without the finger strength needed to hold the wheel.

I follow his tail lights through sheets of rain and tell myself that if anybody could do this, it's him. I go over and over his flawless record of strange and dangerous driving. I've seen him get off a ten-hour airplane ride and drive a rental car through London, unfazed by the clotted streets, the strange traffic signals, or the backwards flow of traffic. I've seen him make his way through Ireland, not even bothered when the road signs were suddenly all in Gaelic. I've ridden beside him down the steep canyon road from Snowbird, Utah in a whiteout storm. I've trusted him to drive when one of our infant daughters was screaming loud enough to erase normal adult thought patterns.

Bruce can do this. He can get himself home with these hand controls, and he does. My temporary stint as the only driver in the family is officially ended. I am only shaking a little when we get home and I pull into my space in the garage.

Day 274

Emily and Heather are not sure whether to be anxious along with me or make fun of me. Bruce has gone to choir practice alone, and we have done our old Thursday night girl-world thing. They've finished their homework, and I've cleaned the kitchen. We've had ice cream and watched the latest poor sod get booted off "Survivor." Now it's time for him to be home, but he isn't here. I'm walking around the house like Rocky does when he needs to get out; I put my hands in the pockets of my jeans to keep from wringing them.

"Chill, Mom," Emily says. "You're making me nervous."

I glance at the clock again. Ten twelve, two minutes later than the last time I looked. "Well," I say, talking super fast to make her laugh. "I just think it's really rude of him not to come right back. Doesn't he know I'm going to worry? Huh? Of course he does, but is he concerned about my feelings? I don't think so. He's just down there going la-la-la, probably hanging around talking with his choir friends, who, by the way, I think are also behaving quite badly. Why haven't they sent him off? Have they no concern for my poor nerves? Wait, is that him?" We all look as a pair of headlights appears far away up the street.

"No," Emily says. "The van's headlights aren't shaped like that."

"Well, I think that's a design flaw. Why wouldn't they be shaped like that? It's a perfectly nice shape." The perfectly nice headlights round the curve in front of our house and vanish.

"Mom, wait, are you joking?" Heather has a tight look around her mouth.

I roll my eyes. "Totally. You know how he is when he gets talking." But I give myself away by glancing again at the clock.

She takes a step toward me. "Should he be here by now?"

Nice going, Kate. Scare the kids. "He has his phone, remember? If anything happened, he has his phone. He'd call us."

"But what if he couldn't?"

Emily has caught the bug, too. "I think that's him." We're all standing in front of the sink, looking out at another pair of headlights. "That is him."

"Daddy!"

It's embarrassing how relieved I am. I follow them outside to welcome him back from his first solo trip.

Day 283

"You can do it."

"Mom——"

"Don't be goofy. This is the Boy Scouts' Christmas Tree sale. Trust me, they're going to be falling all over themselves to help a couple of middle-school girls with their tree." I appeal to Bruce. "Right? You were a boy scout."

He nods. "She's right, you guys. Come on, let's just go get it."

Every year, Bruce and the girls go out to buy the tree; it's their job. I don't want to go because I don't want it to seem like this is just one more thing he can't manage.

"But how will we get it on top of the car?"

Bruce is pulling his fleece jacket over his head. "The Boy Scouts will do it," he says, spinning the wheelchair to face the garage door. "Let's go."

I follow them out and heave the chair into the back of the van. Emily climbs in, resigned, but Heather looks unhappy. She's been talking for weeks about how much she hates our house without its carpet. Back in the garage, I pull down the boxes of ornaments from the shelves above the ramp and think about Heather's complaints. Our house isn't cozy. This isn't going to seem like Christmas. We can't even sit on the floor to open our presents. The wood is too dark; it makes the whole room dark. Everything is ruined.

Emily takes the opposite tack: Daddy is getting better. His cough is even gone. Christmas isn't like it was, but it isn't horrible. Next year will be better. She wants to talk about presents, especially the ones that will have her name on them. I haul the last box up into the living room and start moving the furniture to make a space for the tree.

Our family has an uneasy balance now. Bruce is still doggedly quiet. He goes about his routines with a clumsy gravity, all awkward grit and exhaustion. Heather has staked out an emotional territory that demands brutal honesty. This sucks, and anyone who pretends otherwise is lying. She's not thinking about next year. She's looking at this one, and it's hideous. Emily, by contrast, is all about patience. Her self-imposed task is to watch me and her dad for cues. She wants reasons to be hopeful; I often look up to see her wide blue eyes on me, and she can calibrate my moods with amazing precision.

I only want this season to pass. I want to wake up and have it be next year. I want my kids to stop looking as if they're afraid I will collapse or disappear. I want to stop having to agree with Heather's grim assessment, and then help her find reasons why it's not so bad. I want to see Emily feel safe enough to get mad at me. I want to hear her talk back to her dad. I want Bruce to stand up and put his arms around me. I want to look up at him.

Day 286

I'm at the chiropractor's office, describing what happened to my back this morning. "Bruce was lying in bed, and I was bent over him, trying to put on his socks. Something—I don't know, like, gave, right here." I put one hand in the center of my lower back. I am in serious pain; I can hardly walk. I drove the carpool and came right here. No way am I trying to teach my classes.

Dr. Jim is a short, dark-haired guy whose gifted hands have adjusted all four of our backs at one time or another; Bruce first started going to him before we were married. This is my first time seeing him since the accident, and I'm not in good shape. I give him the quick rundown. (Still hard, getting better, yes, it was terrifying, I'm okay, the girls are coping …) He has me lie on my back and try to push my leg out to the side. I can't do it. I also can't get over how panicky I feel; I ask him about this.

I'm on my stomach with my face in the little padded hole. While he works on my lower spine, he explains that lots of people get that surge of anxiety—a statement that goes a long way toward dissipating it. I leave with a pain prescription, orders to avoid lifting anything, and appointments every day for the rest of the week.

"Uh, Mom."

Heather is standing by my side of the bed, trying to wake me up. It takes me a minute to get oriented. Hurt my back. Took a nap. Evening. Okay. I focus on her face. "What's the matter?"

"There's like, a bulge in the kitchen ceiling."

"A bulge."

"Yeah, like, there's a spot where the ceiling is kind of puffing out." She demonstrates with her cheeks.

My eyes go to the darkened window; it's raining hard. It's been raining hard for weeks. "Where in the kitchen?"

"Over the table ... kind of, on the side by the cupboards."

"How big is it?"

She makes a circle the size of a doughnut with her two hands.

"Tell Daddy I want to talk to him."

"Can't you come down?"

No, dammit. He's the one who never called the roofers. "I don't feel good, Heather. The medicine they gave me for my back makes me dizzy." This is true; even if it didn't hurt so much to move around, I would have a hard time getting up. I also want nothing to do with leaking ceilings.

A few minutes later, the lift grinds, and then he's in the room.

I don't even sit up.

"So, the ceiling." He's wheeled over to his edge of the bed, and he's leaning forward in the chair, his chin on one hand.

"What about it?"

"Well, it doesn't look too good right now." I don't answer. "Did Heather tell you?"

"I can't do anything, Bruce. I can't even get up. Call David or somebody and figure it out."

Now he's pissed at me. Tough. He makes that little pteh noise and stays right where he is. I wait him out. "Whatever," he says finally, and pushes himself out into the hall.

I'm so angry I can hardly speak. "Could you close that, please?" He backs up and shuts the door with a soft click. I lie there, fuming. After a few minutes, I hear him talking to David on the phone. A little ceiling problem, could you come over? Oh, good. Yeah, thanks. See you soon.

In ten minutes, Heather is back. "Mama?"

"What."

"The bulge is getting bigger. It's, like, moving."

"Moving?"

"There are two of them. Mama, can you come down?"

I take a breath. "Heather, get the Christmas presents off the kitchen table. Move everything out from under the bulge that you can. Make Daddy get out from underneath it."

She leaves, closing the door behind herself. Five more minutes pass. The rain is pounding on the roof. I listen for the sound of David's car, but what I hear instead is a huge whooommmphhh! and then, Emily shrieking. I get up at last.

From the stair landing, I can see the three of them in the kitchen, unhurt. There is a ragged hole in our kitchen ceiling, about four feet in diameter. The table, the floor, the windows, and the cupboards are covered with a six-inch-thick layer of soggy grey insulation and rotten drywall. Water has apparently been collecting in the space between our ceiling and the roof. Summer before last, I spent a week painting that kitchen: butter yellow for two walls and the rest eggshell white. I was proud of it. Emily is standing with both hands over her mouth.

"That was actually kind of cool," Bruce says.

"At least I'll have something to tell about in school tomorrow." Heather picks up a wad of dripping grey goop.

"Stay away from there," I say. They all look up. I'm standing at the top of the first flight of stairs. "I'm not cleaning this up," I announce. They stare. Huh? I turn around, slam the door, and limp back to my side of the bed. When Bruce comes in, I don't even open my eyes.

"What was that about?" he says. I can tell by his voice that he thinks I'm being crazy.

"Just what I said. I'm not cleaning it up. You said you'd call somebody to fix the roof. You didn't. You deal with it."

The doorbell rings. Ah, here's David. Fine, Bruce will have help. In the dark, I listen to the two of them laughing, guy-style, about what an unusual sight that was—a ceiling, collapsing! Not something you see every day! I think of Michael, telling me three months ago that I would have to decide whether I wanted to keep doing everything myself, or risk finding out what happens when I don't. Now I know. What happens when I don't do everything myself is that I'm suddenly finished with seeing my husband as a patient. He's just my husband. I'm just his wife, at last.

Day 292

I'm in the candle-lit sanctuary, sitting alone in a huge throng of people. Bruce is in his wheelchair, tucked in among the stringed instruments that crowd the chancel. Emily and Heather are out in the lounge, eating cookies and playing cards with their friend Simone. This is their very first time coming to the late Christmas Eve service; always before, one of us has skipped it and stayed home to put them to bed.

Backed by the orchestra, the choir is singing, full-throated and in four-part harmony, all the verses to "It Came Upon A Midnight Clear." I don't think I've ever heard the language of the third verse: "And you, beneath life's crushing load, whose forms are bending low/Who toil along the climbing way, with painful steps and slow/Look now, for glad and golden hours come swiftly on the wing"— I can't bear to sing it. Glad and golden hours? How swift is "swiftly?" Is this in God's time, or human time? "O, rest, beside the weary road, and hear the angels sing!"

Day 296

"Wait," Bruce says. "Girls, come here."

Emily is fearless. She slips under one parallel bar to stand in front of Bruce. We're all in the rehab gym at the University of Washington, where the girls and I have been hanging around for the last half an hour. Today, they're going to get to see him stand up. Five minutes ago, they were bored and making noises about going down to the cafeteria. Then Andy strapped the canvas safety belt around Bruce's waist and hauled him to his feet. On his right leg, he's wearing a long white plastic brace that goes from beneath his foot to the top of his thigh. He's holding on to the parallel bars for dear life, and his balance is so bad that he has to keep staring straight ahead. Andy is right behind him, holding tight to the canvas belt.

"Hi, Daddy! You're looking very tall, there." Emily is six inches away from his body.

His eyes flick down at her. "Closer," he says.

She takes a step forward. I tell her to give him a hug, and she wraps her arms very carefully around his waist. She lays her head against the part of his stomach where the belt is looped and looks at me and Heather with an expression that clearly says, okay, this is kind of weird. Bruce's clenched right hand comes off the bar and pats her shoulder a couple of times. "I love you, Daddy," she says, and steps away.

Biting her lip, Heather goes gamely in to take her sister's place. She's grown a couple of inches since they last stood up together. Bruce says, "Hey, you."

"Hi, Dad."

Andy stands right behind them, still holding firmly to the safety belt. There is activity and noise all around us. There are newly injured patients, slumped in temporary wheelchairs wearing stiff blue and white collars and hospital pajamas. Some of these people, I know, will not do what Bruce is doing right now until there is a cure. Others will walk out of this hospital in a few weeks' time. Against the backdrop of the windows looking at the Seattle winter sky, there are therapists adjusting equipment, and I can hear a radio playing an old song by the Moody

Blues. If we were in a movie, this scene would play as a big-moment-turning-point. The brave, injured father, finally well enough to stand up and hug his grateful, teary children! Well, yeah. And, no. It doesn't feel like a turning point. It feels, once again, like having to endure a teaspoon-sized dose of hope while awash in the enormity of loss. It feels like trying to balance on the edge of a blade.

Day 314

Bruce and I are sitting in an office downstairs from the one where Heather has been having her sessions with Alice. The building is an old house, remodeled to serve as office space for half a dozen psychologists, and it's just barely accessible. There is no way for Bruce to get up the staircase, so Alice has arranged for us to meet with her in a partner's space. She's been speaking in her low, articulate voice about Heather. I have my journal out, ready to hear what she thinks we need to do now.

She's saying that she perceives that Heather feels as if she and I are in some kind of role reversal. She perceives that Heather sometimes feels as if she has to be the parent because I take the role of child. She says, therefore, that I ought to be focusing—if I'm not already—on my self-esteem and self-confidence in my work with my own therapist.

I carefully write these words down, but I know before they're even on the page that she's got it wrong. I keep quiet, trying to track what she's saying, while I feel around inside myself to be sure.

"Heather sees you as—not strong." Alice is sitting on the edge of her chair with her booted legs crossed. Every so often she shifts her shoulders so that her long curls move. She has a very serious face.

"That doesn't sound right," I say.

"No?"

"I mean—no. It doesn't resonate." My face is getting hot. How exactly do you defend yourself if someone has just said you lack self-esteem? Is arguing the point evidence against you? A sign that you can't take criticism? I don't care. This is about Heather. "I think I'd know it if she felt like she was having to mother me. She doesn't act that way." I turn to Bruce, who is next to me in his wheelchair, his gloved hands nestled in his lap. "Do you think?"

He's silent for a long time. "I'm sure she knows you're stressed," he says finally.

Alice breathes out very slowly.

"Yeah, but that's a different thing." Now we're all quiet. I'm still doing my inner check, thinking of what it's like when I'm alone with Heather. I don't know the rules here. I don't know if I'm supposed to ask why Alice thinks this, or if I'm just supposed to trust that she has a good reason. I look up at her; she's watching me with a completely neutral expression.

"I'll think about it," I say. I pretend to make another note in my journal, but it's just doodling. What I'm actually doing is thinking of what I ought to say to Alice, if I felt like paying her to be educated.

What are you doing after work, Alice? Going home? Stopping at the grocery store to pick up some salad? Meeting your husband for some Thai food? What are you doing next week? Next month? How about this ... how about if you go to a trauma center tonight, and don't make it home at all. How about if your husband doesn't come home until— what is it now, January? Until April.

What if he comes home weak and sick and broken, and you spend the next few months trying to deal with your life while you take care of him. And what if, after all that, you find yourself sitting in some therapist's office, being told that your child sees you as not strong?

What I think is that Heather correctly recognizes there are some problems I can't solve. I think she's been forced to grow up all at once, instead of over time, and that it's been a painful season for her. What I wanted you to give her is a place to say so—a place where she could let her innocence go without knowing that her parents were watching and suffering. If she got that much, I'm in your debt. But please. Please. Don't give me advice about self-esteem.

Day 316

Before we can go to the mall for walking practice, Bruce has to go upstairs and do the catheter. When I hear the lift begin its deep electric groan, I know I have ten minutes to get ready. I'll need his blue backpack, with his extra shoe and heel wedge inside. I'll need the gait-belt, and the collapsible aluminum walker. I'll need Louie the Leg, his custom-made brace. Louie is formed of white plastic molded in the shape of Bruce's right leg, from his thigh to his foot. Louie holds Bruce's foot and ankle in a ninety degree angle; Louie lets Bruce bend his knee, but only if the rectangular metal clip is slipped off the joint. Louie is heavy and awkward; when I hold Louie next to me, the top of him comes to my lower ribs, just like Bruce's thigh.

At the mall, Bruce parks us in the handicapped space, and I get the wheelchair out of the back of the van and set it next to the driver's door. After Bruce lowers himself into the chair, I set the backpack and Louie in his lap, then walk next to him while he pushes himself into Target. He doesn't want to be helped, which is good because it's hard to carry the folded-up walker and push the chair at the same time. We roll through the store and out into the spacious hallway, where I drop the backpack on a wooden bench next to an artificial tree and kneel to take off his shoes.

I set his right foot into Louie, then fasten the Velcro clasps at his shin and thigh. I open his ratty old Adidas running shoe as wide as it will go and slide it over Louie's foot, then push the heel in and tie the laces. I fit the heel wedge into his black left shoe and put it on him; this will compensate for the extra height Louie adds to his right side. I get the gait belt out and wrap it around behind him; he cinches it tightly over his stomach with his left hand. I open the walker and stage it in front of the wheelchair. Time to stand up.

"Ready?"

Bruce is inching himself forward to the edge of his seat cushion. He takes firm hold of the top of the walker. "Okay."

I'm facing his weak side with my left hand clutching the gait belt in the middle of his back and my right one in his armpit. We count to three, just like when we were doing the quad cough, and then both of us heave together. My back is straight, my knees bent and open in a plie position. He's so heavy. There's a moment when it seems impossible; we push through it, and Bruce is on his feet. He supports himself for a minute or so, slowly straightening his back while one leg rattles in a spasm. I reach down to lock Louie's knee joint. A middle-aged couple has stopped to watch us; their faces are anxious. I smile to let them know it's okay, and they move off.

For the next fifteen minutes, I follow him through the mall. He holds himself very straight and looks directly ahead; sometimes he asks me to check his gait. His left foot does an ultra-slow-motion version of its old walk, but his right leg is rigid inside of Louie. I have one hand on the gait belt at his back, and I'm pulling the wheelchair along behind him with the other. This is a good night; he takes one step every five seconds, and his bowels behave. Too often, the effort of standing up is enough to trigger an accident. On those nights, we keep going anyway, but it still feels like a kind of defeat.

After fifteen minutes, Bruce is exhausted. I set the chair behind him, lock the brakes, and we do the whole thing in reverse. For now—and maybe forever—this is walking.

Electrical stimulation has been used to activate muscle
for centuries. Although ... much data indicate that
such stimulation can maintain and increase muscle
bulk and strength, they are still not consistently used in
rehabilitative centers ... in the past decade, however,
many commercial devices are now available for
patients to use at home ...

Dr. Wise Young

TWENTY-FOUR

Day 319

Our computer sits in a corner of the dining room, on a scarred oak desk that once belonged to Bruce's grandfather. The desk is cluttered and dusty. I should sort through the pile of papers next to the mouse pad; I should get out the Murphy's Oil Soap and clean this beautiful, tough wood. I should find the broom and sweep the dog hair from under my feet, and then I should wash the floor. I don't do anything of the sort. Instead, I sit for hours at this desk, lost in the CareCure forums, which have gradually become my shelter from the storm.

When Bruce first discovered this website last summer, I wasn't particularly interested; Bruce is the computer guy. I am a book person. Now, I can't get enough of what these people have to say. They're discussing every single subject I care about, and they're doing it with energy, intelligence and humor, right now. It's astonishing how much information is here. To my amazement, Dr. Wise Young himself is often logged on, answering questions and joking with the members.

The forum called CARE seems to be mostly concerned with B&B. For spinal-cord-people, this shorthand doesn't stand for "bed and breakfast." It means bowel and bladder. I spend a lot of time on these threads, and so does Bruce. Maybe someone out there will know what to do about the strange thing that Bruce calls "butt juice." Butt juice is about a cup's worth of goopy, mucousy stuff that explodes randomly out of him—usually when he's trying to get to his feet, though not always. Sometimes butt juice just happens out of the blue, like the very first time. Bruce was sitting in his wheelchair at our kitchen table, talking to a friend.

At a pause in the conversation, the sound of it was audible to me all the way across the room. I couldn't have said which was the stronger emotion—embarrassment or anxiety. We high-tailed it upstairs to clean him up, only to be surprised by a pile of slimy glop. What is this stuff? The next day, when I described what we found in his jeans to his outpatient nurse, she told me that people who don't have spinal cord injuries probably get it too, but we don't make a habit of examining our waste products so carefully. I told her I thought I'd have noticed if my body ever produced this stuff. Butt juice is mostly odorless, completely colorless, and definitely a nightmare, if only because it attacks without provocation. So far, I haven't found anybody else on any of the forums who suffers from it.

Almost everybody has bladder issues, though. They talk endlessly about catheters. They talk about urinary tract infections, and about drugs that will help keep the sphincter at the tip of the bladder from going into a spasm. These spasms are what make Bruce go the craziest. He has enough sensation now to know when he needs to find a place to cath. Usually, he gets about a two-minute warning—just enough time to roll up onto the lift, take the thirty-second ride up, roll off and into our bathroom, and get organized. About half the time, he makes it. The act of bending over in his chair to push himself onto the lift can cause the bladder to spasm. The vibration of the lift can cause the bladder to spasm. If he's still dry by the time he gets to the bathroom, the exertion of getting his cath set up can cause the bladder to spasm, which is the worst of all possible scenarios.

He's there in front of the toilet, trying frantically to get the dark pink hose in, when—the bladder has a spasm, he gushes all over himself and he is helpless to do anything but swear. People on the CARE forum agree that they would do almost anything to have the B&B issues resolved.

9 pm

The girls have gone to bed, and I'm back at the desk. I've just decided that my very favorite CareCure poster is someone who calls himself Ron. There's no way of knowing his actual name, and it wouldn't matter if there were. Ron is funny. He's a misogynist, his sarcasm is brutal, his sneer is visible, and I love him. He tells a man who asks if it's possible to be happy again after a spinal cord injury to go and find some Brazilian whores and get busy. That will put him on the road to rehabilitation!

Ron makes me laugh until I cry. His jolly crudity is so over the top that I can't resist the ride. He proudly anoints himself the Paralyzed Pimp. His contribution to a long thread about stupid-things-able-bodied–people-have-said involves a graphic description of an encounter with a brainless lap dancer. When a man who has full use of his hands writes to say that his wife is leaving him because she resents having to do his B&B tasks, Ron replies that she should leave him. Ron calls him a pitiful peckerhead; other members jump in to point out that Ron is an immature punk, but I'm calling for Bruce to come and read this thread.

He maneuvers his chair into the space in front of the desk, and I go off to load the dishwasher. In five minutes I turn around to see Bruce pounding the old desk in a fit of silent laughter. It's the kind of laughing that you can't help but join, even if you don't know the joke. Bruce is shaking his head and saying weakly, "Oh, no! Oh, no!"

I knew he'd like this guy.

"Oh, my God. That is fucking hysterical." He's wiping tears from his eyes.

"Which part?"

"He made me wet my pants!"

He leans back so I can see. Sure enough, a dark stain has appeared across Bruce's lap. This time, he doesn't much care. Thanks, Ron.

Day 340

If Bruce comes out of our bathroom in five minutes, it will only be 9:30. He will still have to wash his hands, gather up his pills, and brush his teeth. He will have to put his carafes into their little plastic tub, add a couple of dark pink catheters curled up inside their Ziploc sandwich bags, and toss in a package of baby wipes and some wiener slime. He will ride over to our bed with this gear in his lap, put himself on the bed, and set the carafes on the chair seat where he can reach them. The tub goes on the floor next to the bed; he'll chuck used wipes and catheters into it after the three o'clock draining of the lizard.

"Weiner slime" is Bruce's name for KY lubricant. "Carafe" is Bruce's name for the pee jug. It's a flimsy white plastic affair with a green snap-on top, about the size and shape of a quart of milk. Every night, he goes to sleep lying on his back with this thing tucked between his legs. When he wakes up to cath, it's usually got a few hundred milliliters in it. His bladder leaks when he's asleep, which is a good thing; if it didn't, his urine might back up into his kidneys and damage them. At three am, he caps the carafe that's been between his legs, drains himself into the second one, and puts them both back on the seat of the wheelchair.

Now it's nearly ten o'clock, and he's already in bed with everything done. This won't be one of the nights when I get sleepy and frustrated waiting for him to get here so we can start the e-stim. Sometimes I read while he's getting undressed; once in a while I still help him. Tonight I'm writing in my journal, mostly to pass the time. He goes through the range of motion exercises on his own now. This takes another ten minutes, and then it's time.

Functional electrical stimulation—e-stim—is a way to make muscles contract. I know from reading the posts on the CURE forum that a lot of spinal-cord-people use "stim-bikes" to keep themselves in shape. At least, they do if they have enough money to buy what their insurance won't. A stim-bike has strategically placed electrodes that send jolts of electricity to the appropriate muscles, so that the paralyzed person's legs move the pedals. Others—including Bruce—use e-stim to target specific muscles that are firing but weak. His physical therapists have been doing this to him at the UW, and it's working. Since they started, there's a small but measurable difference in strength.

His hamstrings are the issue. He's trying to learn to walk, but he can't even lie on his stomach and bend his knee to lift his foot off the bed. The problem is that while these muscles are getting a signal through the cord, they're too weak from lack of use to respond. The job of e-stim is to correct this—to provide an artificial boost that will contract and strengthen his hamstrings.

There are four electrodes, each one embedded in circles of gray fabric about the size of soup can lids. Bruce has given me a sketch from his PT that shows where to put them: one pair high on either side of the back of his thigh and another down near the back of his knee. I check the glue that holds them in place; good, it's still sticky as flypaper. I hook up the leads that hang from the circles to wires from a black box that reminds me of a Marlboro package.

"Ready?" Bruce has already set the timing mechanism to deliver the juice in a fifteen-second rhythm.

"Yeah. Could you start it at about seven?"

He's talking about the power setting. I squint at the tiny numbers on the edge of the box and turn it on. "Here you go." His foot flies off the bed. "Whoa!"

"Yeah, turn it down a notch."

I do. For the next ten minutes, I adjust the power as needed. I try to find the perfect height of pillow to set under his foot so that he can help lift it. If he tries when his leg is flat on the bed, he gets an attack of "tone"—a form of spasticity in which all his muscles lock up tight. My job is to manage the current, the pillow, and his leg so that he has to work hard to help the machine.

Once his foot gets going, I stabilize it. The current helps him get it in the air, but there's nothing to keep it from flopping over to the side once it's there. Since he got this machine, his hamstring has gained the tiniest bit of strength, which is what makes the whole routine worth doing. I sit on the edge of the bed, watching the red and green lights on the box that tell me when the foot is going to start drifting up. It's boring because Bruce can't talk to me. Most of the time, it takes all his concentration just to bend his knee. I know I'm supposed to be grateful that this is working, and I am. I'm also wondering exactly when these microscopically incremental gains will stop coming.

On CareCure, we read about a place in San Diego called Project Walk. It's a kind of specialized personal training center for people with damaged spinal cords. Their approach seems to be very close to what the University of Washington PTs have set up for Bruce—a tightly targeted exercise routine designed to work with whatever he's got, gradually building on it. There's no way to know how far this method will take him; for all we know, he's already at the absolute end of recovery. The only way to find out is to keep trying. Adjust the power down a fraction. Put one hand next to his ankle. Wait while he growls into the mattress. Again. Again.

Day 343

"You just walked into a room where I am," I say admiringly. This has not happened in almost a year. Bruce is behind his walker, wearing Louie and clumping very slowly around and around. Out the doorway that leads to the dining room. Into the front hall. Back into the kitchen. I can see his reflection in the window over the sink, where I'm scrubbing the pans from tonight's dinner. The girls have just gone to bed.

"I did," he says, gripping the walker and looking straight ahead. "And I'm going to walk out again, too." He moves the walker forward eight inches and takes two halting steps into it. "But I'll be back."

Five minutes and one trip later. "Kate, bring my chair right now." He sounds desperate.

I flip the locks up and race it out to the rock-lined hallway, where he is standing perfectly straight with his faced squeezed in an expression of anguish. I stage the chair behind him, lock the brakes again, and get ready to help him sit down.

"Oh, Christ. I can't—I'm shitting. Oh, Christ, I can't—God damn it!"

I glance toward the girls' rooms. We're in the hall just below the top of their staircase, and I know they'll come out to see what's wrong if he starts yelling. "Don't yell. Okay? The chair's right here, don't yell." We're both completely helpless. This is definitely not butt juice; it's the real thing, and there's nothing we can do. Finally, it seems to be over. He's standing in his walker. If he sits down, it will make a mess. Okay. I run to get a towel, lay it on the wheelchair, undo his jeans, slip them over his hips, and help him sit. Please, girls, don't come out.

I take off his shoes, then slide the pants over his shins. "Uh, wow." The pants weigh about five pounds. I can't believe all this was in him. "No wonder you couldn't hold it." I get them off his feet without making too big a mess, then shove the chair onto the lift. I leave his pants and shoes sitting on the floor and go ahead of him to set up the shower chair. I don't look at him. In the bathroom, I take off his socks, help him with his shirt, and wait while he moves himself into the shower.

He glances down at himself and winces. "That's disgusting."

"You okay? I'm going to get the pants."

He pulls the curtain shut. "Yeah." I hear the sound of the water, and go to get the pants.

It really is amazing. I've never produced this quantity of shit in my life. The lower leg of his jeans is completely full! I dump it in the toilet and tell him through the curtain that he's got the bowels of a bull moose. I take the dirty things down to the laundry room; by the time I get back, he's swearing again.

"This is fucking unbelievable! I just made a fucking cow pie!"

I pull the edge of the curtain back. On the floor of our shower is—there's no other word for it—a cow pie. I have to bite my cheek to keep from laughing out loud. I know he's upset. I know it's the thing he hates most, not having control of his own shit. But there's so much of it! This is two week's worth of shit! This is a cow pie—this is two cow pies! When I can speak without giggling, I tell him that it's amazing more of it didn't get on the chair. The chair is, in fact, perfectly clean.

An hour later, we're trying to go to sleep. Bruce is lying on his back with his plastic carafe between his thighs. I'm next to him, thinking about Ron and his Brazilian whores fantasy, and then I do start to laugh.

"What?"

I tell him. In a few minutes, we're both laughing so hard we can't breathe. We repeat all of Ron's goofy pronouncements to each other. We cover our mouths with the backs of our hands, as if the girls might hear us. Then he says, very quiet—"I could just as easily be crying."

"Me, too." His hand finds mine under the covers.

"God, I hate this."

"Me, too."

Happy families are all alike …

Leo Tolstoy

TWENTY-FIVE

Day 365: March 7th, 2002

"Go downstairs! I'll call you when it's time, I promise."

"Mama! What's the surprise?"

"You'll see ... now go." I'm trying to get the girls out of the kitchen before the limo shows up, but Emily keeps finding reasons to come back in. This is our day—the first anniversary of the accident, and we've taken Emily and Heather out of school for the afternoon. There it is! A shiny black limousine is rolling grandly down our street; just as it pulls into the driveway, Emily pokes her head into the kitchen again. She sees the car.

"Who's here?"

I take her by the shoulders and hustle her toward the steps that lead to the family room. She keeps twisting around to look over her shoulder through the front door. Okay. "Get Heather," I say.

I open the front door and walk out to say hello to our driver, who turns out to be a courtly man in a sharply pressed uniform. While I'm telling him the plan, the girls come out to stand on the porch, looking confused. I call them over.

"Mama, who is it?"

"It's nobody! It's us. Girls, this is Don. He's our driver today. This limo is for us."

"Oh, my God!"

"Are you kidding?"

"Get in, check it out."

Don opens the door, and we climb inside. Black leather, soft as butter. Tinted windows and a sunroof. A television set and a bar. It's even better than I imagined. I ask Don to take the girls for a ride around the neighborhood while Bruce finishes getting ready. We have to hurry; the shift at Harborview is about to change, and we want to be there in time to see Chris before she leaves for the day.

332

It's my first ride in a limo. I've brought sparkling cider and snacks and even a movie. Don pulls regally into the turnaround area behind the hospital—the same space where I learned to put Bruce into the Prius last May. I get out and let him help me assemble the wheelchair, and then I grab Louie and the walker. Don stands beside the chair while Bruce moves himself into it; he's the movie version of a family chauffeur, all twinkly and respectful. Yes, he'll wait right here until we're finished. Lovely, thank you. The girls, hearing me say this, giggle like five-year-olds

Inside, we have two stops to make. Emily and Heather haven't been here since Bruce was discharged. They walk along beside the wheelchair, subdued now, and murmuring about what they remember.

"Ohhh, I hate this elevator."

"I hate this smell."

Bruce is bent over, spinning himself fast along the halls. When we get to NICU, I call inside and ask if any of the nurses who took care of Bruce Hanson a year ago happen to be working. By the time I have Louie strapped on, the nurse named Karen has come out to say hello. While she watches, I set up the walker, wind the gait belt around his middle, and help him stand up.

It's hard not to cry when other people are crying. Karen is thrilled to see him. She keeps exclaiming that she can't believe it. Has it really been a year? She remembers all of us well. And look at you—you're so tall! While she and Bruce are visiting, I follow Emily and Heather into the lounge, where a whole new set of families are camped out with their sleeping bags. Heather walks over to a bulletin board. There are notices about phone calls, and prayers, and even a letter or two. I move off, keeping my eyes away from the people who sit, stunned, on the couches.

Emily comes to get me.

"Mama, Heather's crying."

She is. "What's wrong, Honey?"

She points at a piece of paper covered with feminine handwriting. The writer is saying thank you to her son's nurses; she knows they did the best they could. She says that she'll always be grateful they made her son's last days comfortable for him, and bearable for her. She says she still misses him. Just as Heather and I are walking away, Emily shows up with Bruce; she's told him that Heather is upset. He's back in the wheelchair.

He asks Heather to show him what she saw, and she leads him back to the board. He holds her hand while he looks up at the note. When he starts asking her if she thought he was going to die, I put my arm around Emily and walk away.

The doors to rehab are wide open. We turn left, toward the gym, and I leave Bruce there with the girls while I go off to find people. Chris, Diva, Nurse Bob, and Josh are all on the floor today. Chris and Diva hug me tight. Good to see you, too.

"You look so relaxed," Diva says to me in her sing-song voice. "So much better!"

The girls are letting Nurse Bob tease them about homework, and Chris is telling Bruce how tall he is. I love seeing her look up at him. I love seeing all of them look up at him. Josh is curious about exactly what muscle groups Bruce has got now; while they're talking, Heather starts to cry again.

I take her over by the standing frame. "Are you okay? Do you want to go?"

She uses my body to hide herself from the rest of the room. "I was so scared here." She struggles for a minute, then gets hold of herself. "I'm okay," she says.

I don't let her go. "We were all scared here. God, I hated to bring you here."

"You had to."

Back in the limo, we pop the sparkling cider and say goodbye to Harborview. The plan was to go from here to Dr. Huseby's office up the street, but it turns out he's got patients. He makes time, though, to talk with Bruce on the cell phone. The girls and I are quiet, looking through the blacked-out windows while Bruce tells him how it's going, and says how glad he was that Dr. Huseby went skiing that day.

Don drives us next to the curb outside our church, where we're going to meet the ski-patroller named Jill. We're in the lounge and Bruce is already standing up when she comes in with her boyfriend, Cedar.

Jill goes right to Heather. "Wow, look at you! You're so big!" It's true. A year ago today, Heather was more than three inches shorter. Jill has brought us presents.

Heather takes hers, and says very seriously, "Thank you so much." She's not talking about the present.

Jill gives her a squeeze. "You're so welcome. I was glad—I was supposed to be there, I guess." She turns to Emily. "Is this your sister?"

Heather introduces them, and then Jill tells us all who Cedar is. He was the one who was scheduled to work that day. Jill was only on the mountain because he was working. When the emergency call came, she was the first one on the scene—by the rules, she was supposed to stay with Bruce until the helicopter lifted off.

"But Cedar was second on the scene, right behind me ... and I saw you. And it seemed like you needed me as much as your dad did."

Heather is looking into the middle distance. After a moment she nods. "I did."

I manage to say thank you to Jill. I've talked with her, but we haven't seen each other since this day last year, when she looked at me in our driveway with an expression I didn't want to read. Bruce and Cedar talk for a few minutes about the snow this year (It's been great. Don't torture me!), and then we all thank them again.

At Jocelyn's house, the twins Peter and Matthew are messing around with a soccer ball in the front yard. We're sitting behind our darkened windows, laughing hysterically at their efforts not to look interested in this stretch limo parked smack in front of their house. Finally the girls open the sunroof and stick their heads out.

The boys say, "What the—" and we all laugh harder.

I go in the house to get Jocelyn, who has been warned we were coming. Her husband, Dan, and I wait while our driver takes Bruce, the girls, Jocelyn and the boys for a ride around the neighborhood.

"So, this is cool," Dan says.

"So far, it's great. Kind of emotional."

"Oh, well. Peter and Matthew'll put a stop to that."

I laugh. "No doubt. God, it's getting nasty out."

He looks at the sky, which is darker than it ought to be for this time of the afternoon. "You know they're forecasting snow."

"Tonight?"

"That's what I heard. And maybe a thunderstorm."

335

"Cool. Oh, man, I hope that happens." Seattle gets snow maybe once a year, and never in March. Snow tonight would be amazing.

By the time we get downtown to the Hilton, the temperature has dropped ten degrees and the rain is feeling icy. Don and I assemble the chair as fast as we can, and then our family rides the elevator to the restaurant at the very top—twenty nine floors above the ground. This is where Dave, Heather and I ate our extraordinary, other-worldly breakfast on the Sunday after the accident. The maitre d' shows us to a table by the window. White linen. Crystal candleholders. Leather-bound menus with no prices. Beyond us, ferry traffic moving silently across Puget Sound, and snow falling through the darkness on the streets far below. When the waiter, with an eye on the weather, asks if we'd like him to call us a taxi, I answer serenely that we have our own driver waiting for us.

Emily laughs out loud. "Our own driver," she says after he leaves. "I love that." She keeps looking around the room, then out at the view, then into my face, and Bruce's, and Heather's. "It's like we're rich," she says solemnly.

Exactly.

It takes forever to get back home, which makes us even happier. On the I-90 bridge, snow is falling so hard that the few cars on the road are keeping their speed to about twenty miles an hour. Don is up in front, cheerfully navigating, and the four of us are lounging in our plush compartment, cozy and well fed. What could be better than this? A thunderstorm, that's what. By the time the limo makes its ponderous way down our street, the sky is booming, and lightning is crackling to the north.

It's almost too much—a made-for-TV-movie-ending to a perfect day. Emily and Heather take Rocky into the front yard and throw snow at him. Bruce sits in the driveway in his wheelchair, snow falling on his upturned face. I pay Don and tell him how to get out of our neighborhood without having to go down any steep hills.

Tomorrow there will be no school. Bruce and I will sleep in, and when I come downstairs the front hall will be littered with soggy snow clothes. The girls will be in the kitchen, making a mess with the hot chocolate and arguing over the television. It will be the start of the second year.

March 13ᵗʰ, 2002

Bruce has pulled his wheelchair right up next to the counter where the television sits in our kitchen. He's leaning forward so far that his face is inches from the screen. He's watching disabled athletes compete in the Men's Giant Slalom at Snow Basin in Utah. This is the 2002 Paralympics. The men are riding on sit-skis. They're carving clean turns, and they appear to be having a wonderful time. "Look at that," he murmurs. "They're ripping down the mountain ..."

Uh oh.

Day 2087: November 22, 2006

It's long past dinnertime. The girls and I are in the kitchen making the grocery list for tomorrow: Granny Smith apples, celery, sage, buttermilk, pumpkin. Earlier today I bought us a fancy free-range turkey from the deluxe grocery store near my office. I'm telling Emily and Heather that this turkey is going to be extra fine because it got to run around free its whole life, and when it went to bed—of course underneath a goose down comforter—it only heard violins and gentle piano music. No heavy metal at all.

Heather gives me her killer that-is-really-stupid-Mom look. Straight mouth. Direct gaze. Flat eyes. I keep talking about the turkey's life of luxury, pretending she will see the humor anytime now. She puts one hand on my shoulder. "Mom. No."

My plan is to have them do most of the cooking so they'll know in their fingers the secrets that make this food taste the way my mother taught it to me, and hers to her. Emily got home last night; her first quarter of college is turning out to be trauma-free. She's on top of her classes, her roommate is her best friend from high school, and she has a boyfriend in the military who is currently in town between assignments. We'll be seeing a lot of him this weekend, which is fine.

The garage door growls open and then Bruce finally appears. He's wearing blue jeans and white sneakers and his new Fender hooded sweatshirt. He looks tired; he's been working on a software product launch for the past few weeks. He drops his backpack, sets his cane next to the refrigerator and walks stiffly across the room. I stand up and put my arms around his waist; I fit just under his chin. Dad's home.

Day 2088: Thanksgiving Morning

I am the first one awake. I lie next to Bruce, who sleeps quietly now, just as he used to. He's curled on his side with one pillow under his head and another on top to shut out light and noise. The wheelchair is parked next to him, exactly as it has been every morning for more than five years. He uses it to get to our bathroom when he wakes up in the night and to simplify his morning and evening routines. He still takes medications for neuropathic pain, bladder management, and osteoporosis.

The pink hoses, the wiener slime, and the carafe are somewhere in the garage, stuffed into a dusty box labeled "Hospital Stuff We Hate." With it are the neck brace, the belly binder, and the fat syringe I once used to squirt liquid food into his stomach.. The equipment to monitor blood pressure is in that box too, along with the old gait belt and a couple of cans of thickened apple juice. The wheelchair itself, though, is still with us. He likes to sit in it while he's in the living room every evening, teaching himself how to play his new bass guitar. He gets along fine, mostly, without it.

Rocky is thrilled to see me coming downstairs with my iPod wires dangling. He's getting to be an old gray-faced dog now, but he still goes into the full-body joy dance over our morning walk. The weather is satisfyingly terrible—sharp wind, steady rain, almost freezing. A perfect day to hang around the house and cook. I'm wearing plenty of layers, walking fast with the Dixie Chicks playing softly, insistently, in my ears. "How long do you want to be loved/Is forever enough, is forever enough?"

While the turkey cooks, the girls and I sit down to watch *Pride and Prejudice*, which we know by heart. Bruce is at the computer next to where the lift used to be, doggedly slaying bugs in his new software. Every once in a while I hear him make his famous God-this-is-so-annoying noise ("Pteh!"). Sometimes he can't resist repeating one of the movie lines in a weird falsetto ("Mr. Bennett! Netherfield has been let at last!"). Heather and Emily shout at him to shut up, but we'd all be disappointed if he didn't hassle us a little. I secretly think that he likes Jane Austen as much as we do, but he can't admit it because he doesn't want to give up this game.

Heather is going skiing tomorrow. Last Sunday Bruce took her out and bought her a pair of cushy Head boots. On Tuesday he took her skis down to the local shop to have them tuned. He's up in our living room with her now, having her stand in the bindings so he can adjust them. They have to be loose enough to let her pop out of the skis if she falls. Heather missed the whole ski season last year after having knee surgery because of a soccer injury. She was on crutches for months and in physical therapy for many months after that. For a brief, strange time last winter she and Bruce were about equally hobbled. They raced each other around the kitchen, and he won.

I am cleaning the carving space on our butcher block table and watching the two of them. He's kneeling at her feet, studying the angle her legs make when the bindings pop; he applies the screwdriver and has her do it again and again until he's satisfied. The other day I heard him ask her if she wanted to learn how to help load him, in his sitski, onto the chair lift. She said yes, which means that probably sometime this year I will be standing in the doorway, watching the two of them drive off to go skiing together. Oh, boy.

It's a simple meal, really. Root vegetables. Seasoned poultry. Bitter bright cranberries, cool and tart. We use the everyday china—our twenty-year-old wedding china—but the table feels special because Emily has set out last year's stubby Christmas candles and turned down the lights. Sitting there with the slow, smooth taste of sage in my mouth, I have an image of our family as a plain and glowing room. We are warm and spare, the four of us—a little like the inside of a church. This makes me smile because right now this kitchen really is a plain and glowing room, but it sits in one corner of a complicated, cluttered house. The image fits. The rest of the universe can get as messy as it likes, but this room, these people, are the place of nourishment. The years of being forced to pay such close attention to Bruce's health—his breath, his skin, his sleep, his body—have somehow cut us a wide green path right through the routines and cynicism. Together, we are as simple as potatoes, as uncomplicated as candlelight. We are as inviolable as love itself.

ACKNOWLEDGMENTS

This book began in 2002 as a disjointed collection of scribbled journal entries and half-remembered emails. As it grew into a coherent narrative, my extraordinary friends Judy Bentley, Susan Starbuck, Deborah Davis, Terri Miller, Christine Castigliano, and Janine Brodine listened patiently, offered sound criticism, and kept the goal of publication always before me. Their encouragement moved me forward in spite of every setback.

In the fall of 2003, Hedgebrook provided twenty-four blessed days of solitude, during which the bulk of these pages came into being. I cannot imagine a better setting than the meadows and gardens and sounds of Whidbey Island for writing about loss and grace and love, and I owe a debt to the women who made my stay possible.

Bob Simmons was an early reader whose careful editing improved the manuscript greatly. His enthusiastic support for the project was a blessing I needed more than he knew.

Dr. Wise Young of Rutgers University has touched the lives of every person affected by spinal cord injury whether they are aware of it or not. His pioneering work in neuroscience, his astounding determination to find a cure, and his generous presence on the CareCure.org web site are among the reasons no simple words of thanks could ever be adequate. Wise, our world is a brighter, more hopeful place because of you.

In 2004, Bruce spent three amazing months at the University of Florida where he underwent a rigorous clinical trial of body-weight-supported treadmill training. Thank you Dr. Andrea Behrman, Mark Bowden, Chetan Phadke, Preeti Nair and Monsoo Ko for the gift of walking. I also want to thank his physical therapy team at the University of Washington: Scott Turnipseed, Andy Hedley and Stacia Lee.

Dave and Miriam Hanson managed, as always, to be both supportive and discreet. Their sturdy faith in me is a well I visit often and a grace I cannot deserve.

Finally, Bruce Hanson is the person most responsible for whatever value these pages hold. Without his generous design work, there would be no book. Without his strength and heart, there would be no story to tell.

BIBLIOGRAPHY

Hanson, Bruce. <u>Approaching the Third Room: A Dream/Memory Journal</u>. MFA Thesis. Vermont College, 2001.

Maddox, Sam. *Paralysis Resource Guide*. Springfield, New Jersey: Christopher Reeve Paralysis Foundation, 2003.

Oliver, Mary. *Wild Geese, New and Selected Poems*. Boston: Beacon Press, 1992.

Reeve, Christopher. *Nothing is Impossible: Reflections on a New Life*. New York: Random House, 2002.

Reeve, Christopher. *Still Me*. New York: Random House, 1998.

Vikhanski, Luba. *In Search of the Lost Cord: Solving the Mystery of Spinal Regeneration*. Washington, DC: Joseph Henry Press, 2001.

Whyte, David. *The Heart Aroused*. New York: Currency Doubleday, 1994.

Young, Wise. *Articles by Dr. Wise Young*. 14 March 2003. Rutgers University. <http://sci.rutgers.edu/index.php?page=articles>.